Samuel Butler

Hudibras
Parts I and II
and Selected Other Writings

Edited by **John Wilders**
and **Hugh de Quehen**

1973 Clarendon Press · Oxford

Oxford University Press *Ely House, London W.1*

Glasgow	Bombay
New York	Calcutta
Toronto	Madras
Melbourne	Karachi
Wellington	Lahore
	Dacca
Cape Town	Delhi
Ibadan	
Nairobi	Kuala Lumpur
Dar es Salaam	Singapore
Lusaka	Hong Kong
Addis Ababa	Tokyo

Made and printed in Great Britain by
Richard Clay (The Chaucer Press) Ltd
Bungay Suffolk

Paul Dundas

b974

Samuel Butler

**Hudibras Parts I and II
and Selected Other Writings**

Contents

Introduction

When the First Part of *Hudibras* made its appearance on the London bookstalls in December 1662 it immediately became the most talked-about poem of its time and brought sudden fame to its author. 'All the world', wrote Pepys, 'cries it up to be the example of wit.'[1] Charles II was himself delighted with it and 'all courtiers, loyal scholars and gentlemen, to the great profit of the author and book-seller'.[2]

Until that moment Samuel Butler had lived in obscurity, earning a living as a clerk to a succession of noblemen. He was born on 14 February 1613, the son of a yeoman farmer who lived in the hamlet of Strensham, a few miles south of Worcester. The family had been farmers in Worcestershire from at least the early part of the six-teenth century. As a boy the poet was sent to one of the best schools in the neighbourhood, King's School, Worcester, and later in-herited from his father a small but impressive collection of books, including poetry, philosophy, logic, rhetoric, law, and the Latin classics, subjects of which he ultimately acquired considerable knowledge but which, paradoxically, he ridiculed in his writings as useless and pedantic.

According to his early biographers his first employment was as a clerk to a Mr. Jefferey, a local Justice of the Peace, who lived in the neighbouring parish of Earl's Croome. How long he remained there is not known but, if the same biographers are to be trusted, he soon advanced in his profession and became secretary to the Dowager Countess of Kent at Wrest Park in Bedfordshire where 'he employed his time much in painting and drawing and also music' and estab-lished a close friendship with a frequent visitor to Wrest, the minia-turist Samuel Cooper, whose portrait of Butler is still in existence.[3] It has until recently been generally believed that Butler later worked as a clerk to the Puritan army officer Sir Samuel Luke, whose home was also in Bedfordshire, at Cople, and who, it was thought, served as a model for the Presbyterian knight who is the hero of Butler's poem. None of the early biographers, however, mentions this association and it is probably legendary.

---

[1] *Diary*, 26 December 1662.
[2] Anthony à Wood, *Athenae Oxonienses*, ed. P. Bliss, 1813–20, iii. 875. The short biographies by Wood and John Aubrey (*Brief Lives*, ed. A. Clark, 2 vols., Oxford, 1898, i. 135–8) are the only sources for much of the information about Butler's life.
[3] It is in the Duke of Buccleuch and Queensberry's collection of miniatures. The portrait is reproduced in *Hudibras*, ed. J. Wilders, Oxford, 1967.

The poet himself declared that the original Hudibras was in fact a West Country knight with whom he lodged for a time in Holborn and there is no reason to doubt his word. Since the internal evidence suggests that he began to write *Hudibras* in about 1658 we can conclude that he was by then living in London where, we are told, he became a familiar figure in Gray's Inn Walk and formed an acquaintance with the lawyers. By 1661, however, he had acquired a post of some responsibility as steward to Richard Vaughan, Earl of Carbery, at Ludlow Castle where his duties included the payment of craftsmen for repairs to the castle which had been damaged during the Civil War. A year later, he had relinquished this post and with the publication of *Hudibras* in December of that year, his obscurity was temporarily at an end.

Such was its popularity that nine editions were printed within twelve months, four of them cheaply produced by a rival and unauthorized printer who was keen to exploit its success. The poem was also plagiarized by an anonymous and much inferior author who brought out a spurious Second Part in the same year which itself went into at least three editions. As the author of a work which had found favour at court and which was strongly anti-Puritan, Butler appears to have expected some tangible reward in the form of a pension or political office. It was not, however, until 1677, fifteen years after the First Part of *Hudibras* had appeared, that he was granted an annual pension of £100 by the King. By then he himself had probably given currency to the complaint that, though a loyal satirist, he was left to waste his old age in poverty. By the time he died he was already regarded as a classic example of poetic genius neglected by the great:

> Unpitied Hudibras, your champion friend,
> Has shown how far your charities extend.
> This lasting verse shall on his tomb be read,
> 'He shamed you living and upbraids you dead'.
> (Dryden, *Hind and the Panther*, iii. 247–50.)

During the last ten years of his life Butler continued to work as a secretary but his last employer was one of the most powerful men in the land, the second Duke of Buckingham. In the summer of 1670 he accompanied the Duke to Versailles where a treaty was being negotiated with Louis XIV. In preparation for this visit he compiled his own English–French dictionary and, in a transcript made by William Longueville,[1] recorded his impressions of French life and

[1] See p. x.

manners. He may also have accompanied Buckingham to the Hague two years later, for he also composed a brief 'Description of Holland' and remarked in a commonplace book on the cleanliness of the Dutch houses. By June 1673 he was acting as secretary for the Duke's affairs as Chancellor of Cambridge University and may have continued to do so until a year later when Buckingham ceased to be Chancellor. He is said to have collaborated with the Duke in the composition of his satirical play *The Rehearsal*.

The Second Part of *Hudibras* had appeared in print almost exactly a year after the first. Although we do not know how many copies were printed, the fact that it went into only two editions, both in the same year, suggests that it may have been less popular than its predecessor. In 1674 Butler published a revised version of the first two parts, adding the satirical and explanatory notes which are included in the present text. The Third and Last Part, which has not been included in this present volume, came out at the end of 1677. It was far less successful than the previous two parts, partly, no doubt, because the Civil War was no longer a topical subject, partly because the writing was disappointingly feeble and verbose. Before embarking on *Hudibras* Butler had written a few minor works but the rest of his writings were composed after the Second Part, including his best short satirical poem, 'The Elephant in the Moon', and his only other substantial work, the prose *Characters*, written, according to their first editor, Robert Thyer, mainly between 1667 and 1669.

In spite of his success as the author of what was, for a time, the most popular poem in England, Butler spent his last years a lonely, embittered man. 'He might have had preferments at first', says Aubrey, 'but would not accept any but very good ones, so that at last he had none at all, and died in want.' His last home was a room in Rose Alley, Covent Garden, where he died on 25 September 1680. He was buried in the churchyard of St. Paul's, Covent Garden. Physically he was, according to Aubrey, 'of a middle stature, strong set, high coloured, a head of sorel hair'. Temperamentally he could be sociable and high-spirited, but his wit and animation, like those of Swift and Samuel Johnson, both of whom greatly admired him, were a reaction against, or escape from, an essential pessimism. This combination of vitality and gloom, which also appears in his writings, was shrewdly observed by a physician from Plymouth, James Yonge, who came across him by chance in a coffee house in Covent Garden in 1678 and fortunately recorded his impression in a diary.[1] 'I saw the famous old Mr. Butler,' wrote Yonge, 'an old paralytic claret

---

[1] *The Journal of James Yonge*, ed. F. N. L. Poynter, 1963, p. 157.

drinker, a morose, surly man, except elevated with claret, when he becomes very brisk and incomparable company.'

Towards the end of his life he was befriended by an eminent lawyer, William Longueville, and on Butler's death his manuscripts became Longueville's property. After passing through several hands, they reached Robert Thyer, the Keeper of the Public Library in Manchester. As far as we know, the manuscript of *Hudibras* is no longer in existence but many of those which Thyer acquired, including some of Butler's commonplace books and many miscellaneous sketches in verse and prose, have survived and are now in the British Museum (Add. MS. 32625). Thyer himself transcribed a substantial portion of the manuscripts and his transcription is also in the British Museum (Add. MS. 32626). In 1759 he published a generous selection from the *Characters*, miscellaneous poems, and commonplace books under the title of *The Genuine Remains in Verse and Prose of Mr. Samuel Butler*. Another commonplace book, which includes Butler's English–French dictionary, is now in the library of the Rosenbach Foundation in Philadelphia. Although the texts of the other manuscripts have been published in full, the contents of the Rosenbach volume have remained unpublished.

Butler's peculiar temperament is consistently reflected in his writings which are almost entirely satirical attacks on the social and intellectual follies of his time, written in the highly ingenious, allusive, 'witty' style of his contemporaries, Cleveland and Cowley. His works are related to one another, moreover, not simply by their distinctive style but by the moral and philosophical convictions which Butler seems to have held throughout his mature life. He lived during a period in which long-established beliefs, many of them unchallenged since their formulation by the Greeks and Romans, were being shown to be false and when a theological view of the world, supported by the Bible and the scholastic philosophers, was being replaced by a scientific view supported by observation and experience. The contradictions which arose from the collision of these views led men more intellectually distinguished than Butler to inquire into the nature of knowledge itself and the means by which it is acquired. The question of 'human understanding' was a central preoccupation of Bacon, Descartes, and Hobbes, with whose writings Butler was familiar, and of Locke whose *Essay* on the subject appeared ten years after the poet's death. Butler shared with the most enlightened thinkers of his time a scepticism towards established philosophy, particularly that of Aristotle, a mistrust of purely theoretical ideas, especially those of the schoolmen, and a belief that truth could be found only in 'the right observation of nature'. Butler's empiricism and his contempt for abstract philosophy can be recognized throughout his work but is most plainly stated in his commonplace books, a selection from which is included in this volume.

His central conviction is that 'the opinions and judgements of men can have no better nor other foundation than that of nature'. It is only by the dispassionate observation of the physical world that they may discover what is true. The faculty by which they may do so is their reason which 'puts the notions and images of things ... that are confused in the understanding, into the same order and condition in which they are really disposed by nature'. Hence the mind, when it functions properly, resembles a mirror which contains an accurate representation of the physical objects set before it: 'notions are but pictures of things in the imagination of man and, if they agree with their originals in nature they are true, and if not false'. Butler believed that empirical observation was the only means of acquiring not only what we now call 'scientific' knowledge but also knowledge of God. The Bible, since it was written by fallible human beings, was not the 'immediate word of God', but the unreliable testimony of men. Nature, on the other hand, is the creation of God himself and Butler agreed with the scientifically minded clergy of his day that God manifested himself in his own handiwork. The diversity and perfection of the universe was an expression of God's own nature, 'a copy which the divine wisdom has drawn of itself'. The study of creation was 'the nearest visible access to his divine presence humanity is capable of'.

Although he believed that men could discover truth, he was much more preoccupied with their habitual failure to do so. 'There are but few truths in the world', he noted, 'but millions of errors and falsities which prevail with the opinion of the world.' The ultimate source of error lay in the imperfection of man and his tendency to be deceived by irrational forces within himself. Perhaps the most misleading of these was the imagination which 'cheats the senses', 'raises the passions to a prodigious height', and, if allowed to flourish without control, 'becomes the most disordered and ungoverned thing in the world'. Individual men are deceived by their own private imaginations, passions, and prejudices and also by the false philosophies and pseudo-sciences devised by others. Aristotle's philosophy is fallacious because he had less concern for 'truth and nature' than for 'the metaphysics of his own brain'; the mystic can never apprehend the truth because he mistakenly 'puts out his own eyes that he might contemplate the better'; logic, since it is preoccupied with words rather than things, cannot teach 'solid and substantial' knowledge but 'only little tricks and evasions'. The irrational impulses in men prevail most strongly, however, when they turn their minds to religion, for theology is an era of inquiry in which there is no empirical evidence: God cannot be apprehended at first hand but only as he reveals himself in his creation. Theology is 'a speculative science of finding out reasons of things that are not within the reach of reason'. The intellectualism of pedants like Hudibras and the visions of sectarian mystics like Ralpho are equally unprofitable: we can no more define the nature of God than we can 'draw a true map of *terra incognita* by mere imagination'.

Butler's concern about the prevalence of error was not purely intellectual: he also believed it had practical consequences, attributing the violence of his age to the attempts of deluded men to impose their errors on other people. Many of the representative figures who appear in the prose *Characters* are of this kind: the 'Hypocritical Nonconformist' whose 'little petulant differences ... produce and continue animosities among the rabble', the 'Fifth-Monarchy Man, who 'groans sedition' and 'hums and hahs high treason', the 'Fanatic' whose religion 'tends only to faction and sedition'. Less destructive, though just as hypocritical, is the 'Astrologer' whose trade depends on his own pretensions to wisdom and the credulity of his customers. The *Characters* are, incidentally, closely related to the commonplace books in that observations on specific social types develop into statements about human conduct generally, as when, considering the 'Romance Writer', Butler is led to remark that 'Truth herself has little or nothing to do in the affairs of the world, although all matters of the greatest weight and moment are pretended and done in her name'. Another moralist, Dr. Johnson, remarked that Butler 'had watched with great diligence the operations of human nature, and traced the effects of opinion, humour, interest and passion'. This comment on *Hudibras* applies just as well to Butler's other writings.

In asserting that truth was to be found only in the right observation of nature, Butler expressed an opinion which was heard increasingly in his lifetime and which proved favourable for the development of science. Yet he had no sympathy for the newly founded Royal Society and in some of his minor works, such as 'The Elephant in the Moon', held up their experiments to ridicule. The 'virtuosi' who appear in his writings are as easily deceived as other men and are even less able to see truth through their telescopes than with their unaided eyes. The learned gentlemen who peer through the 'optic glass', having once believed they see an elephant on the moon, are unwilling to admit it is actually a mouse. The poem ends not with a specific attack on science but with a complaint, repeated in the notebooks, against men generally who 'explicate appearances, not as they are, but as they please'. Butler was also unimpressed by the scientists because they seemed to devote themselves to trivial speculations. The unfinished 'Satire on the Royal Society' is largely a list of useless experiments (some of which were actually attempted) such as weighing the air or observing the sleeping habits of fish, and in the 'Occasional Reflection' we are treated to the spectacle of the 'diligent and solert' Dr. Charleton, the royal physician, feeling the pulse of a dog. In his contempt for such occupations Butler anticipated Pope's and Swift's attacks on scientific pedantry.

His literary theories were an extension of his philosophical principles. He objected to the misrepresentation of truth not only by religious fanatics but by writers of poetry and romances. One of the faults of the 'Small Poet' is that he will not apply himself to 'the imitation of nature' with the result that 'the account he gives of things deserves no regard'. The same principle lies behind his objection to those 'Critics who Judge Modern Plays by the Rules of the Ancients'. A play should be judged not by its conformity to the practice of antiquity but by the extent to which it 'draws true images of all mankind'. Such truth to nature was to be found neither in epic poetry, which perpetuated old superstitions such as the belief in classical deities and the inspiration of the muse, nor in the romances, which upheld outmoded ideals of chivalry which would prove ridiculous if actually put into practice. It is not surprising that Butler admired *Don Quixote* and used it as a major source for *Hudibras*. Yet although he saw the function of literature as primarily realistic and representational, Butler did allow some scope for the imagination in so far as it served to illuminate reality, as in the case of allegories which may be useful 'when they serve as instances to illustrate some obscure truth'. The use of satire, conversely, was to expose error. It is 'a kind of knight-errant, that goes upon adventures to relieve . . . oppressed Truth and Reason out of the captivity of giants and magicians'. His own most ambitious poem is a satirical allegory in which he attempted to free truth and reason from the captivity of contemporary superstition and hypocrisy. It is also written in the form of a mock-heroic poem which is itself a criticism of epic and romance.

Butler was entirely consistent with his own principles when he

chose to create, as the principal characters in *Hudibras*, a knight who
is a Presbyterian and an Aristotelian, a squire who is a Baptist and
a Hermetic philosopher, and an astrologer who dabbles in experimental science. Hudibras is well versed in logic, rhetoric, and ancient
languages, and the scholastic philosophy. Yet in practical life his
learning is an impediment rather than a help. It either enables him
dimly to perceive the obvious or prevents him from seeing things
which are apparent to common sense. His mathematical skill in-
duces him to calculate the time by algebra and his classical learning
persuades him that a village procession is a Roman triumph.
Whereas Hudibras is encumbered by excessive learning, Ralpho
prides himself on his ignorance. As a neo-Platonist and a disciple of
Thomas Vaughan he claims to perceive intuitively the truths which
elude the knight's intelligence. He pretends to be divinely inspired
and to know things beyond the scope of empirical experience. He is,
however, shrewder than Hudibras and his relationship to his master
is somewhat like that of Sancho Panza to Don Quixote who, as
Butler remarked, is the less 'wise and politic' of the two in spite of
'all his studied and acquired abilities'. The immediate cause of their
quarrels is theological: Ralpho's assertion that Presbyterian synods
are nothing more than bear gardens provokes Hudibras to defend
his own church. But whereas the squire's accusation is based on the
intuitive conviction that a synod is a 'type' or symbol of a bear
garden, the knight's defence is conducted by the cumbersome pro-
cesses of formal logic. The opponents confront each other as rep-
resentatives not simply of conflicting religious factions but of different modes of 'human understanding', the mystical and the intellectual. When, at the end of the First Part, they become aware that
their disagreement is philosophical, their debate terminates. Since
the principles from which they argue are incompatible it could not
possibly continue. Neither realizes, however, that he has been prevented by his principles from recognizing the truth. That discovery is
left to the reader.

With the appearance of Sidrophel in the Second Part Butler returns to the question of intellectual delusion. The astrologer, like
the knight, is a scholar who has 'been long towards mathematics,
optics, philosophy and statics'. But his education again proves an
encumberance, and when he sees a boy's kite through his telescope,
he mistakes it for a comet. As well as being a pedant he is also a
charlatan, living on the credulity of his clients to whom he sells
useless charms and horoscopes. The knight's dispute with him, like
his earlier one with Ralpho, develops into an examination of basic

principles in which Hudibras points out that the astrologers have themselves disagreed about the exact location of the stars and the extent of their influence on human life. This debate is also inconclusive and the increasing frustration of the disputants leads to a fight, a demonstration of the way in which intellectual misapprehensions cause physical violence.

Hudibras has sometimes been dismissed as a clever attack on the Puritans designed to solicit the royal favour. Seen in relation to Butler's other writings it is obviously very much more than this, but its success at the Restoration court was well deserved and it is often brilliantly comic at the same time as it is serious. The means by which Butler achieved his comic effects cannot, ultimately, be explained. They grew naturally out of his bizarre inventiveness and his vision of mankind as absurdly ignorant and hypocritical. Something can be said, however, about his comic mode which, as Johnson pointed out, 'consists of a disproportion between the style and the sentiments'. Sometimes trivial objects are described in the exalted manner of an epic poem, and sometimes respectable sentiments are expressed in deliberately low, colloquial language. The poem is a mixture of mock-heroic and burlesque. The mock-heroic passages occur most frequently in the First Part which, in accordance with epic convention, enters *in medias res* with the description of the two chief characters before the muse is invoked and the scene is set. The hero, whose name is taken from *The Faerie Queene*, is a modern-day knight errant, setting out on horseback to remedy anti-Christian wrongs. He addresses the mob in words adapted from Lucan and courts his mistress in poetry adapted from Lucretius. When the rabble appear they are described like epic combatants, each member bearing a high-sounding name appropriate to his trade. They are also ironically compared to ancient heroes—Crowdero, the bear-keeper, to Chiron, Talgol, the butcher, to Ajax, and Colon, the farmer, to Hercules. The effect of this discrepancy between tone and subject is both to emphasize the absurdity of the characters and to cast doubt on the ideals of the epic heroes to whom they are compared.

Butler's most characteristic weapon, however, is his intentionally clumsy verse, slangy diction, and comic rhymes. He deliberately commits the faults of which he elsewhere accuses the 'Small Poet' in a style which is both ironically amusing and a means whereby religious and intellectual pretensions are made to appear gross and commonplace:

> Beside 'tis known he could speak Greek
> As naturally as pigs squeak;
> That Latin was no more difficile
> Than to a blackbrid 'tis to whistle.

The flat, colloquial language is an expression of the matter-of-fact point of view from which Butler regarded mankind.

Although he has been largely neglected for two centuries—his popularity had waned even by Johnson's time—Butler deserves some attention as a literary innovator. Throughout his work we can glimpse the Augustan ideals of 'nature', 'use', and 'common sense' in the process of evolution and thereby may better understand why they evolved. *Hudibras* is the first comic poem in English which simultaneously attacks contemporary follies and the heroic form in which it is cast. Without its example *Absalom and Achitophel*, *A Tale of a Tub*, and *The Dunciad* could probably not have been written. The poem itself is distinguished by its brilliantly inventive wit and the sporadic violence of its invective. Butler is at his best when he creates a string of images of increasing absurdity which, while serving his satirical purpose, delight the reader by their sheer abundance and ingenuity. Ralpho's extended 'proof' that synods are indistinguishable from bear-gardens is the most sustained example, but the poem is full of shorter passages of a similar kind:

> He could raise scruples dark and nice
> And after solve 'em in a trice;
> As if divinity had catched
> The itch of purpose to be scratched,
> Or, like a mountebank, did wound
> And stab herself with doubts profound
> Only to show with how small pain
> The sores of faith are cured again;
> Although by woeful proof we find
> They always leave a scar behind.

The disillusioned final couplet is typical of Butler. In spite of its many brilliant passages, however, *Hudibras* is only a partial success. The deliberately commonplace style and regular, unvaried octosyllabics eventually become monotonous. There are signs, moreover, that Butler's ability to create ingenious images was becoming exhausted even during the writing of the Second Part. Much of the Third Part is so verbose and tired that it is scarcely readable. Butler was most at ease in relatively short, formal exercises such as the prose or verse character and the debate and he never really managed to work such passages into a coherent long poem. None of the three parts is really complete in itself and it is hard to imagine a successful conclusion to the whole. Some of the abuses he attacked have disappeared but others, such as academic pedantry and religious intolerance, have not. His desire for clear-sightedness, tolerance, and good sense are still relevant and the energy and ingenuity of his best writing can still arouse pleasure and astonishment.

A Note on the Text

The text of *Hudibras* is a modernized version of the one edited by John Wilders (Oxford, 1967). The texts of 'Upon Critics who Judge of Modern Plays', 'A Ballad', and 'Miscellaneous Observations' are modernized versions of Butler's own manuscripts (British Museum Add. MS. 32625). The remaining texts have been modernized from those in *The Genuine Remains of Mr. Samuel Butler*, edited by Robert Thyer, 1759 (see p. x).

The spelling used both in the manuscripts and printed texts of Butler's verse writings indicates that he was anxious to preserve strict rhyme and rhymical stress. For this reason he used the spelling 'conquerer' to rhyme with 'confer' and 'conquerours' to rhyme with 'ours'. Similarly he used either the spelling 'squire' or 'squier' depending on whether the metre required one or two syllables. These peculiarities have been retained in the text of the verse. Elisions at the ends of words have also been preserved as a guide to metrical stress. The explanatory notes which Butler added to the 1674 edition of *Hudibras* are printed at the bottom of the relevant pages. Where Butler's notes and editorial notes occur on the same page, they are separated by a rule. A superior n in the text indicates a note at the end of the book, pp. 289 ff.

References to the sources on which the biography of Butler is based may be found in the Introduction to the 1967 edition of *Hudibras* which also has a more fully documented commentary. The surviving Butler manuscripts together with editions and transcriptions of his works other than *Hudibras* are discussed by A. H. de Quehen in *Editing Seventeenth-Century Prose*, edited by D. I. B. Smith, 1972.

Reading List

EARLY EDITIONS

Hudibras, the First Part, 1663.
Hudibras, the Second Part, 1664.
Hudibras, the First and Second Parts (revised by Butler), 1674.
Hudibras, the Third and Last Part, 1678.
Hudibras in Three Parts, 1684; 1704 (including a biography); 1710 (with illustrations); 1726 (with illustrations by Hogarth); ed. Zachary Grey, 2 vols., 1744; ed. T. R. Nash, 3 vols., 1793.
Posthumous Works in Prose and Verse, 3 vols., 1715–17 (largely spurious).
Genuine Remains in Verse and Prose, ed. Robert Thyer, 2 vols., 1759.

MODERN EDITIONS

Works, ed. A. R. Waller and René Lamar, 3 vols., 1905–28.
Three Poems, ed. A. C. Spence, 1961.
Hudibras, ed. John Wilders, 1967.
Characters, ed. C. W. Daves, 1970.

IMPORTANT BOOKS

BOND, R. P. *English Burlesque Poetry*, 1932.
HAZLITT, W. *The English Comic Writers*, 1819 (Lecture III).
JACK, I. *Augustan Satire*, 1952.
JOHNSON, SAMUEL. *Lives of the Poets*, 1779–81.
RICHARDS, E. A. *Hudibras in the Burlesque Tradition*, 1937.

IMPORTANT ARTICLES

DE BEER, E. S. 'The Later Life of Samuel Butler', *R.E.S.* iv, 1928.
BENTLEY, NORMA E. '*Hudibras* Butler Abroad', *Modern Language Notes*, lx, 1945. 'Another Butler Manuscript', *Modern Philology*, xlvi, 1948.
CRAIG, HARDIN. '*Hudibras* and the Politics of 1647', *Manly Anniversary Studies*, 1923.
QUINTANA, RICARDO. 'The Butler–Oxenden Correspondence', *Modern Language Notes*, xlviii, 1933. 'Samuel Butler', *E.L.H.* xviii, 1951.
WASSERMAN, GEORGE R. 'Samuel Butler and the Problem of Unnatural Man', *Modern Language Quarterly*, xxxi, 1970.
WILDING, MICHAEL. 'The Last of the Epics', in *Restoration Literature: Critical Approaches*, ed. Harold Love, 1972.

Hudibras

The First Part

THE ARGUMENT

Sir Hudibras[n] his passing worth,
The manner how he sallied forth,
His arms and equipage are shown,
His horse's virtues and his own.
The adventure of the bear and fiddle
Is sung but breaks off in the middle.

When civil fury first grew high
And men fell out they knew not why,
When hard words, jealousies and fears[n]
Set folks together by the ears
And made them fight like mad or drunk   5
For Dame Religion as for punk,
Whose honesty they all durst swear for,
Though not a man of them knew wherefore,
When gospel-trumpeter, surrounded
With long-eared rout, to battle sounded   10
And pulpit, drum ecclesiastic,
Was beat with fist instead of a stick,
Then did Sir Knight abandon dwelling
And out he rode a-colonelling.

A wight he was whose very sight would   15
Entitle him Mirror of Knighthood,
That never bent his stubborn knee
To anything but chivalry,
Nor put up blow but that which laid
Right worshipful on shoulder-blade;   20

3 *jealousies*: suspicions.
16 *Mirror of Knighthood*: the title of a popular Spanish romance.
19 *put up*: to submit to.

Chief of domestic knights and errant
Either for chartel or for warrant,
Great on the bench, great in the saddle,
That could as well bind o'er as swaddle.
Mighty he was at both of these   25
And styled of war as well as peace
(So some rats of amphibious nature
Are either for the land or water).
But here our authors make a doubt
Whether he were more wise or stout.   30
Some hold the one and some the other,
But, howsoe'er they make a pother,
The difference was so small, his brain
Outweighed his rage but half a grain,
Which made some take him for a tool   35
That knaves do work with, called a fool,
And offer to lay wagers that,
As Montaigne, playing with his cat,
Complains she thought him but an ass,
Much more she would Sir Hudibras   40
(For that's the name our valiant knight
To all his challenges did write),
But they're mistaken very much:
'Tis plain enough he was no such.
We grant, although he had much wit,   45
H'was very shy of using it,
As being loath to wear it out,
And therefore bore it not about
Unless on holy days or so,
As men their best apparel do.   50
Beside 'tis known he could speak Greek
As naturally as pigs squeak;
That Latin was no more difficile
Than to a blackbird 'tis to whistle.
Being rich in both, he never scanted   55
His bounty unto such as wanted,

---

24 Bind over to the sessions as being a justice of the peace in his county as well
  as a colonel of a regiment of foot in the parliament's army and a committee-
  man.
38 Montaigne in his *Essays* supposes his cat thought him a fool for losing his
  time in playing with her.[n]

---

22 *chartel*: challenge.
24 *swaddle*: beat soundly.

But much of either would afford
To many that had not one word.
For Hebrew roots, although they're found
To flourish most in barren ground,   60
He had such plenty as sufficed
To make some think him circumcised;
And truly so, perhaps, he was:
'Tis many a pious Christian's case.

He was in logic a great critic,[n]   65
Profoundly skilled in analytic.
He could distinguish and divide
A hair 'twixt south and south-west side,
On either which he would dispute,
Confute, change hands and still confute.   70
He'd undertake to prove by force
Of argument a man's no horse;[n]
He'd prove a buzzard is no fowl,
And that a lord may be an owl,
A calf an alderman, a goose a justice,   75
And rooks committee-men and trustees.[n]
He'd run in debt by disputation
And pay with ratiocination.
All this by syllogism, true
In mood and figure, he would do.   80

For rhetoric, he could not ope
His mouth but out there flew a trope,
And when he happened to break off
I'th' middle of his speech, or cough,
He'd hard words ready to show why,   85
And tell what rules he did it by,

---

66 Analytic is a part of logic that teaches to decline and construe reason as
grammar does words.

---

66 *analytic*: the principles of logic established by Aristotle.
73 *buzzard*: a fool (colloquial).
74 *owl*: a colloquialism for a stupid person, as is also 'calf' in the following line.
75 *goose*: a simpleton (colloquial).
76 *rooks*: cheats (colloquial).
80 *in mood and figure*: in due logical form.

Else when with greatest art he spoke
You'd think he talked like other folk;
For all a rhetorician's rules
Teach nothing but to name his tools.   90
His ordinary rate of speech
In loftiness of sound was rich,
A Babylonish dialect
Which learned pedants much affect.
It was a particoloured dress   95
Of patched and piebald languages;
'Twas English cut on Greek and Latin,
Like fustian heretofore on satin.
It had an odd, promiscuous tone,
As if he'd talked three parts in one,   100
Which made some think, when he did gabble
They'd heard three labourers of Babel,
Or Cerberus himself pronounce
A leash of languages at once.
This he as volubly would vent   105
As if his stock would ne'er be spent,
And truly to support that charge
He had supplies as vast and large;
For he could coin or counterfeit
New words with little or no wit;   110
Words so debased and hard, no stone
Was hard enough to touch them on,
And when with hasty noise he spoke 'em
The ignorant for current took 'em;
That had the orator, who once   115
Did fill his mouth with pebble stones
When he harangued, but known his phrase
He would have used no other ways.

---

93 A confusion of languages such as some of our modern virtuosi use to express
themselves in.
115 Demosthenes, who is said to have had a defect in his pronunciation, which
he cured by using to speak with little stones in his mouth.

---

98 Clothes made of cheap fustian were slashed and lined with satin.
102 Genesis 11: 6–9.
103 *Cerberus*: the three-headed dog which guarded the entrance to Hades.
104 *leash*: a set of three.

In mathematics he was greater
Than Tycho Brahe or Erra Pater;   120
For he by geometric scale
Could take the size of pots of ale,
Resolve by sines and tangents straight
If bread or butter wanted weight,
And wisely tell what hour o'th' day   125
The clock does strike by algebra.

Beside he was a shrewd philosopher
And had read every text and gloss over.
What e'er the crabbed'st author hath
He understood b'implicit faith;   130
What ever sceptic could inquere for
For every why he had a wherefore;
Knew more than forty of them do,
As far as words and terms could go.
All which he understood by rote   135
And, as occasion served, would quote,
No matter whether right or wrong;
They might be either said or sung.
His notions fitted things so well
That which was which he could not tell,   140
But oftentimes mistook the one
For th'other, as great clerks have done.
He could reduce all things to acts
And knew their natures by abstracts,
Where entity and quiddity,   145
The ghosts of defunct bodies, fly;

143 The old philosophers thought to extract notions out of natural things, as
chemists do spirits and essences, and when they had refined them into the
nicest subtleties, gave them as insignificant names as those operators do their
extractions. But (as Seneca says)[n] the subtler things are rendered they are but
the nearer to nothing. So are all their definitions of things by acts the nearer to
nonsense.

120 *Tycho Brahe*: (1546–1601) a celebrated Danish astronomer. *Erra Pater*: a
pseudonym used by the authors of almanacs published in the sixteenth and
seventeenth centuries.
132 Proverbial (*Oxford Dictionary of English Proverbs*, 1970, p. 886) (*ODEP*
hereafter).
139 *notions*: cf. p. 272.

Where truth in person does appear,
Like words congealed in northern air.
He knew what's what, and that's as high
As metaphysic wit can fly.   150
In school divinity as able
As he that hight irrefragable;
Profound in all the nominal
And real ways beyond them all,
And with as delicate a hand   155
Could twist as tough a rope of sand,
And weave fine cobwebs, fit for skull
That's empty when the moon is full,
Such as take lodgings in a head
That's to be let unfurnished.   160
He could raise scruples dark and nice
And after solve 'em in a trice;
As if divinity had catched
The itch, of purpose to be scratched,
Or, like a mountebank, did wound   165
And stab herself with doubts profound
Only to show with how small pain
The sores of faith are cured again;
Although by woeful proof we find
They always leave a scar behind.   170
He knew the seat of paradise,
Could tell in what degree it lies,
And, as he was disposed, could prove it
Below the moon or else above it;

147 Some authors have mistaken truth for a real thing, when it is nothing but a
   right method of putting those notions or images of things in the understanding
   of man into the same state and order that their originals hold in nature,[n] and
   therefore Aristotle says *unum quodque sicut se habet secundum esse ita se habet
   secundum veritatem.* Met. L. 2.
148 Some report that in Nova Zembla and Greenland men's words are wont to
   be frozen in the air, and at the thaw, may be heard.
171 There is nothing more ridiculous than the various opinions of authors
   about the seat of paradise. Sir Walter Raleigh has taken great pains to collect
   them in the beginning of his *History of the World*, where those who are unsatisfied may be fully informed.[n]

---

152 *irrefragable*: the medieval philosopher Alexander of Hales was known as
   the *Doctor Irrefragabilis.*
156 *rope of sand*: a proverbial expression meaning 'an incoherent argument'.
147 note *unum quodque*: 'as each thing is in respect of being, so is it in respect of
   truth' (Aristotle, *Metaphysics*, 993[b] 30).
148 note *Nova Zembla*: a group of islands in the Arctic Ocean.

What Adam dreamt of when his bride   175
Came from her closet in his side;
Whether the devil tempted her
By a High Dutch interpreter;
If either of them had a navel;
Who first made music malleable;   180
Whether the serpent at the fall
Had cloven feet, or none at all.
All this, without a gloss or comment,
He would unriddle in a moment
In proper terms, such as men smatter   185
When they throw out and miss the matter.

For his religion, it was fit
To match his learning and his wit:
'Twas Presbyterian true blue,
For he was of that stubborn crew   190
Of errant saints whom all men grant
To be the true church militant,
Such as do build their faith upon
The holy text of pike and gun,
Decide all controversies by   195
Infallible artillery,
And prove their doctrine orthodox
By apostolic blows and knocks;
Call fire and sword and desolation
A 'godly thorough reformation'   200
Which always must be carried on
And still be doing, never done,
As if religion were intended
For nothing else but to be mended.

178 Goropius Becanus endeavours to prove that High Dutch was the language
   that Adam and Eve spoke in paradise.[n]
179 Adam and Eve being made, and not conceived and formed in the womb, had
   no navels, as some learned men have supposed,[n] because they had no need of
   them.
180 Music is said to be invented by Pythagoras, who first found out the proportion of notes from the sounds of hammers upon an anvil.

191 *errant*: (i) thoroughgoing; (ii) wandering, as in 'knight errant'.
192 *church militant*: an expression used of the church on earth in contradistinc-
   tion to the 'church triumphant' in heaven.
201 'Carrying on the work' was an expression used by the Puritans to describe
   the furtherance of their own religious convictions.

A sect whose chief devotion lies   205
In odd, perverse antipathies;
In falling out with that or this,
And finding somewhat still amiss;
More peevish, cross and splenetic
Than dog distract or monkey sick;   210
That with more care keep holy day
The wrong, than others the right way;
Compound for sins they are inclined to
By damning those they have no mind to;
Still so perverse and opposite,   215
As if they worshipped God for spite.
The self-same thing they will abhor
One way, and long another for.
Free will they one way disavow,
Another, nothing else allow.[n]   220
All piety consists therein
In them, in other men all sin.
Rather than fail, they will defy
That which they love most tenderly,
Quarrel with minced pies, and disparage   225
Their best and dearest friend plum-porridge;[n]
Fat pig and goose itself oppose,
And blaspheme custard through the nose.
Th'apostles of this fierce religion,
Like Mahomet's, were ass and widgeon,[n]   230
To whom our knight, by fast instinct
Of wit and temper, was so linked,
As if hypocrisy and nonsense
Had got th'advowson of his conscience.

Thus was he gifted and accoutred,   235
We mean on the inside, not the outward:
That next of all we shall discuss.
Then listen, sirs, it followeth thus:

---

230 Mahomet had a tame dove that used to pick seeds out of his ear that it
   might be thought to whisper and inspire him. His ass was so intimate with
   him that the Mahometans believe it carried him to heaven and stays there with
   him to bring him back again.

---

228 The puritan preachers adopted a characteristic nasal tone of voice. Cf. p. 244.

His tawny beard was th'equal grace
Both of his wisdom and his face;   240
In cut and dye so like a tile,
A sudden view it would beguile.
The upper part thereof was whey,
The nether orange mixed with grey.
This hairy meteor did denounce   245
The fall of sceptres and of crowns;
With grizzly type did represent
Declining age of government,
And tell with hieroglyphic spade
Its own grave and the state's were made.   250
Like Samson's heart-breakers, it grew
In time to make a nation rue,
Though it contributed its own fall
To wait upon the public downfall.
It was canonic, and did grow   255
In holy orders by strict vow;
Of rule as sullen and severe
As that of rigid cordelier.
'Twas bound to suffer persecution
And martyrdom with resolution;   260
T'oppose itself against the hate
And vengeance of th'incensed state,
In whose defiance it was worn,
Still ready to be pulled and torn,
With red-hot irons to be tortured,   265
Reviled and spit upon and martyred.
Maugre all which, 'twas to stand fast
As long as monarchy should last,
But when the state should hap to reel,
'Twas to submit to fatal steel,   270
And fall, as it were consecrate
A sacrifice to fall of state,
Whose thread of life the fatal sisters
Did twist together with its whiskers,

256 He made a vow never to cut his beard until the Parliament had subdued the
King, of which order of fanatic votaries there were many in those times.

251 *heart-breakers*: love-locks, curled locks of hair.
258 *cordelier*: a Franciscan friar of strict rule.
267 *Maugre*: in spite of.
273 *sisters*: the three fates.

And twine so close that time should never,   275
In life or death, their fortunes sever,
But with his rusty sickle mow
Both down together at a blow.

So learned Taliacotius,[n] from
The brawny part of porter's bum,   280
Cut supplemental noses which
Would last as long as parent breech,
But when the date of nock was out,
Off dropped the sympathetic snout.

His back, or rather burthen, showed   285
As if it stooped with its own load;
For, as Æneas bore his sire
Upon his shoulders through the fire,[n]
Our knight did bear no less a pack
Of his own buttocks on his back,   290
Which now had almost got the upper-
Hand of his head, for want of crupper.
To poise this equally, he bore
A paunch of the same bulk before,
Which still he had a special care   295
To keep well crammed with thrifty fare,
As white-pot, butter-milk and curds,
Such as a country house affords,
With other victual, which anon
We further shall dilate upon   300
When of his hose we come to treat,
The cupboard where he kept his meat.

His doublet was of sturdy buff,
And though not sword-, yet cudgel-proof,
Whereby 'twas fitter for his use   305
That feared no blows but such as bruise.

---

279 Taliacotius was an Italian chirurgeon that found out a way to repair lost
   and decayed noses.

---

283 *nock*: the buttocks.
297 *white-pot*: a milk pudding formerly made in Devonshire.
303 *buff*: leather used for making military uniforms.

His breeches were of rugged woollen
And had been at the Siege of Bullen,
To old King Harry so well known,
Some writers held they were his own.   310
Through they were lined with many a piece
Of ammunition-bread and cheese,
And fat black-puddings, proper food
For warriors that delight in blood;
For, as we said, he always chose   315
To carry victual in his hose.
That often tempted rats and mice
The ammunition to surprise,
And, when he put a hand but in
The one or th'other magazine,   320
They stoutly in defence on't stood
And from the wounded foe drew blood,
And, till th'were stormed, and beaten out,
Ne'er left the fortified redoubt.
And though knights errant, as some think,   325
Of old did neither eat nor drink,[n]
Because, when thorough deserts vast
And regions desolate they passed,
Where belly-timber above ground
Or under was not to be found,   330
Unless they grazed, there's not one word
Of their provision on record,
Which made some confidently write
They had no stomachs but to fight,
'Tis false: for Arthur wore in hall   335
Round table, like a farthingal,
On which, with shirt pulled out behind
And eke before, his good knights dined;
Though 'twas no table, some suppose,
But a huge pair of round trunk-hose,   340
In which he carried as much meat
As he and all his knights could eat,

308 *Bullen*: the Siege of Boulogne in which Henry VIII led the British troops; also a punning reference to Anne Boleyn.
329 *belly-timber*: food.
334 *stomachs*: courage.
340 *trunk-hose*: a kind of breeches, often padded, covering the hips and upper thighs.

When, laying by their swords and truncheons,
They took their breakfasts or their nuncheons.
But let that pass at present, lest   345
We should forget where we digressed,
As learned authors use, to whom
We leave it, and to th'purpose come.

His puissant sword unto his side
Near his undaunted heart was tied,   350
With basket-hilt that would hold broth,
And serve for fight and dinner both.
In it he melted lead for bullets,
To shoot at foes, and sometimes pullets,
To whom he bore so fell a grutch,   355
He ne'er gave quarter t'any such.
The trenchant blade, Toledo trusty,
For want of fighting was grown rusty
And ate into itself, for lack
Of somebody to hew and hack.   360
The peaceful scabbard where it dwelt
The rancour of its edge had felt;
For of the lower end two handful
It had devoured, 'twas so manful,
And so much scorned to lurk in case   365
As if it durst not show its face.
In many desperate attempts
Of warrants, exigents, contempts,
It had appeared with courage bolder
Than sergeant Bum invading shoulder.   370
Oft had it ta'en possession,
And prisoners too, or made them run.

This sword a dagger had his page,
That was but little for his age,
And therefore waited on him so   375
As dwarfs upon knights errant do.

344 *nuncheons*: a light refreshment formerly taken in the afternoon; lunch.
355 *grutch*: grudge.
368 *warrants, exigents*: warrants were issued by justices of the peace. An exigent
   is a writ commanding a defendant to appear in court.
370 *sergeant Bum*: the bum-bailiff; a bailiff employed in making arrests.

It was a serviceable dudgeon
Either for fighting or for drudging.
When it had stabbed, or broke a head
It would scrape trenchers or chip bread,   380
Toast cheese or bacon, though it were
To bait a mouse trap, 'twould not care.
'Twould make clean shoes, and in the earth
Set leeks and onions, and so forth.
It had been prentice to a brewer,   385
Where this and more it did endure,
But left the trade, as many more
Have lately done on the same score.

In th'holsters at his saddle-bow
Two aged pistols he did stow   390
Among the surplus of such meat
As in his hose he could not get.
They were upon hard duty still,
And every night stood sentinel
To guard the magazine i'th' hose   395
From two-legged and from four-legged foes.

Thus clad and fortified, Sir Knight
From peaceful home set forth to fight
But first with nimble, active force
He got on th'outside of his horse;   400
For having but one stirrup, tied
T'his saddle, on the further side,
It was so short he'd much ado
To reach it with his desperate toe.
But after many strains and heaves   405
He got up to the saddle eaves,
From whence he vaulted into th'seat
With so much vigour, strength and heat
That he had almost tumbled over
With his own weight, but did recover   410
By laying hold on tail and mane
Which oft he used instead of rein.

387 Oliver Cromwell and Colonel Pride had been both brewers.

---

377 *dudgeon*: a dagger with a wooden hilt.
402 *further*: the 'off' or right-hand side.

But now we talk of mounting steed,
Before we further do proceed
It doth behove us to say something   415
Of that which bore our valiant bumkin.
The beast was sturdy, large and tall,
With mouth of meal and eyes of wall
(I would say eye, for he'd but one,
As most agree, though some say none).   420
He was well stayed and in his gait
Preserved a grave, majestic state.
At spur or switch no more he skipped
Or mended pace than Spaniard whipped,[n]
And yet so fiery, he would bound   425
As if he grieved to touch the ground,
That Caesar's horse who, as fame goes,
Had corns upon his feet and toes,
Was not by half so tender hoofed
Nor trod upon the ground so soft.   430
And, as that beast would kneel and stoop
(Some write) to take his rider up,
So Hudibras his ('tis well known)
Would often do to set him down.
We shall not need to say what lack   435
Of leather was upon his back,
For that was hidden under pad,
And breech of knight galled full as bad.
His strutting ribs on both sides showed,
Like furrows he himself had ploughed;   440
For underneath the skirt of panel,
'Twixt every two there was a channel.
His draggling tail hung in the dirt,
Which on his rider he would flirt
Still as his tender side he pricked   445
With armed heel, or with unarmed kicked;

---

427 Julius Caesar had a horse with feet like a man's. *Utebatur equo insigni,
pedibus prope humanis, et in modum digitorum ungulis fissis.* Sueton. *in Jul.*
Cap. 61.

---

416 *bumkin*: bumpkin, lout.
418 'Mealy-mouthed and wall-eyed'.
439 *strutting*: protruding.
427 note: 'He rode a remarkable horse with feet that were almost human, for its
hoofs were cloven like toes' (Suetonius, *Julius*, lxi).

For Hudibras wore but one spur,
As wisely knowing, could he stir
To active trot one side of's horse,
The other would not hang an arse.   450

A squire he had whose name was Ralph
That in th'adventure went his half.
Though writers, for more stately tone,
Do call him Ralpho, 'tis all one,
And when we can with metre safe   455
We'll call him so, if not plain Ralph
(For rhyme the rudder is of verses,
With which like ships they steer their courses).
An equal stock of wit and valour
He had laid in, by birth a tailor.   460
The mighty Tyrian queen that gained
With subtle shreds a tract of land,
Did leave it with a castle fair
To his great ancestor, her heir.
From him descended cross-legged knights,   465
Famed for their faith and warlike fights
Against the bloody cannibal,
Whom they destroyed, both great and small.
This sturdy squier had as well
As the bold Trojan knight, seen hell,   470
Not with a counterfeited pass
Of golden bough, but true gold lace.
His knowledge was not far behind
The knight's, but of another kind,
And he another way came by 't: 475
Some call it 'gifts' and some 'new light';
A liberal art that costs no pains
Of study, industry or brains.

---

461 Dido, Queen of Carthage, who bought as much land as she could compass
with an ox's hide, which she cut into small thongs, and cheated the owner of
so much ground as served her to build Carthage upon.[n]
470 Æneas, whom Virgil reports to use a golden bough for a pass to hell, and
tailors call that place 'hell' where they put all they steal.[n]

---

450 *hang an arse*: hold back.
465 *cross-legged*: an allusion to the effigies on medieval tombs. Tailors also sat
cross-legged at their work.
476 *'gifts'* and *'new light'*: terms used by the protestant sectarians to signify
divine inspiration. Cf. pp. 244, 250.

His wits were sent him for a token,
But in the carriage cracked and broken. 480
Like commendation ninepence, crooked
With 'to and from my love', it looked.[n]
He ne'er considered it, as loath
To look a gift-horse in the mouth,
And very wisely would lay forth 485
No more upon it than 'twas worth,
But as he got it freely, so
He spent it frank and freely too
(For saints themselves will sometimes be
Of gifts that cost them nothing, free). 490
By means of this, with hem and cough,
Prolongers to enlightened snuff,
He could deep mysteries unriddle
As easily as thread a needle;
For, as of vagabonds we say 495
That they are ne'er beside their way,
What'er men speak by this new light,
Still they are sure to be i'th' right.
'Tis a dark-lantern of the spirit
Which none see by but those that bear it; 500
A light that falls down from on high
For spiritual trades to cozen by;
An *ignis fatuus* that bewitches,
And leads men into pools and ditches,
To make them dip themselves, and sound 505
For Christendom in dirty pond,
To dive like wild-fowl for salvation,
And fish to catch regeneration.
This light inspires, and plays upon
The nose of saint, like bagpipe drone, 510
And speaks through hollow, empty soul,
As through a trunk, or whispering-hole,

479 *token*: (i) a sign of God's providence; (ii) a piece of metal used as a coin by
  a private company.
488 Cf. p. 254.
489 *saints*: the term used by the Puritans to denote the elect of God.
492 *snuff*: a candle end.
499 *dark-lantern*: a lantern designed so that its light may be concealed.
510 *bagpipe*: see note to I. i. 228.
512 *trunk*: a speaking-tube.

Such language as no mortal ear
But spiritual eavesdroppers can hear.
So Phoebus, or some friendly muse,   515
Into small poets, song infuse,
Which they at second-hand rehearse
Through reed or bagpipe, verse for verse.

Thus Ralph became infallible
As three- or four-legged oracle,   520
The ancient cup, or modern chair;
Spoke truth point-blank, though unaware;
For mystic learning wondrous able[n]
In magic, talisman and cabal,
Whose primitive tradition reaches   525
As far as Adam's first green breeches;[n]
Deep-sighted in intelligences,
Ideas, atoms, influences;[n]
And much of *Terra Incognita*,
Th'intelligible world, could say;   530
A deep occult philosopher,

---

524 Talisman is a device to destroy any sort of vermin by casting their images in
    metal, in a precise minute when the stars are perfectly inclined to do them all
    the mischief they can. This has been experimented by some modern virtuosi
    upon rats, mice and fleas, and found, as they affirm, to produce the effect
    with admirable success.
       Raymond Lully[n] interprets *cabal* out of the Arabic to signify *scientia super-
    abundans*, which his commentator Cornelius Agrippa,[n] by over magnifying,
    has rendered a very superfluous foppery.
526 The author of *Magia Adamica*[n] endeavours to prove the learning of the
    ancient *Magi* to be derived from that knowledge which God himself taught
    Adam in paradise before the fall.
530 The intelligible world is a kind of *Terra del Fuego* or *Psittacorum Regio*,
    discovered only by the philosophers, of which they talk, like parrots, what they
    do not understand.

---

520 *oracle*: the priestess of Apollo at Delphi sat on a three-legged stool. The
    'four-legged oracle' is the chair used by the Pope when making *ex cathedra*
    statements.
521 *cup*: the vessel containing liquid which was examined in order to predict
    future events, in the form of divination known as lekanomancy.
529 *Terra Incognita*: 'unknown land', a term formerly used in maps to describe
    land as yet unexplored.
530 note *Terra del Fuego*: the archipelago at the southern tip of South America.
    Although it had been discovered by Magellan in 1520 it remained unexplored
    until 1670. *Psittacorum Regio*: 'land of parrots'.

As learned as the wild Irish are,
Or Sir Agrippa, for profound
And solid lying much renowned.
He Anthroposophus and Fludd   535
And Jacob Behmen understood,[n]
Knew many an amulet and charm
That would do neither good nor harm;
In Rosicrucian lore[n] as learned
As he that *vere adeptus* earned.   540
He understood the speech of birds
As well as they themselves do words;
Could tell what subtlest parrots mean,
That speak and think contrary clean;
What member 'tis of whom they talk   545
When they cry 'Rope', and 'Walk, knave, walk'.
He'd extract numbers out of matter
And keep them in a glass, like water,
Of sovereign power to make men wise;
For, dropped in blear, thick-sighted eyes,   550
They'd make them see in darkest night,
Like owls, though purblind in the light.
By help of these, as he professed,
He had first matter[n] seen undressed.
He took her naked, all alone,   555
Before one rag of form was on.
The chaos[n] too he had descried,
And seen quite through, or else he lied;
Not that of pasteboard which men show
For groats at fair of Barthol'mew,   560

532 No nation in the world is more addicted to this occult philosophy than the
   wild Irish, as appears by the whole practice of their lives, of which see Camden
   in his description of Ireland.[n]
539 The fraternity of the Rosicrucians is very like the sect of the ancient *Gnostici*
   who called themselves so from the excellent learning they pretended to,
   although they were really the most ridiculous sots of all mankind.
540 *vere adeptus* is one that has commenced in their fanatic extravagance.

---

533 *Agrippa*: see p. 290.
545 *member*: i.e. of the secret fraternity of the Rosicrucians.
546 '*Rope*', and '*Walk, knave, walk*': words commonly taught to parrots (see
   John Lyly, *Midas*, I. ii).
559 *pasteboard*: used to make scenery for the puppet theatres at Bartholomew
   Fair, where the creation and history of the world were depicted.
540 note *vere adeptus*: 'truly adept'; the term used to describe a man skilled in
   alchemy. 'Commenced' is used in the sense of 'graduated'.

But its great-grandsire, first o'th' name,
Whence that and Reformation came;
Both cousin-germans, and right able
T'inveigle and draw in the rabble
(But Reformation was, some say,   565
O'th' younger house to puppet play).
He could foretell whats'ever was
By consequence to come to pass,
As death of great men, alterations,
Diseases, battles, inundations;   570
All this without th'eclipse of sun
Or dreadful comet he hath done
By inward light, a way as good
And easy to be understood;
But with more lucky hit than those   575
That use to make the stars depose,
Like knights o'th' post, and falsely charge
Upon themselves what others forge;
As if they were consenting to
All mischief in the world men do;   580
Or, like the devil, did tempt and sway 'em
To rogueries, and then betray 'em.
They'll search a planet's house to know
Who broke and robbed a house below;
Examine Venus and the Moon   585
Who stole a thimble or a spoon;
And though they nothing will confess,
Yet by their very looks can guess,
And tell what guilty aspect bodes,
Who stole, and who received the goods.   590
They'll question Mars, and by his look
Detect who 'twas that nimmed a cloak;
Make Mercury confess and peach
Those thieves which he himself did teach.
They'll find i'th' physiognomies   595
O'th' planets all men's destinies,

---

577 *knights of the post*: men who earned a living by giving false evidence.
583 Astrologers claimed to be able to discover thieves. A 'house' was a sign of
    the zodiac in which a planet was found.
589 *aspect*: the relative positions of the planets.
592 *nimmed*: stole.
593 *peach*: inform against.

Like him that took the doctor's bill,
And swallowed it instead o'th' pill;
Cast the nativity o'th' question,
And, from positions to be guessed on,   600
As sure as if they knew the moment
Of native's birth, tell what will come on't.
They'll feel the pulses of the stars
To find out agues, coughs, catarrhs,
And tell what crisis does divine   605
The rot in sheep, or mange in swine;
In men what gives or cures the itch,
What makes them cuckolds, poor or rich;
What gains or loses, hangs or saves;
What makes men great, what fools or knaves;   610
But not what wise, for only of those
The stars, they say, cannot dispose,
No more than can the astrologians.
There they say right, and like true Trojans.
This Ralpho knew, and therefore took   615
The other course, of which we spoke.

Thus was th'accomplished squire endued
With gifts and knowledge parlous shrewd.
Never did trusty squire with knight
Or knight with squier jump more right.   620
Their arms and equipage did fit,
As well as virtues, parts and wit.
Their valours too were of a rate,
And out they sallied at the gate.
Few miles on horseback had they jogged,   625
But fortune unto them turned dogged:
For they a sad adventure met
Of which we now prepare to treat.
But ere we venture to unfold
Achievements so resolved and bold,   630
We should, as learned poets use,
Invoke th'assistance of some muse

599 *cast the nativity*: draw up the horoscope.
602 *native*: person born under a particular planet.
605 *crisis*: conjunction of the planets.
614 *true Trojans*: good fellows (colloquial).
620 *jump*: coincide; agree.
626 *dogged*: cruel.

(However critics count it sillier
Than jugglers talking t'a familiar).[n]
We think 'tis no great matter which: 635
They're all alike; yet we shall pitch
On one that fits our purpose most,
Whom therefore thus do we accost:

Thou that with ale, or viler liquors,
Didst inspire Withers, Prynne and Vickars,[n]   640
And force them, though it were in spite
Of nature and their stars, to write;
Who, as we find in sullen writs,
And cross-grained works of modern wits,
With vanity, opinion, want,   645
The wonder of the ignorant,
The praises of the author, penned
By himself, or wit-ensuring friend,
The itch of picture in the front,
With bays, and wicked rhyme upon't,   650
All that is left o'th' forked hill
To make men scribble without skill,
Canst make a poet, spite of fate,
And teach all people to translate,
Though out of languages in which   655
They understand no part of speech,
Assist me but this once, I 'mplore,
And I shall trouble thee no more.

In western clime there is a town
To those that dwell therein well known;   660
Therefore there needs no more be said here,
We unto them refer our reader
(For brevity is very good
When w'are, or are not, understood).

640 This Vickars was a man of as great interest and authority in the late reformation as Prynne or Withers, and as able a poet. He translated Virgil's *Æneides*
into as horrible travesty in earnest as the French Scarron did in burlesque,
and was only outdone in his way by the politic author of *Oceana*.[n]

634 *jugglers*: magicians. *familiar*: attendant spirit or demon.
648 Cf. p. 259.
649 *itch of*: restless desire for.
651 *the forked hill*: Parnassus, the mountain sacred to the muses, which has two
prominent peaks.

To this town people did repair   665
On days of market or of fair,
And to cracked fiddle and hoarse tabor
In merriment did drudge and labour.
But now a sport more formidable
Had raked together village rabble.   670
'Twas an old way of recreating,
Which learned butchers call bear-baiting;
A bold, adventurous exercise,
With ancient heroes in high prize;
For authors do affirm it came   675
From Isthmian or Nemean game;
Others derive it from the bear
That's fixed in northern hemisphere,
And round about the pole does make
A circle, like a bear at stake,   680
That at the chain's end wheels about,
And overturns the rabble-rout.
For, after solemn proclamation
In the bear's name (as is the fashion,
According to the law of arms,   685
To keep men from inglorious harms)
That none presume to come so near
As forty foot of stake of bear;[n]
If any yet be so foolhardy
T'expose themselves to vain jeopardy;   690
If they come wounded off and lame,
No honour's got by such a maim;
Although the bear gain much, being bound
In honour to make good his ground
When he's engaged, and take no notice   695
If any press upon him, who 'tis,
But let them know at their own cost
That he intends to keep his post.
This to prevent, and other harms
Which always wait on feats of arms   700
(For in the hurry of a fray
'Tis hard to keep out of harm's way),
Thither the knight his course did steer,
To keep the peace 'twixt dog and bear,

676 *Isthmian or Nemean game*: games formerly held by the Greeks at Corinth
and Nemea in honour of the gods.

As he believed h'was bound to do   705
In conscience and commission too,
And therefore thus bespoke the squire:

'We that are wisely mounted higher
Than constables, in curule wit,
When on tribunal bench we sit,   710
Like speculators should foresee,
From pharos of authority,
Portended mischiefs, farther then
Low, proletarian tithing-men.
And therefore, being informed by bruit   715
That dog and bear are to dispute;
For so of late men fighting name,
Because they often prove the same
(For where the first does hap to be,
The last does *coincidere*);   720
Quantum in nobis, have thought good
To save th'expense of Christian blood,
And try if we by mediation
Of treaty and accommodation
Can end the quarrel, and compose   725
The bloody duel without blows.
Are not our liberties, our lives,
The laws, religion and our wives[n]
Enough at once to lie at stake
For Covenant and the cause's sake;[n]   730
But in that quarrel dogs and bears,
As well as we, must venture theirs?
This feud, by Jesuits invented,
By evil counsel is fomented.[n]

708 This speech is set down as it was delivered by the knight in his own words.
But, since it is below the gravity of heroical poetry to admit of humour, but all
men are obliged to speak wisely alike, and too much of so extravagant a folly
would become tedious and impertinent, the rest of his harangues have only his
sense expressed in other words, unless in some few places where his own words
could not be so well avoided.

706 *in conscience and commission*: as a Puritan and a Justice of the Peace.
711 *speculators*: watchmen; sentries.
712 *pharos*: lighthouse; originally an island off Alexandria where a famous
lighthouse stood.
713 *then*: than (the spelling generally used by Butler).
714 *tithing-men*: petty constables; parish officers.
721 *Quantum in nobis*: as far as lies in our power.

There is a Machiavellian plot   735
(Though every *nare olfact* it not),
A deep design in 't, to divide
The well-affected that confide,
By setting brother against brother
To claw and curry one another.   740
Have we not enemies *plus satis*,
That *cane et angue peius* hate us?
And shall we turn our fangs and claws
Upon our own selves without cause?
That some occult design doth lie   745
In bloody cynarctomachy,
Is plain enough to him that knows
How saints lead brothers by the nose.
I wish myself a pseudo-prophet,
But sure some mischief will come of it,   750
Unless by providential wit
Or force we averruncate it.
For what design, what interest
Can beast have to encounter beast?
They fight for no espoused cause,[n]   755
Frail privilege, fundamental laws,
Nor for a thorough reformation,
Nor Covenant, nor Protestation,
Nor liberty of consciences,
Nor lords' and commons' ordinances,   760
Nor for the church, nor for church lands,
To get them in their own no hands,

---

746 Cynarctomachy signifies nothing in the world but a fight between dogs and
bears, though both the learned and ignorant agree that in such words very
great knowledge is contained, and our knight as one, or both, of those was of
the same opinion.
752 Another of the same kind which, though it appear ever so learned and profound, means nothing else but the weeding of corn.

---

736 *nare olfact*: nose does not scent it.
738 *well-affected*: a term used by the Puritans to describe those sympathetic to
their cause, who were also known as persons in whom one could 'confide'.
740 *claw and curry*: beat and thrash.
741 *plus satis*: 'more than enough.'
742 *cane et angue peius*: 'worse than dog and snake' (proverbial).
762 *no hands*: i.e. paws.

Nor evil counsellors to bring
To justice that seduce the king,
Nor for the worship of us men,   765
Though we have done as much for them.
Th'Egyptians worshipped dogs, and for
Their faith made fierce and zealous war;
Others adored a rat, and some
For that church suffered martyrdom;   770
The Indians fought for the truth
Of th'elephant, and monkey's tooth,
And many, to defend that faith,
Fought it out *mordicus* to death;
But no beast ever was so slight   775
For man, as for his god, to fight.
They have more wit, alas, and know
Themselves and us better than so.
But we, we only, do infuse
The rage in them like *boutefeus*.   780
'Tis our example that instils
In them th'infection of our ills.
For, as some late philosophers[n]
Have well observed, beasts that converse
With man, take after him, as hogs   785
Get pigs all th'year, and bitches dogs.
Just so by our example cattle
Learn to give one another battle.

771 The history of the white elephant and the monkey's tooth, which the Indians adored, is written by Monsieur le Blanc. This monkey's tooth was taken by the Portuguese from those that worshipped it and, though they offered a vast ransom for it, yet the Christians were persuaded by their priests rather to burn it. But as soon as the fire was kindled, all the people present were not able to endure the horrible stink that came from it, as if the fire had been made of the same ingredients with which seamen use to compose that kind of granadoes which they call stinkards.

780 *Boutefeus* is a French word and therefore it were uncivil to suppose any English person (especially of quality) ignorant of it or so ill-bred as to need an exposition.

---

763 *evil counsellors*: see note to I. i. 734, p. 291.

767 *dogs*: The Egyptian god Anubis was represented as a man with the head of a dog.

769 *rat*: The Egyptians are also said to have worshipped the ichneumon, a kind of mongoose.

774 *mordicus*: 'with the teeth'; tenaciously.

780 *boutefeus*: incendiaries.

771 note *le Blanc*: Vincent le Blanc, author of *Les Voyages fameux*, Paris, 1648, published in English as *The World Surveyed*, 1660. *granadoes*: grenades.

We read in Nero's time, the heathen,
When they destroyed the Christian brethren,   790
They sewed them in the skins of bears,
And then set dogs about their ears;[n]
From whence, no doubt, th'invention came
Of this lewd, anti-Christian game.'

To this, quoth Ralpho, 'Verily,   795
The point seems very plain to me.
It is an anti-Christian game,
Unlawful both in thing and name.
First for the name: the word "bear baiting"
Is carnal, and of man's creating;   800
For certainly there's no such word
In all the scripture on record;
Therefore unlawful and a sin.
And so is, secondly, the thing:
A vile assembly 'tis, that can   805
No more be proved by scripture than
Provincial, classic, national,
Mere human creature-cobwebs all.
Thirdly, it is idolatrous;
For when men run a-whoring thus   810
With their inventions, whatsoe'er
The thing be, whether dog or bear,
It is idolatrous and pagan
No less than worshipping of Dagon.'

Quoth Hudibras, 'I smell a rat.   815
Ralpho, thou dost prevaricate.
For though the thesis which thou lay'st
Be true *ad amussim* as thou say'st
(For that bear-baiting should appear
Jure divino lawfuller   820
Than synods are, thou dost deny,
Totidem verbis so do I),

---

807 *Provincial, classic, national*: the names of the various assemblies which the
  Presbyterians proposed to establish for the administration of the Church.
810–11 An allusion to Psalm 106: 39.
814 *Dagon*: a god worshipped by the Philistines of the Old Testament.
818 *ad amussim*: 'according to the rule'; exactly.
820 *Jure divino*: 'according to divine law'.
822 *totidem verbis*: 'in so many words'.

Yet there's a fallacy in this;
For if by sly homoeosis
Thou wouldst sophistically imply   825
Both are unlawful, I deny.'

'And I', quoth Ralpho, 'do not doubt
But bear-baiting may be made out
In gospel times as lawful as is
Provincial or parochial classis;   830
And that both are so near of kin,
And like in all, as well as sin,
That, put them in a bag and shake 'em,
Yourself o'th' sudden would mistake 'em,
And not know which is which, unless   835
You measure by their wickedness;
For 'tis not hard t'imagine whether
O'th' two is worst, though I name neither.'

Quoth Hudibras, 'Thou offerest much,
But art not able to keep touch.   840
Mira de lente, as 'tis i'th' adage,
Id est, to make a leek a cabbage.
Thou canst at best but overstrain
A paradox, and th'own hot brain.
For what can synods have at all   845
With bears that's analogical?
Or what relation has debating
Of church affaiers with bear-baiting?
A just comparison still is
Of things *eiusdem generis*.   850
And then what genus rightly doth
Include and comprehend them both?
If animal, both of us may
As justly pass for bears as they;

824 *homoeosis*: 'a making like'; the substitution of a similar thing for the thing
   itself.
830 *Provincial or parochial classis*: assembly of the Presbyterian Church drawn
   from a province or a parish.
840 *keep touch*: stick to the truth.
841 *Mira de lente*: a proverb, the original meaning of which is obscure but was
   probably 'to serve a pea as if it were a feast'.
850 *eiusdem generis*: 'of the same genus'.

For we are animals no less,   855
Although of different specieses.
But, Ralpho, this is no fit place
Nor time to argue out the case;
For now the field is not far off
Where we must give the world a proof   860
Of deeds, not words, and such as suit
Another manner of dispute;
A controversy that affords
Actions for arguments, not words,
Which we must manage at a rate   865
Of prowess and conduct adequate
To what our place and fame doth promise,
And all the godly expect from us.
Nor shall they be deceived, unless
We're slurred and outed by success: 870
Success, the mark no mortal wit
Or surest hand can always hit;
For, whatsoe'er we perpetrate,
We do but row; we're steered by fate,
Which in success oft disinherits,   875
For spurious causes, noblest merits.
Great actions are not always true sons
Of great and mighty resolutions;
Nor do the bold'st attempts bring forth
Events still equal to their worth,   880
But sometimes fail, and in their stead
Fortune and cowardice succeed.
Yet we have no great cause to doubt:
Our actions still have borne us out,
Which, though they're known to be so ample,   885
We need not copy from example.
We're not the only person durst
Attempt this province, nor the first:
In northern clime a valorous knight
Did whilom kill his bear in fight   890
And wound a fiddler.[n] We have both
Of these the objects of our wroth,
And equal fame and glory from
Th'attempt or victory to come.

---

870 *slurred*: cheated. *success*: the outcome.

'Tis sung, there is a valiant Mameluke 895
In foreign land, ycleped ——,[n]
To whom we have been oft compared
For person, parts, address and beard;
Both equally reputed stout,
And in the same cause both have fought. 900
He oft in such attempts as these
Came off with glory and success;
Nor will we fail in th'execution
For want of equal resolution.
Honour is, like a widow, won 905
With brisk attempt and putting on;
With entering manfully and urging;
Not slow approaches, like a virgin.'

This said, as once the Phrygian knight,
So ours with rusty steel did smite 910
His Trojan horse, and just as much
He mended pace upon the touch;
But from his empty stomach groaned,
Just as that hollow beast did sound,
And angry answered from behind 915
With brandished tail and blast of wind.
So have I seen with armed heel
A wight bestride a commonweal;
While still the more he kicked and spurred,
The less the sullen jade has stirred. 920

909 *Phrygian knight*: Laocoon, who attempted to warn the Trojans of the danger of the wooden horse (Virgil, *Aenid*, ii. 50–3).
918 *wight*: presumably Oliver Cromwell who rose to power and ruled the country with the help of the 'armed heel' of the army.

CANTO II

THE ARGUMENT

The catalogue and character
Of th'enemy's best men of war,
Whom, in a bold harangue, the knight
Defies and challenges to fight.
H'encounters Talgol, routs the bear
And takes the fiddler prisoner;
Conveys him to enchanted castle,
There shuts him fast in wooden bastille.

There was an ancient, sage philosopher[n]
That had read Alexander Ross over,
And swore the world, as he could prove,
Was made of fighting and of love:
Just so romances are, for what else   5
Is in them all but love and battels?
O'th' first of these we've no great matter
To treat of, but a world o'th' latter,
In which to do the injured right
We mean, in what concerns just fight.   10
Certes our authors are to blame,
For to make some well-sounding name
A pattern fit for modern knights
To copy out in frays and fights
(Like those that a whole street do raze   15
To build a palace in the place).
They never care how many others
They kill, without regard of mothers,
Or wives, or children, so they can
Make up some fierce, dead-doing man,   20

---

2 *Alexander Ross:* a prolific writer of theological and historical works (1590–1654).
20 *dead-doing:* murderous.

Composed of many ingredient valours,
Just like the manhood of nine tailors.
So a wild Tartar, when he spies
A man that's handsome, valiant, wise,
If he can kill him, thinks t'inherit   25
His wit, his beauty and his spirit,
As if just so much he enjoyed
As in another is destroyed.[n]
For, when a giant's slain in fight,
And mowed o'erthwart, or cleft downright,   30
It is a heavy case, no doubt,
A man should have his brains beat out
Because he's tall and has large bones,
As men kill beavers for their stones.
But as for our part, we shall tell   35
The naked truth of what befell,
And, as an equal friend to both
The knight and bear, but more to troth,[n]
With neither faction shall take part,
But give to each his due desert,   40
And never coin a formal lie on't
To make the knight o'ercome the giant.
This being professed we hope 's enough,
And now go on where we left off.

They rode, but authors having not   45
Determined whether pace or trot
(That is to say, whether 'tollutation',
As they do term 't, or 'succussation'),[n]
We leave it, and go on, as now
Suppose they did, no matter how   50
(Yet some from subtle hints have got
Mysterious light it was a trot.
But let that pass). They now begun
To spur their living engines on.
For, as whipped tops and bandied balls,   55
The learned hold, are animals,[n]

22 An allusion to the proverb 'Nine tailors make but one man'.
34 An oily substance known as castoreum was formerly extracted from the
   testicles of beavers and used as a medicine (Pliny, *Natural History*, xxxii. iii.
   13).

So horses they affirm to be
Mere engines made by geometry,[n]
And were invented first from engines,
As Indian Britons were from penguins.   60
So let them be. And, as I was saying,
They their live engines plied, not staying
Until they reached the fatal champaign
Which th'enemy did then encamp on,
The dire Pharsalian plain[n] where battle   65
Was to be waged 'twixt puissant cattle
And fierce auxiliary men
That came to aid their bretheren,
Who now began to take the field
As from his steed the knight beheld.   70
For, as our modern wits behold,
Mounted a pick-back on the old,
Much further off, much further he,
Raised on his aged beast could see,
Yet not sufficient to descry   75
All postures of the enemy.
And therefore orders the bold squire
T'advance and view their body nigher
That, when their motions he had known,
He might know how to fit his own.   80
Meanwhile he stopped his willing steed
To fit himself for martial deed.
Both kinds of metal he prepared,
Either to give blows or to ward,
Courage within and steel without,   85
To give or to receive a rout.
His death-charged pistols he did fit well,
Drawn out from life-preserving victual.
These being primed, with force he laboured
To free sword from retentive scabbard   90

60 The American Indians call a great bird they have, with a white head, a
penguin, which signifies the same thing in the British tongue; from whence,
with other words of the same kind, some authors[n] have endeavoured to prove
that the Americans are originally derived from the Britons.

60 and note *Britons*: Welshmen. *British*: Welsh.
65 *Pharsalian*: the plain on which Julius Caesar won a final battle against
Pompey.
83 *both kinds*: metal and mettle.

And, after many a painful pluck,
He cleared at length the rugged tuck,
Then shook himself to see that prowess
In scabbard of his arms sat loose,
And, raised upon his desperate foot,   95
On stirrup side he gazed about,
Portending blood, like blazing star,
The beacon of approaching war.
The squire advanced with greater speed
Than could b'expected from his steed,   100
But far more in returning made,
For now the foe he had surveyed,
Ranged, as to him they did appear,
With van, main battle, wings and rear.

In th'head of all this warlike rabble   105
Crowdero marched, expert and able:
Instead of trumpet and of drum
That makes the warrior's stomach come,
Whose noise whets valour sharp, like beer
By thunder turned to vinegar   110
(For if a trumpet sound or drum beat,
Who has not a month's mind to combat?),
A squeaking engine he applied
Unto his neck on north-east side,
Just where the hangman does dispose   115
To special friends the fatal noose
(For 'tis great grace when statesmen straight
Dispatch a friend, let others wait).
His warped ear hung o'er the strings,
Which was but souse to chitterlings;   120
For guts, some write, ere they are sodden,
Are fit for music or for pudden,
From whence men borrow every kind
Of minstrelsy by string or wind.
His grizzly beard was long and thick,   125
With which he strung his fiddle stick,

92 *tuck*: sword.
106 *Crowdero*: a fiddler, so called because he plays on a 'crowd' or fiddle.
110 *by thunder*: it was believed that wine was turned sour by thunder.
119 *warped*: shrivelled.
121 *sodden*: boiled.

For he to horse tail scorned to owe
For what on his own chin did grow.
Chiron, the four-legged bard, had both
A beard and tail of his own growth,   130
And yet by authors 'tis averred
He made use only of his beard.
In Staffordshire, where virtuous worth
Does raise the minstrelsy, not birth;
Where bulls do choose the boldest king   135
And ruler o'er the men of string[n]
(As once in Persia, 'tis said,
Kings were proclaimed by a horse that neighed),[n]
He, bravely venturing at a crown,
By chance of war was beaten down   140
And wounded sore. His leg, then broke,
Had got a deputy of oak;
For when a shin in fight is cropped,
The knee with one of timber's propped;
Esteemed more honourable than the other,   145
And takes place, though the younger brother.

Next marched brave Orsin, famous for
Wise conduct, and success in war;
A skilful leader, stout, severe,
Now marshal to the champion bear.   150
With truncheon tipped with iron head
The warrior to the lists he led,
With solemn march and stately pace,
But far more grave and solemn face;
Grave as the Emperor of Pegu,[n]   155
Or Spanish potentate Don Diego.
This leader was of knowledge great,
Either for charge or for retreat;
Knew when t'engage his bear pell-mell
And when to bring him off as well.   160

---

129 *Chiron*: the most famous of the centaurs, celebrated for his skill in music as
   well as the other arts.
132 This curious piece of mythology was apparently invented by Butler.
146 *place*: precedence.
147 *Orsin*: a bear-warden. His name is coined from Latin *ursus*, Italian *orso*, a
   bear.
156 *Don Diego*: a colloquialism for a foreigner, especially a Spaniard.

So lawyers, lest the bear defendant
And plaintiff dog should make an end on 't,
Do stave and tail with writs of error,
Reverse of judgement and demurrer,[n]
To let them breathe awhile, and then   165
Cry 'Whoop!' and set them on again.
As Romulus a wolf did rear,
So he was dry-nursed by a bear
That fed him with the purchased prey
Of many a fierce and bloody fray;   170
Bred up where discipline most rare is
In military Garden Paris.
For soldiers heretofore did grow
In gardens, just as weeds do now,
Until some splay-foot politicians[n]   175
T'Apollo offered up petitions
For licensing a new invention
They'd found out, of an antique engine,
To root out all the weeds that grow
In public garden at a blow   180
And leave th'herbs standing. Quoth Sir Sun,
'My friends, that is not to be done'.
'Not done?' quoth statesmen, 'Yes, an't please ye.
When 'tis once known you'll say 'tis easy.'
'Why then, let's know it!' quoth Apollo.   185
'We'll beat a drum and they'll all follow.'
'A drum?' quoth Phoebus, 'Troth that's true;
A pretty invention, quaint and new.
But though of voice and instrument
We are, 'tis true, chief president,   190
We such loud music do not profess:
The devil's master of that office,
Where it must pass, if 't be a drum.
He'll sign it with *Cler. Parl. Dom. Com.*

163 *stave and tail*: terms used in bear-baiting; to hold back a bear or dog with a
staff and to pull a dog by the tail.
167 *Romulus*: the legendary founder of Rome who, with his brother Remus,
was said to have been abandoned at birth and to have been suckled and kept
alive by a she-wolf.
172 *Garden Paris*: Paris Garden was an arena in Southwark used for bear-
baiting.
194 *Cler. Parl. Dom. Com.*: the abbreviation of the Latin title of the Clerk to
the House of Commons, who signed Ordinances and correspondence published
in the name of the Commons.

To him apply yourselves, and he   195
Will soon dispatch you for his fee.'
They did so, but it proved so ill,
They'd better have let them grow there still.

But to resume what we discoursing
Were on before, that is stout Orsin: 200
That which so oft by sundry writers
Has been applied t'almost all fighters
More justly may b'ascribed to this
Than any other warrior, *viz*:
None ever acted both parts bolder,   205
Both of a chieftain and a soldier.
He was of great descent and high
For splendour and antiquity,
And from celestial origine
Derived himself in a right line;   210
Not as the ancient heroes did,
Who, that their base births might be hid
(Knowing they were of doubtful gender
And that they came in at a windore),
Made Jupiter himself and others   215
O'th' gods gallants to their own mothers,
To get on them a race of champions
(Of which old Homer first made lampoons).
Arctophylax in northern sphere
Was his undoubted ancestor;   220
From him his great forefathers came,
And in all ages bore his name.
Learned he was in med'cinal lore,
For by his side a pouch he wore,
Replete with strange hermetic powder   225
That wounds nine miles point-blank would
     solder,[n]
By skilful chemist with great cost
Extracted from a rotten post,

213 *gender*: birth.
214 *at a windore*: were illegitimate (proverbial). Butler's spelling is preserved
here for the sake of the rhyme.
219 *Arctophylax*: 'the bear-keeper'; the name of a northern constellation situ-
ated at the tail of the Great Bear.

But of a heav'nlier influence
Than that which mountebanks dispense,   230
Though by Promethean fier made,
As they do quack that drive that trade.
For, as when slovens do amiss
At others' doors by stool or piss,
The learned write, a red-hot spit,   235
Being prudently applied to it,
Will convey mischief from the dung
Unto the part that did the wrong,[n]
So this did healing, and as sure
As that did mischief, this would cure.   240

Thus virtuous Orsin was endued
With learning, conduct, fortitude
Incomparable; and, as the prince
Of poets, Homer, sung long since,
A skilful leech is better far   245
Than half a hundred men of war,
So he appeared, and by his skill,
No less than dint of sword, could kill.

The gallant Bruin marched next him,
With visage formidably grim,   250
And rugged as a Saracen
Or Turk of Mahomet's own kin,
Clad in a mantle *della guer*
Of rough, impenetrable fur,
And in his nose, like Indian king,   255
He wore for ornament a ring;
About his neck a three-fold gorget,
As tough as trebled leathern target;
'Armed', as heralds cant, and 'langued',
Or, as the vulgar say, sharp-fanged.   260
For, as the teeth in beasts of prey
Are swords with which they fight in fray,
So swords in men of war are teeth
Which they do eat their victual with.

245 *leech*: doctor. The allusion is to Homer, *Iliad*, xi. 514–15.
258 *target*: shield.
259 *armed* and *langued*: When, in heraldry, a beast is represented with teeth or
   a tongue of a different tincture from its body, it is said to be armed or langued.

He was by birth, some authors write,   265
A Russian, some a Muscovite,
And 'mong the Cossacks had been bred,
Of whom we in diurnals read,
That serve to fill up pages here
As with their bodies ditches there.[n]   270
Scrimansky was his cousin-german,
With whom he served and fed on vermin,
And when these failed he'd suck his claws
And quarter himself upon his paws.
And though his countrymen, the Huns,   275
Did use to stew between their bums
And their warm horses' backs their meat,
And every man his saddle eat,
He was not half so nice as they,
But ate it raw when't came in 's way.   280
He had traced countries far and near
More than le Blanc, the traveller,
Who writes, he spoused in India
Of noble house a lady gay,
And got on her a race of worthies   285
As stout as any upon earth is.
Full many a fight for him between
Talgol and Orsin oft had been,

275 This custom of the Huns is described by Ammianus Marcellinus. *Hunii
    semicruda cuiusvis pecoris carne vescuntur, quam inter femora sua et equorum
    terga subsertam, fotu calefaciunt brevi.* Pag. 686.
283 This story in le Blanc, of a bear that married a king's daughter, is no more
    strange than many others in most travellers that pass with allowance, for if
    they should write nothing but what is possible or probable they might appear
    to have lost their labour and observed nothing but what they might have done
    as well at home.

---

268 *diurnals*: newspapers.
271 *Scrimansky*: possibly the name of a well-known bear. The name suggests
    Latin *scrimatur*, 'roars'.
273 Young bears were popularly supposed to feed themselves on their own
    paws (Pliny, *Natural History*, VIII. xxxvi. 54).
279 *nice*: refined.
282 *le Blanc*: see note to I. i. 771.
288 *Talgol*: a butcher. His name means 'cutthroat' from Italian *tagliare* and
    gola.
275 note: 'The Huns feed on the half-raw flesh of any beast, which they place
    between their own thighs and the backs of their horses and give them a short
    heating' (Ammianus Marcellinus, xxxi. 2).

Each striving to deserve the crown
Of a saved citizen.[n] The one　　　　　　290
To guard his bear, the other fought
To aid his dog, both made more stout
By several spurs of neighbourhood,
Church fellow-membership, and blood.
But Talgol, mortal foe to cows,　　　　　　295
Never got ought of him but blows;
Blows hard and heavy, such as he
Had lent, repayed with usury.

Yet Talgol was of courage stout,
And vanquished oftener than he fought;　　300
Inured to labour, sweat and toil,
And, like a champion, shone with oil.
Right many a widow his keen blade,
And many fatherless, had made.
He many a boar and huge dun cow　　　　305
Did, like another Guy, o'erthrow;
But Guy with him in fight compared
Had like the boar or dun cow fared.
With greater troops of sheep he'd fought
Than Ajax or bold Don Quixote,[n]　　　　310
And many a serpent of fell kind,
With wings before and stings behind
Subdued, as poets say long agone
Bold Sir George Saint George did the dragon.
Nor engine, nor device polemic,　　　　　315
Disease, nor doctor epidemic,
Though stored with deletery medicines
(Which whosoever took is dead since),
E'er sent so vast a colony
To both the underworlds as he.　　　　　　320
For he was of that noble trade
That demigods and heroes made,
Slaughter and knocking on the head,
The trade to which they all were bred,
And is, like others, glorious when　　　　　325
'Tis great and large, but base if mean.

---

306 *another Guy*: Guy of Warwick, a hero of popular ballads and romances,
whose exploits included the killing of a boar and a huge cow.

The former rides in triumph for it,
The latter in a two-wheeled chariot,
For daring to profane a thing
So sacred, with vile bungleing.   330

Next these the brave Magnano came,
Magnano, great in martial fame;
Yet, when with Orsin he waged fight,
'Tis sung he got but little by't.
Yet he was fierce as forest boar,   335
Whose spoils upon his back he wore,
As thick as Ajax' seven-fold shield,
Which o'er his brazen arms he held.
But brass was feeble to resist
The fury of his armed fist,   340
Nor could the hardest iron hold out
Against his blows, but they would through't.

In magic he was deeply read
As he that made the brazen head;
Profoundly skilled in the black art   345
As English Merlin[n] for his heart,
But far more skilful in the spheres
Than he was at the sieve and shears.[n]
He could transform himself in colour
As like the devil as a collier;   350
As like as hypocrites in show
Are to true saints, or crow to crow.

Of warlike engines he was author,
Devised for quick despatch of slaughter.
The cannon, blunderbuss and saker   355
He was th'inventor of and maker.
The trumpet and the kettle-drum
Did both from his invention come.

328 *chariot*: the cart in which prisoners were taken to the gallows.
331 *Magnano*: Italian for a locksmith. It is clear from the poem, however, that
he is a tinker.
337 *shield*: *Iliad*, vii. 222.
344 *brazen head* made, according to popular legend, by the philosopher Roger
Bacon.
350 The devil was popularly thought to be black in colour. Cf. II. i. 399–400.
355 *saker*: small cannon.

He was the first that e'er did teach
To make, and how to stop a breach.   360
A lance he bore with iron pike;
Th'one half would thrust, the other strike,
And when their forces he had joined
He scorned to turn his parts behind.

He Trulla loved, Trulla more bright   365
Than burnished armour of her knight;
A bold virago, stout and tall
As Joan of France or English Mall.
Through perils both of wind and limb,
Through thick and thin she followed him   370
In every adventure h'undertook
And never him or it forsook.
At breach of wall or hedge-surprise
She shared in th'hazard and the prize;
At beating quarters up or forage   375
Behaved herself with matchless courage,
And laid about in fight more busily
Than th'Amazonian dame Penthesile.
And, though some critics here cry shame[n]
And say our authors are to blame   380
That (spite of all philosophers
Who hold no females stout but bears,[n]
And heretofore did so abhor
Their women should pretend to war,
They would not suffer the stout'st dame   385
To swear by Hercules his name)
Make feeble ladies in their works
To fight like termagants and Turks;

---

385 The old Romans had particular oaths for men and women to swear by and
therefore Macrobius says *Viri per Castorem non iurabant antiquitus nec mulieres
per Herculem, Aedepol autem ijuramentum erat tam mulieribus quam viris
commune &c.*

---

365 *Trulla*: coined from 'trull', a whore.
368 *Mall*: probably Mary Ambree, the Amazonian heroine of an English ballad
(*Percy's Reliques*, ed. Wheatley, 1910, ii. 232).
378 *Penthesile*: Penthesilea, Queen of the Amazons, who fought in the Trojan
War (*Aeneid*, i. 490).
385 note: 'Men did not formerly swear by Castor nor women by Hercules but
the oath "edepol" was used by women and men alike.' Butler's source is not
Macrobius but Aulus Gellius, xi. vi.

To lay their native arms aside,
Their modesty, and ride astride;   390
To run a-tilt at men, and wield
Their naked tools in open field;
As stout Armida, bold Thalestris,
And she that would have been the mistress
Of Gondibert, but he had grace   395
And rather took a country lass;
They say 'tis false, without all sense,
But of pernicious consequence
To government, which they suppose
Can never be upheld in prose;[n]   400
Strip nature naked to the skin,[n]
You'll find about her no such thing.
It may be so, yet what we tell
Of Trulla that's improbable
Shall be deposed by those have seen't,   405
Or, what's as good, produced in print,
And if they will not take our word,
We'll prove it true upon record.

The upright Cerdon next advanced,
Of all his race the valiant'st,   410
Cerdon the great, renowned in song,
Like Herc'les, for repair of wrong.
He raised the low and fortified
The weak against the strongest side.
Ill has he read that never hit   415
On him in muse's deathless writ.
He had a weapon keen and fierce
That through a bull-hide shield would pierce

---

393 Two formidable women at arms in romances that were cudgelled into love
   by their gallants.

---

393 *Armida*: the enchantress in Tasso's *Gerusalemme Liberata*, who fought
   against the Christians.
393 *Thalestris*: a queen of the Amazons.
395 *Gondibert*: the hero of Davenant's poem of this name falls in love with a
   country girl, having previously been a suitor to Rhodalind, the heir to the
   throne.
409 *Cerdon*: a cobbler, from Latin *cerdo*, a craftsman. An 'upright' shoe was one
   which would fit either foot.

And cut it in a thousand pieces,
Though tougher than the knight of Greece his,   420
With whom his black-thumbed ancestor
Was comrade in the ten years war.
For when the restless Greeks sat down
So many years before Troy town,
And were renowned, as Homer writes,   425
For well-soled boots no less than fights,
They owed that glory only to
His ancestor that made them so.
Fast friend he was to reformation
Until 'twas worn quite out of fashion;   430
Next rectifier of wry law,
And would make three to cure one flaw;
Learned he was and could take note,
Transcribe, collect, translate and quote;
But preaching was his chiefest talent,   435
Or argument, in which being valiant,
He used to lay about and stickle,
Like ram or bull, at conventicle:
For disputants, like rams and bulls,
Do fight with arms that spring from skulls.   440

Last Colon came, bold man of war,
Destined to blows by fatal star;
Right expert in command of horse,
But cruel and without remorse.
That which of centaur long ago   445
Was said, and has been wrested to
Some other knights, was true of this:
He and his horse were of a piece.
One spirit did inform them both,
The self-same vigour, fury, wroth;   450
Yet he was much the rougher part
And always had a harder heart,
Although his horse had been of those
That fed on man's flesh, as fame goes.

420 *knight of Greece*: Ajax. See I. ii. 337.
426 *boots*: Homer refers to the Greeks as 'well-greaved'.
437 *stickle*: to be energetic.
441 *Colon*: from Latin *colonus*, a farmer.
454 The horses of Diomedes, King of Thrace. He was killed by Hercules and his
     body devoured by his own horses.

Strange food for horse! and yet, alas,   455
It may be true, for flesh is grass.
Sturdy he was, and no less able
Than Hercules to cleanse a stable;
As great a drover, and as great
A critic too in hog or neat.   460
He ripped the womb up of his mother,
Dame Tellus, 'cause she wanted fother
And provender wherewith to feed
Himself and his less cruel steed.
It was a question whether he   465
Or 's horse were of a family
More worshipful, till antiquaries
(After they'd almost pored out their eyes)
Did very learnedly decide
The business on the horse's side,   470
And proved not only horse, but cows,
Nay pigs were of the elder house:
For beasts, when man was but a piece
Of earth himself, did th'earth possess.

These worthies were the chief that led   475
The combatants, each in the head
Of his command, with arms and rage
Ready and longing to engage.
The numerous rabble was drawn out
Of several countries round about,   480
From villages remote and shires
Of east and western hemispheres.
From foreign parishes and regions,
Of different manners, speech, religions
Came men and mastiffs, some to fight   485
For fame and honour, some for sight.
And now the field of death, the lists,
Were entered by antagonists,
And blood was ready to be broached,
When Hudibras in haste approached   490

456 *flesh is grass*: Isaiah 40:6.
458 *Hercules*: his labours included the cleansing of the stables of Augeas where
   three thousand oxen had been kept.
459–60 Further allusions to the labours of Hercules in which he captured the
   Cretan bull and overcame a wild boar.
462 *Dame Tellus*: the earth.

With squire and weapons to attack them,
But first thus from his horse bespake them:

'What rage, O citizens, what fury
Doth you to these dire actions hurry?
What oestrum, what phrenetic mood   495
Makes you thus lavish of your blood,
While the proud Vies your trophies boast
And unrevenged walks —— ghost?[n]
What towns, what garrisons might you
With hazard of this blood subdue,   500
Which now you're bent to throw away
In vain, untriumphable fray?
Shall saints in civil bloodshed wallow
Of saints, and let the cause lie fallow?
The cause, for which we fought and swore   505
So boldly, shall we now give o'er?
Then because quarrels still are seen
With oaths and swearing to begin,
The Solemn League and Covenant
Will seem a mere god-damn-me rant,   510
And we that took it and have fought,
As lewd as drunkards that fall out.
For as we make war for the King
Against himself,[n] the self-same thing
Some will not stick to swear we do   515
For God and for religion too.
For if bear-baiting we allow,
What good can reformation do?
The blood and treasure that's laid out
Is thrown away and goes for nought.   520
Are these the fruits o'th' Protestation,
The prototype of reformation,
Which all the saints, and some since martyrs,

493–502 These lines are a parody of Lucan, *Pharsalia*, i. 8–14.
495 *oestrum*: a gadfly; hence, an irrational passion.
497 *Vies*: the old name for the town of Devizes in Wiltshire where in 1643 the
   Royalists won a celebrated victory.
502 *untriumphable*: after a victory in a civil war Roman leaders were not awarded
   the customary triumph.
509 *League*: see note p. 291.
521 *Protestation*: see note p. 292.

Wore in their hats like wedding-garters
When 'twas resolved by either house   525
Six Members' quarrel to espouse?[n]
Did they for this draw down the rabble[n]
With zeal and noises formidable,
And make all cries about the town
Join throats to cry the bishops down?   530
Who, having round begirt the palace
(As once a month they do the gallows),
As Members gave the sign about,
Set up their throats with hideous shout;
When tinkers bawled aloud to settle   535
Church discipline, for patching kettle;
No sow-gelder did blow his horn
To geld a cat, but cried "Reform";
The oyster-women locked their fish up
And trudged away to cry "No bishop";   540
The mousetrap-men laid save-alls by
And 'gainst ev'l counsellors did cry;
Botchers left old clothes in the lurch
And fell to turn and patch the church;
Some cried "The Covenant", instead   545
Of "Pudding-pies and gingerbread",
And some for broom, old boots and shoes,
Bawled out to purge the Commons' House;
Instead of "Kitchen-stuff", some cry
"A gospel-preaching ministry",   550
And some for old suits, coats or cloak,
"No surplices nor service book".[n]
A strange harmonious inclination
Of all degrees to reformation!

524 Some few days after the King had accused the five Members of treason in
the House of Commons, great crowds of the rabble came down to Westminster
Hall with printed copies of the Protestation tied in their hats like favours.

---

524 *wedding-garters*: lengths of ribbon worn by guests at a wedding.
537 *horn*: The sow-gelder announced his arrival by playing a tune on his horn.
541 *save-alls*: a type of candlestick which allowed the candle to burn away
and leave no waste. The same tradesmen sold both mousetraps and save-
alls.
542 *counsellors*: see note to I. i. 734, p. 291.
543 *botchers*: tailors who repair clothes.
545 *Covenant*: taken in 1638 by the Scottish Presbyterians in defence of their
Church against Laud's attempts to introduce the Anglican liturgy.

And is this all? Is this the end   555
To which these carryings on did tend?
Hath public faith[n] like a young heir
For this tak'n up all sorts of ware,
And run int' every tradesman's book
Till both turned bankrupts and are broke?   560
Did saints for this bring in their plate
And crowd as if they came too late?
For when they thought the cause had need on't,
Happy was he that could be rid on't.
Did they coin piss-pots, bowls and flagons   565
Int'officers of horse and dragoons,
And into pikes and musketeers
Stamp beakers, cups and porringers?
A thimble, bodkin and a spoon
Did start up living men as soon   570
As in the furnace they were thrown,
Just like the dragon's teeth b'ing sown.
Then was the cause all gold and plate,
The brethren's off'rings, consecrate
Like th'Hebrew calf, and down before it   575
The saints fell prostrate to adore it.
So say the wicked—and will you
Make that sarcasmous scandal true,
By running after dogs and bears,
Beasts more unclean than calves or steers?   580
Have pow'rful preachers plied their tongues
And laid themselves out and their lungs;
Used all means, both direct and sinister,
I'th' power of gospel-preaching minister?
Have they invented tones to win   585
The women, and make them draw in
The men, as Indians with a female
Tame elephant inveigle the male?[n]

---

578 'Abusive' or 'insulting' had been better, but our knight believed the learned
languages more convenient to understand in than his own mother tongue.

---

572 *dragon's teeth*: sown in the ground by Jason. They grew up as armed men
and attacked him (Apollonius Rhodius, *Argonautica*, iii. 1326–1407).
578 *sarcasmous*: coined from Latin *sarcasmos*, a gibe.
580 *unclean*: Leviticus, 11:26.
582 *laid themselves out*: expended themselves; a Puritan expression.
585 *tones*: see I. i. 228 and note.

Have they told prov'dence what it must do,
Whom to avoid and whom to trust to?   590
Discovered th'enemy's design,
And which way best to countermine;
Prescribed what ways it hath to work,
Or it will ne'er advance the kirk;
Told it the news o'th' last express,   595
And, after good or bad success,
Made prayers, not so like petitions
As overtures and propositions
(Such as the army did present
To their creator, th'parliament)ⁿ   600
In which they freely will confess
They will not, cannot acquiesce
Unless the work be carried on
In the same way they have begun,
By setting church and commonweal   605
All on a flame bright as their zeal
On which the saints were all agog—
And all this for a bear and dog?

'The parliament drew up petitionsⁿ
T'itself, and sent them, like commissions,   610
To well-affected persons down
In every city and great town,
With power to levy horse and men,
Only to bring them back again.
For this did many, many a mile,   615
Ride manfully in rank and file
With papers in their hats that showed
As if they to the pillory rode.
Have all these courses, these efforts,
Been tried by people of all sorts,   620
Velis et remis, omnibus nervis,
And all t'advance the cause's service?
And shall all now be thrown away
In petulant intestine fray?
Shall we that in the Covenantⁿ swore   625
Each man of us to run before

---

596 *success*: outcome.
621 *Velis et remis*: literally 'with sails and oars'; *omnibus nervis*: literally 'with
all strength'. Both expressions were proverbial.

Another still in reformation,
Give dogs and bears a dispensation?
How will dissenting brethren relish it?
What will malignants say? *Videlicet,*   630
That each man swore to do his best
To damn and perjure all the rest,
And bid the devil take the hinmost,
Which at this race is like to win most.
They'll say our business to reform   635
The church and state is but a worm;
For to subscribe, unsight, unseen,
T'an unknown church's discipline[n]
What is it else but beforehand
T'engage, and after understand?   640
For when we swore to carry on
The present reformation
According to the purest mode
Of churches best-reformed abroad,
What did we else but make a vow   645
To do we know not what nor how?
For no three of us will agree
Where, or what churches these should be,
And is, indeed, the self-same case
With theirs that swore Etceteras,[n]   650
Or the French League, in which men vowed
To fight to the last drop of blood.

650 The convocation in one of the short parliaments that ushered in the long one (as dwarfs are wont to do knights errant) made an oath to be taken by the clergy for observing of canonical obedience, in which they enjoined their brethren, out of the abundance of their consciences, to swear to articles with etcetera.

651 The Holy League in France, designed and made for the extirpation of the protestant religion, was the original out of which the Solemn League and Covenant here was (with difference only of circumstances) most faithfully transcribed. Nor did the success of both differ more than the intent and purpose; for after the destruction of vast numbers of people of all sorts, both ended with the murders of two kings whom they had sworn to defend, and, as our covenanters swore every man to run before another in the way of reformation, so did the French in the Holy League to fight to the last drop of blood.

629 *dissenting brethren*: members of the Puritan sects.
630 *malignants*: a term of abuse applied by the Puritans to the Royalists. See note to I. i. 734, p. 291.
636 *worm*: whim.

These slanders will be thrown upon
The cause and work we carry on,
If we permit men to run headlong   655
T'exorbitancies fit for Bedlam,
Rather than gospel-walking times
When slightest sins are greatest crimes.
But we the matter so shall handle
As to remove that odious scandal.   660
In name of king and parliament
I charge ye all, no more foment
This feud, but keep the peace between
Your brethren and your countrymen,
And to those places straight repair   665
Where your respective dwellings are.
But, to that purpose, first surrender
The fiddler, as the prime offender,
Th'incendiary vile that is chief
Author and engineer of mischief,   670
That makes division between friends
For profane and malignant ends.
He and that engine of vile noise
On which illegally he plays
Shall (*dictum factum*) both be brought   675
To condign punishment, as th'ought.
This must be done, and I would fain see
Mortal so sturdy as to gainsay;
For then I'll take another course,
And soon reduce you all by force.'   680
This said, he clapped his hand on sword
To show he meant to keep his word.

But Talgol, who had long suppressed
Enflamed wrath in glowing breast,
Which now began to rage and burn as   685
Implacably as flame in furnace,
Thus answered him: 'Thou vermin wretched
As e'er in measled pork was hatched!
Thou tail of worship that dost grow
On rump of justice as of cow!   690

656 *exorbitancies*: fits of madness.
671 *division*: meaning both 'dissension' and 'a musical descant'.
675 *dictum factum*: 'no sooner said than done'.

How darest thou, with that sullen luggage
O'thyself, old iron and other baggage,
With which thy steed of bones and leather
Has broke his wind in halting hither,
How darest th', I say, adventure thus   695
T'oppose thy lumber against us?
Could thine impertinence find out
No work t'employ itself about,
Where thou, secure from wooden blow,
Thy busy vanity might'st show?   700
Was no dispute afoot between
The caterwauling bretheren?
No subtle question raised among
Those out o'their wits and those i'th' wrong?
No prize between those combatants   705
O'th' times, the land and water saints,
Where thou might'st stickle without hazard
Of outrage to thy hide and mazard,
And not for want of business come
To us to be thus troublesome;   710
To interrupt our better sort
Of disputants, and spoil our sport?
Was there no felony, no bawd,
Cutpurse nor burglary abroad?
No stolen pig nor plundered goose   715
To tie thee up from breaking loose?
No ale unlicensed, broken hedge,
For which thou statute might'st allege,
To keep thee busy from foul evil
And shame due to thee from the devil?   720
Did no committee sit, where he
Might cut out journey-work for thee,
And set th'a task with subornation
To stitch up sale and sequestration,[n]
To cheat with holiness and zeal   725
All parties and the commonweal?
Much better had it been for thee
He'd kept thee where th'art used to be,
Or sent th'on business any whither,
So he had never brought thee hither.   730

706 An allusion to the controversy among the Puritan sects concerning the need for baptism by total immersion.

But if thou'st brain enough in skull
To keep within its lodging whole,
And not provoke the rage of stones
And cudgels to thy hide and bones,
Tremble, and vanish while thou may'st,   735
Which I'll not promise if thou stay'st.'

At this the knight grew high in wroth
And, lifting hands and eyes up both,
Three times he smote on stomach stout,
From whence at length these words broke out: 740

'Was I for this entitled Sir,
And girt with trusty sword and spur,
For fame and honour to wage battle,
Thus to be braved by foe to cattle?
Not all that pride that makes thee swell   745
As big as thou dost blown-up veal;
Nor all thy tricks and sleights to cheat,
And sell thy carrion for good meat;
Not all thy magic to repair
Decayed old age in tough, lean ware,   750
Make natural death appear thy work,
And stop the gangrene in stale pork;
Not all that force that makes thee proud,
Because by bullock ne'er withstood,
Though armed with all thy cleavers, knives   755
And axes made to hew down lives,
Shall save or help thee to evade
The hand of justice or this blade,
Which I, her sword-bearer, do carry
For civil deed and military;   760
Nor shall these words of venom base,
Which thou hast from their native place,
Thy stomach, pumped to fling on me,
Go unrevenged, though I am free.
Thou down the same throat shalt devour 'em,   765
Like tainted beef, and pay dear for 'em.
Nor shall it e'er be said that wight
With gauntlet blue and bases white,

764 *free*: guiltless.
768 *bases*: skirt of mail. Presumably he wears a butcher's apron.

And round, blunt dudgeon by his side,
So great a man at arms defied 770
With words far bitterer than wormwood,
That would in Job or Grizel stir mood.
Dogs with their tongues their wounds do heal,
But men with hands, as thou shalt feel.'

This said, with hasty rage he snatched 775
His gun-shot, that in holster watched,
And, bending cock, he levelled full
Against th'outside of Talgol's skull,
Vowing that he should ne'er stir further,
Nor henceforth cow or bullock murther. 780
But Pallas came in shape of rust,
And 'twixt the spring and hammer thrust
Her Gorgon shield, which made the cock
Stand stiff, as if 'twere turned t'a stock.
Meanwhile fierce Talgol, gath'ring might, 785
With rugged truncheon charged the knight,
And he his rusty pistol held
To take the blow on, like a shield.
The gun recoiled, as well it might,
Not used to such a kind of fight, 790
And shrunk from its great master's gripe,
Knocked down and stunned with mortal stripe.
Then Hudibras with furious haste
Drew out his sword, yet not so fast
But Talgol first with hardy thwack 795
Twice bruised his head and twice his back.
But when his nut-brown sword was out,
Courageously he laid about,
Imprinting many a wound upon
His mortal foe, the truncheon. 800
The trusty cudgel did oppose
Itself against dead-doing blows,

772 *Job or Grizel*: both Job and Griselda, the heroine of medieval romance, were
celebrated for their patience.
781 *Pallas*: the goddess Athene whose interventions in the action of Homer's
Iliad are here parodied.
783 *Gorgon shield*: the shield of Athene which bore the head of the Gorgon
Medusa and turned all who saw it into stone.
792 *stripe*: blow.

To guard its leader from fell bane,
And then revenged itself again.
And though the sword, some understood,   805
In force had much the odds of wood,
'Twas nothing so: both sides were ballanced
So equal, none knew which was valiant'st.
For wood with honour being engaged
Is so implacably enraged,   810
Though iron hew and mangle more,
Wood wounds and bruises honour more.
And now both knights were out of breath,
Tired in the hot pursuit of death,
While all the rest, amazed, stood still,   815
Expecting which should take or kill.
This Hudibras observed, and fretting
Conquest should be so long a-getting,
He drew up all his force into
One body, and that into one blow.   820
But Talgol wisely avoided it
By cunning sleight; for, had it hit,
The upper part of him the blow
Had slit, as sure as that below.

Meanwhile th'incomparable Colon   825
To aid his friend began to fall on.
Him Ralph encountered, and straight grew
A fierce dispute betwixt them two,
Th'one armed with metal, th'other wood;
This fit for bruise and that for blood.   830
With many a stiff thwack, many a bang,
Hard crab-tree and old iron rang,
While none that saw them could divine
To which side conquest would incline,
Until Magnano, who did envy   835
That two should with so many men vie,
By subtle stratagem of brain
Performed what force could ne'er attain.
For he, by foul hap having found
Where thistles grew on barren ground,   840
In haste he drew his weapon out
And, having cropped them from the root,

He clapped them under th'horse's tail
With prickles sharper than a nail.

The angry beast did straight resent   845
The wrong done to his fundament,
Began to kick and fling and wince,
As if he'd been beside his sense,
Striving to disengage from smart
And raging pain th'afflicted part.   850
Instead of which he threw the pack
Of squire and baggage from his back,
And, blund'ring still, with smarting rump,
He gave the champion's steed a thump
That staggered him. The knight did stoop   855
And sat on further side aslope.
This Talgol viewing, who had now
By flight escaped the fatal blow,
He rallied, and again fell to't;
For, catching him by nearer foot,   860
He lifted with such might and strength
As would have hurled him thrice his length
And dashed his brains (if any) out.
But Mars, that still protects the stout,
In pudding-time came to his aid   865
And under him the bear conveyed;
The bear, upon whose soft fur gown
The knight with all his weight fell down.
The friendly rug preserved the ground
And headlong knight from bruise or wound,   870
Like feather bed betwixt a wall
And heavy brunt of cannon-ball.
As Sancho on a blanket fell
And had no hurt,[n] ours fared as well
In body, though his mighty spirit,   875
B'ing heavy, did not so well bear it.
The bear was in a greater fright,
Beat down and worsted by the knight.
He roared and raged and flung about
To shake off bondage from his snout.   880
His wrath, enflamed, boiled o'er, and from
His jaws of death he threw the foam.

865 *pudding-time*: a lucky time (a proverbial phrase).

Fury in stranger postures threw him,
And more, than ever herald drew him.
He tore the earth, which he had saved   885
From squelch of knight, and stormed and raved,
And vexed the more, because the harms
He felt were 'gainst the Law of Arms;
For men he always took to be
His friends, and dogs the enemy,   890
Who never so much hurt had done him
As his own side did falling on him.
It grieved him to the guts that they
For whom he'd fought so many a fray,
And served with loss of blood so long,   895
Should offer such inhuman wrong,
Wrong of unsoldier-like condition,
For which he flung down his commission,
And laid about him, till his nose
From thrall of ring and cord broke loose.   900
Soon as he felt himself enlarged,
Through thickest of his foes he charged,
And made way through th'amazed crew.
Some he o'erran and some o'erthrew,
But took none; for, by hasty flight,   905
He strove t'avoid the conquering knight,
From whom he fled with as much haste
And dread as he the rabble chased.
In haste he fled, and so did they,
Each and his fear a several way.   910

Crowdero only kept the field,
Not stirring from the place he held,
Though beaten down and wounded sore
I'th' fiddle, and a leg that bore
One side of him, not that of bone,   915
But, much its betters, th'wooden one.
He, spying Hudibras lie strowed
Upon the ground like log of wood,
With fright of fall, supposed wound,
And loss of urine, in a swound,   920
In haste he snatched the wooden limb
That, hurt in th'ankle, lay by him,

And, fitting it for sudden fight,
Straight drew it up t'attack the knight.
For, getting up on stump and huckle, 925
He with the foe began to buckle,
Vowing to be revenged for breach
Of crowd and shin upon the wretch,
Sole author of all detriment
He and his fiddle underwent. 930

But Ralpho (who had now begun
T'adventure resurrection
From heavy squelch, and had got up
Upon his legs with sprained crup),
Looking about, beheld the bard 935
To charge the knight entranced prepared.
He snatched his whinyard up, that fled
When he was falling off his steed
(As rats do from a falling house)
To hide itself from rage of blows, 940
And, winged with speed and fury, flew
To rescue knight from black and blue.
Which e'er he could achieve, his sconce
The leg encountered twice and once,
And now 'twas raised to smite again, 945
When Ralpho thrust himself between.
He took the blow upon his arm
To shield the knight from further harm
And, joining wrath with force, bestowed
On th'wooden member such a load 950
That down it fell, and with it bore
Crowdero, whom it propped before.
To him the squire right nimbly run
And, setting his bold foot upon
His trunk, thus spoke: 'What desperate frenzy 955
Made thee, thou whelp of sin, to fancy
Thyself and all that coward rabble
T'encounter us in battle able?
How durst th', I say, oppose thy curship
'Gainst arms, authority and worship? 960

928 *crowd*: fiddle.
937 *whinyard*: a short sword.
944 *twice and once*: once or twice.

And Hudibras or me provoke,
Though all thy limbs were heart of oak,
And th'other half of thee as good
To bear out blows as that of wood?
Could not the whipping-post prevail   965
With all its rhetoric, nor the gaol,
To keep from flaying scourge thy skin,
And ankle free from iron gin?
Which now thou shalt —— but first our care
Must see how Hudibras doth fare.'   970

This said, he gently raised the knight
And set him on his bum upright.
To rouse him from lethargic dump,
He tweaked his nose with gentle thump,
Knocked on his breast, as if't had been   975
To raise the spirits lodged within.
They, wakened with the noise, did fly
From inward room to window eye
And, gently opening lid, the casement,
Looked out, but yet with some amazement.   980
This gladded Ralpho much to see,
Who thus bespoke the knight: quoth he,
Tweaking his nose, 'You are, great sir,
A self-denying conqueror,[n]
As high, victorious and great   985
As e'er fought for the churches yet,
If you will give yourself but leave
To make out what y'already have,
That's victory. The foe, for dread
Of your nine-worthiness,[n] is fled,   990
All save Crowdero, for whose sake
You did th'espoused cause undertake,
And he lies prisoner at your feet,
To be disposed as you think meet,
Either for life, or death, or sale,   995
The gallows, or perpetual gaol;
For one wink of your powerful eye
Must sentence him to live or die.
His fiddle is your proper purchase,
Won in the service of the churches,   1000

999 *proper purchase*: rightful booty.

And by your doom must be allowed
To be or be no more a crowd.
For though success did not confer
Just title on the conquerer;
Though dispensations were not strong   1005
Conclusions whether right or wrong;
Although outgoings did not confirm,
And owning were but a mere term;
Yet, as the wicked have no right
To th'creature, though usurped by might,   1010
The property is in the saint,
From whom th'injuriously detain 't.
Of him they hold their luxuries,
Their dogs, their horses, whores and dice,
Their riots, revels, masques, delights,   1015
Pimps, buffoons, fiddlers, parasites,
All which the saints have title to,
And ought t'enjoy, if they'd their due.
What we take from them is no more
Than what was ours by right before.   1020
For we are their true landlords still,
And they our tenants but at will.'

At this the knight begun to rouse
And by degrees grow valorous.
He stared about, and seeing none   1025
Of all his foes remain but one,
He snatched his weapon that lay near him,
And from the ground began to rear him,
Vowing to make Crowdero pay
For all the rest that ran away.   1030

But Ralpho now in colder blood
His fury mildly thus withstood:
'Great sir,' quoth he, 'your mighty spirit
Is raised too high. This slave does merit
To be the hangman's business, sooner   1035
Than from your hand to have the honour

1005 *dispensations*: interventions of divine providence.
1007 *outgoings*: another Puritan term for the intervention of providence.
1010 *creature*: material comforts; derived from New Testament usage.
1011 *in the saint*: legally invested in him.

Of his destruction. I that am
So much below in deed and name,
Did scorn to hurt his forfeit carcass,
Or ill entreat his fiddle or case.   1040
Will you, great sir, that glory blot
In cold blood which you gained in hot?
Will you employ your conquering sword
To break a fiddle and your word?
For though I fought and overcame   1045
And quarter gave, 'twas in your name.
For great commanders always own
What's prosperous by the soldier done.
To save, where you have power to kill,
Argues your power above your will,   1050
And that your will and power have less
Than both might have of selfishness.
This power, which now alive with dread
He trembles at, if he were dead
Would no more keep the slave in awe   1055
Than if you were a knight of straw:
For death would then be his conqueror,
Not you, and free him from that terror.
If danger from his life accrue,
Or honour from his death to you,   1060
'Twere policy and honour too
To do as you resolved to do.
But, sir, 'twould wrong your valour much
To say it needs or fears a crutch.
Great conquerors greater glory gain   1065
By foes in triumph led than slain.
The laurels that adorn their brows
Are pulled from living, not dead boughs,
And living foes. The greatest fame
Of cripple slain can be but lame.   1070
One half of him's already slain,
The other is not worth your pain.
Th'honour can but on one side light,
As worship did when y'were dubbed knight.
Wherefore I think it better far   1075
To keep him prisoner of war,
And let him fast in bonds abide,
At court of justice to be tried,

Where, if h'appear so bold or crafty,
There may be danger in his safety.   1080
If any member there dislike
His face, or to his beard have pike;
Or if his death will save, or yield,
Revenge, or fright, it is revealed.
Though he has quarter, ne'ertheless   1085
You've power to hang him when you please.
This hath been often done by some
Of our great conquerors (you know whom),[n]
And has by most of us been held
Wise justice, and to some revealed.   1090
For words and promises that yoke
The conqueror are quickly broke,
Like Samson's cuffs, though by his own
Direction and advice put on.
For if we should fight for the cause   1095
By rules of military laws,
And only do what they call just,
The cause would quickly fall to dust.
This we among ourselves may speak,
But to the wicked or the weak   1100
We must be cautious to declare
Perfection truths, such as these are.'

This said, the high outrageous mettle
Of knight began to cool and settle.
He liked the squire's advice, and soon   1105
Resolved to see the business done,
And therefore charged him first to bind
Crowdero's hands on rump behind,
And to its former place and use
The wooden member to reduce,   1110
But force it take an oath before
Ne'er to bear arms against him more.

Ralpho despatched with speedy haste,
And having tied Crowdero fast,

1082 *pike*: pique.
1084 *revealed*: i.e. as the will of God.
1093 *Samson's cuffs*: Judges 16:21.

He gave Sir Knight the end of cord 1115
To lead the captive of his sword
In triumph, while the steeds he caught,
And them to further service brought.
The squire in state rode on before,
And on his nut-brown whinyard bore 1120
The trophy fiddle and the case,
Placed on his shoulder like a mace.
The knight himself did after ride,
Leading Crowdero by his side,
And towed him if he lagged behind, 1125
Like boat against the tide and wind.
Thus grave and solemn they march on
Until quite through the town they'd gone,
At further end of which there stands
An ancient castle that commands 1130
Th'adjacent parts. In all the fabric
You shall not see one stone nor a brick,
But all of wood, by powerful spell
Of magic made impregnable.
There's neither iron bar, nor gate, 1135
Portcullis, chain, nor bolt, nor grate,
And yet men durance there abide
In dungeon scarce three inches wide,
With roof so low that under it
They never stand, but lie or sit; 1140
And yet so foul that whoso is in
Is to the middle leg in prison,
In circle magical confined
With walls of subtle air and wind,
Which none are able to break thorough 1145
Until they're freed by head of borough.
Thither arrived, th'advent'rous knight
And bold squire from their steeds alight
At th'outward wall, near which there stands
A bastille built t'imprison hands, 1150
By strange enchantment made to fetter
The lesser parts, and free the greater.
For, though the body may creep through,
The hands in grate are fast enough.
And when a circle 'bout the wrist 1155
Is made by beadle exorcist,

The body feels the spur and switch
As if 'twere ridden post by witch
At twenty miles an houer pace,
And yet ne'er stirs out of the place.   1160
On top of this there is a spire
On which Sir Knight first bids the squire
The fiddle and its spoils, the case,
In manner of a trophy place.
That done, they ope the trap-door gate   1165
And let Crowdero down thereat.
Crowdero making doleful face,
Like hermit poor in pensive place,[n]
To dungeon they the wretch commit,
And the survivor of his feet.   1170
But th'other, that had broke the peace,
And head of knighthood, they release.
Though a delinquent false and forged,
Yet, being a stranger, he's enlarged,[n]
While his comrade that did no hurt   1175
Is clapped up fast in prison for't.
So Justice, while she winks at crimes,
Stumbles on Innocence sometimes.

1163 *spoils*: the armour of a defeated enemy stripped off by the victor.
1174 *stranger*: foreigner.

CANTO III
THE ARGUMENT
The scattered rout return and rally,
Surround the place; the knight does sally
And is made prisoner. Then they seize
Th'enchanted fort by storm, release
Crowdero, and put the squire in's place.
I should have first said 'Hudibras'.

Ay me! What perils do environ
The man that meddles with cold iron![n]
What plaguy mischiefs and mishaps
Do dog him still with after-claps!
For though Dame Fortune seem to smile   5
And leer upon him for a while,
She'll after show him, in the nick
Of all his glories, a dog-trick.
This any man may sing or say
I'th' ditty called 'What if a day'.[n]   10
For Hudibras, who thought he'd won
The field as certain as a gun,
And, having routed the whole troop,
With victory was cock-a-hoop;
Thinking he'd done enough to purchase   15
Thanksgiving Day among the churches,
Wherein his mettle and brave worth
Might be explained by holder-forth,
And registered by fame eternal
In deathless pages of diurnal;   20

---

2 *cold iron*: a sword (colloquial).
8 *dog trick*: dirty trick (colloquial).
12 *certain as a gun*: beyond question (*ODEP* 789).
16 *Thanksgiving Day*: declared by Parliament in celebration of a victory or other event favourable to their cause.
18 *holder-forth*: preacher.
20 *diurnal*: newspaper.

Found in few minutes, to his cost,
He did but count without his host,
And that a turnstile is more certain
Than, in events of war, Dame Fortune.

For now the late faint-hearted rout,   25
O'erthrown and scattered round about,
Chased by the horror of their fear
From bloody fray of knight and bear
(All but the dogs, who in pursuit
Of the knight's victory, stood to 't,   30
And most ignobly sought to get
The honour of his blood and sweat),
Seeing the coast was free and clear
O'th' conquered and the conquerer,
Took heart again and faced about,   35
As if they meant to stand it out.
For now the half-defeated bear,
Attacked by th'enemy i'th' rear,
Finding their number grew too great
For him to make a safe retreat,   40
Like a bold chieftain faced about;
But, wisely doubting to hold out,
Gave way to fortune, and with haste
Faced the proud foe, and fled, and faced,
Retiring still until he found   45
He'd got th'advantage of the ground;
And then as valiantly made head
To check the foe, and forthwith fled,
Leaving no art untried, nor trick
Of warrior stout and politic;   50
Until, in spite of hot pursuit,
He gained a pass to hold dispute
On better terms, and stop the course
Of the proud foe. With all his force
He bravely charged, and for a while   55
Forced their whole body to recoil;
But still their numbers so increased,
He found himself at length oppressed,

---

22 *count without his host*: 'He that reckons without his host must reckon again'
   (*ODEP* 667).

And all evasions so uncertain
To save himself for better fortune,   60
That he resolved, rather than yield,
To die with honour in the field,
And sell his hide and carcass at
A price as high and desperate
As e'er he could. This resolution   65
He forthwith put in execution
And bravely threw himself among
The enemy i'th' greatest throng.
But what could single valour do
Against so numerous a foe?   70
Yet much he did, indeed too much
To be believed, where th'odds was such:
But one against a multitude
Is more than mortal can make good.
For while one party he opposed,   75
His rear was suddenly enclosed,
And no room left him for retreat
Or fight against a foe so great.
For now the mastiffs, charging home,
To blows and handy-grips were come,   80
While manfully himself he bore,
And, setting his right foot before,
He raised himself to show how tall
His person was above them all.
This equal shame and envy stirred   85
In th'enemy, that one should beard
So many warriors and so stout
As he had done, and stand it out,
Disdaining to lay down his arms
And yield on honourable terms.   90
Enraged thus, some in the rear
Attacked him, and some everywhere,
Till down he fell, yet, falling, fought,
And being down still laid about,
As Witherington in doleful dumps   95
Is said to fight upon his stumps.[n]
But all, alas, had been in vain,
And he inevitably slain,

95 *dumps*: mournful songs.

If Trulla and Cerdon in the nick
To rescue him had not been quick.   100
For Trulla, who was light of foot
As shafts which long-field Parthians shoot
(But not so light as to be borne
Upon the ears of standing corn,[n]
Or trip it o'er the water quicker   105
Than witches when their staves they liquor,
As some report), was got among
The foremost of the martial throng,
Where, pitying the vanquished bear,
She called to Cerdon who stood near,   110
Viewing the bloody fight, to whom,
'Shall we,' quoth she, 'stand still hum drum,
And see stout Bruin all alone
By numbers basely overthrown?
Such feats already he's achieved,   115
In story not to be believed,
And 'twould to us be shame enough
Not to attempt to fetch him off.'

'I would,' quoth he, 'venture a limb
To second thee and rescue him;   120
But then we must about it straight
Or else our aid will come too late.
Quarter he scorns, he is so stout,
And therefore cannot long hold out.'

This said, they waved their weapons round   125
About their heads to clear the ground,
And, joining forces, laid about
So fiercely that th'amazed rout
Turned tail again, and straight begun
As if the devil drove, to run.   130
Meanwhile th'approached the place where Bruin
Was now engaged to mortal ruin.

---

102 *Parthians*: an ancient kingdom whose soldiers shot their arrows backwards
as they rode away from the enemy.
106 *witches*: were popularly thought to ride through the air on staves or broom-
sticks by means of a magical ointment with which they anointed themselves or
their sticks.
112 *hum drum*: undecided.

The conquering foe they soon assailed;
First Trulla staved and Cerdon tailed
Until the mastiffs loosed their hold,   135
And yet, alas, do what they could,
The worsted bear came off with store
Of bloody wounds, but all before.
For as Achilles, dipped in pond,
Was anabaptized free from wound,[n]   140
Made proof against dead-doing steel
All over but the pagan heel,
So did our champion's arms defend
All of him but the other end,
His head and ears, which in the martial   145
Encounter lost a leathern parcel.
For, as an Austrian archduke once
Had one ear (which in ducatoons
Is half the coin) in battle pared
Close to his head, so Bruin fared;   150
But tugged and pulled on th'other side,
Like scrivener newly crucified,
Or like the late-corrected leathern
Ears of the circumcised brethren.[n]
But gentle Trulla into th'ring   155
He wore in 's nose conveyed a string,
With which she marched before, and led
The warrior to a grassy bed,
As authors write,[n] in a cool shade
Which eglantine and roses made,   160
Close by a softly-murmuring stream
Where lovers used to loll and dream.

---

134 Staving and tailing are terms of art used in the bear-garden and signify
there only the parting of dogs and bears, though they are used metaphorically
in several other professions for moderating, as law, divinity, hectoring, etc.
154 Prynne, Bastwick, and Burton, who laid down their ears as proxies for three
professions of the godly party, who not long after maintained their right and
title to the pillory to be as good and lawful as theirs who first of all took
possession of it in their names.

---

147 *archduke*: the Archduke Albert, Archbishop of Toledo, later sovereign of
the Low Countries. During the Battle of Nieuport, in which he led the Spanish
forces, he was wounded in the ear.
148 *ducatoons*: Venetian silver coins on one side of which a figure of St. Justina
is stamped, carrying an ear of corn which covers half the coin.
152 *crucified*: a man convicted of forging legal documents used to be punished
by standing in the pillory and having his ears cut off.

There leaving him to his repose,
Secured from pursuit of foes,
And wanting nothing but a song,   165
And a well-tuned theorbo hung
Upon a bough, to ease the pain
His tugged ears suffered, with a strain,
They both drew up to march in quest
Of his great leader and the rest.   170

For Orsin (who was more renowned
For stout maintaining of his ground
In standing fights than for pursuit,
As being not so quick of foot)
Was not long able to keep pace   175
With others that pursued the chase,
But found himself left far behind,
Both out of heart and out of wind;
Grieved to behold his bear pursued
So basely by a multitude,   180
And like to fall, not by the prowess,
But numbers of his coward foes.
He raged and kept as heavy a coil as
Stout Hercules for loss of Hylas,
Forcing the valleys to repeat   185
The accents of his sad regret.
He beat his breast and tore his hair
For loss of his dear crony bear,
That Echo from the hollow ground
His doleful wailings did resound   190
More wistfully by many times
Than in small poets' splay-foot rhymes,
That make her in their ruthful stories
To answer to inter'gatories,[n]
And most unconscionably depose   195
To things of which she nothing knows,
And when she has said all she can say,
'Tis wrested to the lover's fancy.

166 *theorbo*: a large lute with two necks and two sets of strings.
184 *Hylas*: the close companion of Hercules. He was drawn into a fountain by
 enamoured nymphs, leaving Hercules to complain of his loss (Apollonius
 Rhodius, *Argonautica*, i. 1207–72).

Quoth he, 'O whither, wicked Bruin,
Art thou fled to my ——' Echo: 'Ruin?'   200
'I thought thou'dst scorned to budge a step
For fear.' Quoth Echo, 'Marry guep!'
'Am not I here to take thy part?
Then what has quailed thy stubborn heart?
Have these bones rattled, and this head   205
So often in thy quarrel bled?
Nor did I ever winch or grudge it
For thy dear sake.' Quoth she, 'Mum budget!'
'Think'st thou 'twill not be laid i'th' dish
Thou turn'dst thy back?' Quoth Echo, 'Pish!'   210
'To run from those thou'dst overcome
Thus cowardly?' Quoth Echo, 'Mum!'
'But what a vengeance makes thee fly
From me too, as thine enemy?
Or, if thou hast no thought of me,   215
Nor what I have endured for thee,
Yet shame and honour might prevail
To keep thee thus from turning tail.
For who would grudge to spend his blood in
His honour's cause?' Quoth she, 'A puddin!'   220

This said, his grief to anger turned
Which in his manly stomach burned.
Thirst of revenge, and wrath, in place
Of sorrow now began to blaze.
He vowed the authors of his woe   225
Should equal vengeance undergo,
And with their bones and flesh pay dear
For what he suffered, and his bear.
This being resolved, with equal speed
And rage he hasted to proceed   230
To action straight, and giving o'er
To search for Bruin any more,
He went in quest of Hudibras,

202 *Marry   guep*: an   exclamation   of   surprise;   originally 'By Mary
    gypsy'.
207 *winch*: wince.
208 *Mum budget*: 'shut up!'
209 *laid i'th' dish*: held against you.

To find him out, where e'er he was,
And if he were above ground, vowed   235
He'd ferret him, lurk where he would.

But scarce had he a furlong on
This resolute adventure gone,
When he encountered with that crew
Whom Hudibras did late subdue.   240
Honour, revenge, contempt and shame
Did equally their breasts inflame.
'Mong these the fierce Magnano was,
And Talgol, foe to Hudibras,
Cerdon and Colon, warriors stout   245
And resolute as ever fought,
Whom furious Orsin thus bespoke:

'Shall we,' quoth he, 'thus basely brook
The vile affront that paltry ass
And feeble scoundrel Hudibras,   250
With that more paltry ragamuffin
Ralpho, with vapouring and huffing,
Have put upon us like tame cattle
As if they'd routed us in battle?
For my part, it shall ne'er be said   255
I for the washing gave my head,
Nor did I turn my back for fear
Of them, but losing of my bear,
Which now I'm like to undergo;
For whether these fell wounds, or no,   260
He has received in fight are mortal,
Is more than all my skill can fortell.
Nor do I know what is become
Of him, more than the Pope of Rome.
But if I can but find them out   265
That caused it (as I shall, no doubt,
Where'er th'in hugger-mugger lurk),
I'll make them rue their handiwork,
And wish that they had rather dared
To pull the devil by the beard.'   270

252 *vapouring and huffing*: boasting.
256 *for the washing gave my head*: yielded without resistance.

Quoth Cerdon, 'Noble Orsin, thou'st
Great reason to do as thou say'st,
And so has everybody here
As well as thou hast, or thy bear.
Others may do as they see good,   275
But, if this twig be made of wood
That will hold tack, I'll make the fur
Fly 'bout the ears of that old cur,
And th'other mongrel vermin, Ralph,
That braved us all in his behalf.   280
Thy bear is safe and out of peril,
Though lugged indeed and wounded very ill.
Myself and Trulla made a shift
To help him out at a dead lift,
And, having brought him bravely off,   285
Have left him where he's safe enough.
There let him rest; for if we stay,
The slaves may hap to get away.'

This said, they all engaged to join
Their forces in the same design   290
And forthwith put themselves in search
Of Hudibras upon their march;
Where leave we them awhile, to tell
What the victorious knight befell;
For such, Crowdero being fast   295
In dungeon shut, we left him last.

Triumphant laurels seemed to grow
Nowhere so green as on his brow.
Laden with which, as well as tired
With conquering toil, he now retired   300
Unto a neighboring castle by
To rest his body, and apply
Fit medicines to each glorious bruise
He got in fight, reds, blacks and blues,
To mollify th'uneasy pang   305
Of every honourable bang.

---

277 *hold tack*: last out; be strong enough.
282 *lugged*: a pun, meaning both 'baited' and 'hurt in the ear'.
284 *at a dead lift*: as a last resort.

Which being by skilful midwife dressed,
He laid him down to take his rest.

But all in vain. He'd got a hurt
O'th' inside, of a deadlier sort,   310
By Cupid made, who took his stand
Upon a widow's jointure-land
(For he in all his amorous battles,
No 'dvantage finds like goods and chattels),
Drew home his bow, and aiming right,   315
Let fly an arrow at the knight.
The shaft against a rib did glance
And gall him in the purtenance.
But time had somewhat 'swaged his pain,
After he found his suit in vain;   320
For that proud dame, for whom his soul
Was burnt in 's belly like a coal
(That belly that so oft did ache
And suffer griping for her sake,
Till purging comfits and ants' eggs   325
Had almost brought him off his legs),
Used him so like a base rascallion,
That old Pyg-(what d'y' call him?) malion,
That cut his mistress out of stone,
Had not so hard-a-hearted one.   330
She had a thousand jadish tricks,
Worse than a mule that flings and kicks,
'Mong which one cross-grained freak she had,
As insolent as strange and mad:
She could love none but only such   335
As scorned and hated her as much.
'Twas a strange riddle of a lady!
Not love, if any loved her? Hey day!
So cowards never use their might
But against such as will not fight;   340

311 *stand*: the place from which a hunter shoots game.
325 *ants' eggs*: according to Thomas Moffet (*Theater of Insects*, II. xvi. 1080)
    these could restore decayed sexual powers.
327 *rascallion*: wretch.
328 *Pygmalion*: in classical myth, a sculptor who fell in love with one of his own
    statues. In answer to his prayers, she was changed by the gods into a living
    woman.

So some diseases have been found
Only to seize upon the sound.
He that gets her by heart must say her
The back way, like a witch's prayer.
Meanwhile the knight had no small task   345
To compass what he durst not ask.
He loves, but dares not make the motion;
Her ignorance is his devotion.
Like caitiff vile, that for misdeed
Rides with his face to rump of steed,   350
Or rowing scull, he's fain to love,
Look one way and another move;
Or like a tumbler, that does play
His game and look another way
Until he seize upon the coney,   355
Just so does he by matrimony.
But all in vain: her subtle snout
Did quickly wind his meaning out,
Which she returned with too much scorn
To be by man of honour borne.   360
Yet much he bore, until the distress
He suffered from his spiteful mistress
Did stir his stomach, and the pain
He had endured from her disdain
Turned to regret so resolute   365
That he resolved to waive his suit
And either to renounce her quite,
Or for a while play least in sight.
This resolution being put on,
He kept some months, and more had done,   370
But being brought so nigh by fate,
The victory he achieved so late
Did set his thoughts agog, and ope
A door to discontinued hope
That seemed to promise he might win   375
His dame too, now his hand was in,

344 *witch's prayer*: witches were said to repeat prayers backwards as an incantation.
348 An allusion to the proverb 'Ignorance is the mother of devotion' (*ODEP* 396).
350 Ralpho and Hudibras are carried to the stocks in this way (i. iii. 963–4).
353 *tumbler*: a dog like a small greyhound, formerly used to catch rabbits.

And that his valour and the honour
He'd newly gained might work upon her.
These reasons made his mouth to water
With amorous longings to be at her.   380

Thought he unto himself, 'Who knows
But this brave conquest o'er my foes
May reach her heart, and make that stoop,
As I but now have forced the troop?
If nothing can oppugne love,   385
And virtue invious ways can prove,
What may not he confide to do
That brings both love and virtue too?
But thou bring'st valour too and wit,
Two things that seldom fail to hit.   390
Valour's a mousetrap, wit a gin,
Which women oft are taken in.
Then, Hudibras, why should'st thou fear
To be, that art a conquerer?
Fortune th'audacious doth *iuvare*   395
But lets the timidous miscarry.
Then while the honour thou hast got
Is spick and span-new, piping hot,
Strike her up bravely thou hadst best,
And trust thy fortune with the rest.'   400

Such thoughts as these the knight did keep,
More than his bangs or fleas, from sleep,
And as an owl that in a barn
Sees a mouse creeping in the corn,
Sits still, and shuts his round, blue eyes,   405
As if he slept, until he spies
The little beast within his reach,
Then starts, and seizes on the wretch,
So from his couch the knight did start
To seize upon the widow's heart,   410
Crying with hasty tone and hoarse,
'Ralpho, despatch! To horse! To horse!'

385 *oppugne*: overcome (Latin *oppugnare*, to besiege).
386 *invious*: pathless. This couplet is a parody of Horace, *Carmina*, III. ii.
395 An allusion to the Latin proverb *Audentes fortuna iuvat* ('Fortune favours the bold', Virgil, *Aeneid*, x. 284).

And 'twas but time, for now the rout
We left engaged to seek him out
By speedy marches were advanced   415
Up to the fort where he ensconced,
And had all th'avenues possessed
About the place from east to west.

That done, awhile they made a halt
To view the ground, and where t'assault;   420
Then called a council which was best,
By siege or onslaught, to invest
The enemy, and 'twas agreed
By storm and onslaught to proceed.
This being resolved, in comely sort   425
They now drew up t'attack the fort,
When Hudibras, about to enter
Upon another-gates adventure,
To Ralpho called aloud to arm,
Not dreaming of approaching storm.   430
Whether Dame Fortune, or the care
Of angel bad or tutelar
Did arm, or thrust him on a danger,
To which he was an utter stranger;
That foresight might, or might not blot   435
The glory he had newly got;
Or to his shame it might be said
They took him napping in his bed,
To them we leave it to expound,
That deal in sciences profound.   440

His courser scarce he had bestrid,
And Ralpho that on which he rid,
When setting ope the postern gate
To take the field and sally at,
The foe appeared, drawn up and drilled,   445
Ready to charge them in the field.
This somewhat startled the bold knight,
Surprised with th'unexpected sight.
The bruises of his bones and flesh
He thought began to smart afresh,   450

428 *another-gates*: of another kind.

Till, recollecting wonted courage,
His fear was soon converted to rage,
And thus he spoke: 'The coward foe,
Whom we but now gave quarter to,
Look, yonder's rallied, and appears,   455
As if they had outrun their fears.
The glory we did lately get,
The fates command us to repeat,
And to their wills we must succumb.
Quocunque trahunt, 'tis our doom.   460
This is the same numeric crew
Which we so lately did subdue,
The self-same individuals that
Did run as mice do from a cat
When we courageously did wield   465
Our martial weapons in the field
To tug for victory; and when
We shall our shining blades again
Brandish in terror o'er our heads,
They'll straight resume their wonted dreads.   470
Fear is an ague that forsakes
And haunts by fits those whom it takes.
And they'll opine they feel the pain
And blows they felt today, again.
Then let us boldly charge them home   475
And make no doubt to overcome.'

This said, his courage to enflame,
He called upon his mistress' name.
His pistol next he cocked anew,
And out his nut-brown whinyard drew,   480
And, placing Ralpho in the front,
Reserved himself to bear the brunt,
As expert warriors use; then plied
With iron heel his courser's side,
Conveying sympathetic speed   485
From heel of knight to heel of steed.

460 *Quocunque trahunt*: 'to whatever place they may draw us' (proverbial).
461 *numeric*: identical.
467 *tug*: strive.
480 *whinyard*: short sword.
485–6 Another allusion to belief in sympathetic magic. Cf. I. i. 283–4; I. ii. 233 ff.

Meanwhile the foe with equal rage
And speed advancing to engage,
Both parties now were drawn so close
Almost to come to handy-blows,   490
When Orsin first let fly a stone
At Ralpho; not so huge a one
As that which Diomed did maul
Aeneas on the bum withall,
Yet big enough, if rightly hurled,   495
T'have sent him to another world;
Whether above ground or below,
Which saints twice-dipped are destined to.
The danger startled the bold squire
And made him some few steps retire,   500
But Hudibras advanced to's aid
And roused his spirits half-dismayed.
He, wisely doubting lest the shot
Of th' enemy, now growing hot,
Might at a distance gall, pressed close,   505
To come, pell-mell, to handy-blows;
And, that he might their aim decline,
Advanced still in an oblique line,
But prudently forbore to fire
Till breast to breast he had got nigher,   .   510
As expert warriors use to do
When hand to hand they charge the foe.
This order the adventurous knight
Most soldierlike observed in fight,
When Fortune (as she's wont) turned fickle   515
And for the foe began to stickle.
The more shame for her goody-ship,
To give so near a friend the slip.
For Colon, choosing out a stone,
Levelled so right it thumped upon   520
His manly paunch with such a force
As almost beat him off his horse.

---

493 *Diomed*: the Greek warrior who, in the *Iliad*, hurls a huge stone at Aeneas, wounding him on the hip (*Iliad*, v. 302).
498 *saints twice-dipped*: the Baptists, who believed in the efficacy of adult baptism, even of those who had been baptized in childhood.
516 *stickle*: strive.

He loosed his weapon and the rein,
But, laying fast hold on the mane,
Preserved his seat, and as a goose   525
In death contracts his talons close,
So did the knight, and with one claw
The tricker of his pistol draw.
The gun went off and as it was
Still fatal to stout Hudibras,   530
In all his feats of arms, when least
He dreamt of it, to prosper best,
So now he fared. The shot, let fly
At random 'mong the enemy,
Pierced Talgol's gaberdine, and grazing   535
Upon his shoulder, in the passing
Lodged in Magnano's brass habergeon,
Who straight 'A surgeon!' cried, 'A surgeon!'
He tumbled down and as he fell,
Did 'Murder, murder, murder!' yell.   540
This startled their whole body so
That if the knight had not let go
His arms, but been in warlike plight,
He'd won, the second time, the fight;
As if the squire had but fall'n on,   545
He had inevitably done.
But he, diverted with the care
Of Hudibras his wound, forbare
To press th'advantage of his fortune,
While danger did the rest dishearten.   550
He had with Cerdon been engaged
In close encounter, which both waged
So desperately 'twas hard to say
Which side was like to get the day.
And now the busy work of death   555
Had tired them so, th'agreed to breath,
Preparing to renew the fight,
When the disaster of the knight
And th'other party did divert
And force their sullen rage to part.   560
Ralpho pressed up to Hudibras,
And Cerdon where Magnano was,

528 *tricker*: trigger.

Each striving to confirm his party
With stout encouragements and hearty.

Quoth Ralpho, 'Courage, valiant sir,   565
And let revenge and honour stir
Your spirits up! Once more fall on!
The shattered foe begins to run;
For if but half so well you knew
To use your victory as subdue,   570
They durst not, after such a blow
As you have giv'n them, face us now,
But from so formidable a soldier
Had fled like crows when they smell powder.
Thrice have they seen your sword aloft   575
Waved o'er their heads, and fled as oft.
But if you let them recollect
Their spirits, now dismayed and checked,
You'll have a harder game to play
Than yet you've had, to get the day.'   580

Thus spoke the stout squire, but was heard
Of Hudibras with small regard.
His thoughts were fuller of the bang
He lately took, than Ralph's harangue;
To which he answered, 'Cruel fate   585
Tells me thy counsel comes too late.
The knotted blood within my hose
That from my wounded body flows,
With mortal crisis doth portend
My days to appropinque an end.   590
I am for action now unfit,
Either of fortitude or wit.
"Fortune my foe" begins to frown,
Resolved to pull my stomach down.
I am not apt, upon a wound   595
Or trivial basting, to despond.
Yet I'd be loath my days to curtal;
For if I thought my wounds not mortal,

590 *appropinque*: approach.
593 *Fortune my foe*: the opening lines of a very popular ballad (William Chappell,
    Old English Popular Music, 2 vols., 1893, i. 76).
597 *curtal*: curtail; so spelled for the sake of the rhyme.

Or that we'd time enough as yet
To make an honourable retreat,   600
'Twere the best course. But if they find
We fly, and leave our arms behind
For them to seize on, the dishonour
And danger too is such, I'll sooner
Stand to it boldly and take quarter,   605
To let them see I am no starter.
In all the trade of war, no feat
Is nobler than a brave retreat.
For those that run away and fly
Take place at least of th'enemy.'   610

This said, the squire with active speed
Dismounted from his bony steed
To seize the arms which by mischance
Fell from the bold knight in a trance.
These being found out, and restored   615
To Hudibras, their natural lord,
The active squire with might and main
Prepared in haste to mount again.
Thrice he assayed to mount aloft,
But by his weighty bum as oft   620
He was pulled back till, having found
Th'advantage of the rising ground,
Thither he led his warlike steed,
And having placed him right, with speed
Prepared again to scale the beast,   625
When Orsin, who had newly dressed
The bloody scar upon the shoulder
Of Talgol with Promethean powder,
And now was searching for the shot
That laid Magnano on the spot,   630
Beheld the study squire aforesaid
Preparing to climb up his horse-side.
He left his cure, and laying hold
Upon his arms, with courage bold
Cried out, ' 'Tis now no time to dally!   635
The enemy begins to rally.

606 *starter*: coward.
610 *take place*: precede.
628 *powder*: see I. ii. 225.

Let us that are unhurt and whole
Fall on, and happy man be's dole!'

This said, like to a thunderbolt
He flew with fury to th'assault,   640
Striving the enemy to attack
Before he reached his horse's back.
Ralpho was mounted now and gotten
O'erthwart his beast with active vauting,
Wriggling his body to recover   645
His seat, and cast his right leg over,
When Orsin rushing in, bestowed
On horse and man so heavy a load,
The beast was startled, and begun
To kick and fling like mad and run,   650
Bearing the tough squire like a sack,
Or stout King Richard[n] on his back,
Till, stumbleing, he threw him down,
Sore bruised and cast into a sown.

Meanwhile the knight began to rouse   655
The sparkles of his wonted prowess.
He thrust his hand into his hose
And found both by his eyes and nose
'Twas only choler and not blood
That from his wounded body flowed.   660
This, with the hazard of the squire,
Enflamed him with despiteful ire.
Courageously he faced about
And drew his other pistol out,
And now had half-way bent the cock,   665
When Cerdon gave so fierce a shock
With sturdy truncheon 'thwart his arm
That down it fell and did no harm;
Then, stoutly pressing on with speed,
Assayed to pull him off his steed.   670
The knight his sword had only left
With which he Cerdon's head had cleft,

638 Proverbial: 'Let each one's lot be to be a happy man.'
644 *vauting*: vaulting; a spelling introduced for the rhyme.
654 *sown*: swoon.

Or at the least cropped off a limb,
But Orsin came and rescued him.
He with his lance attacked the knight   675
Upon his quarters opposite.
But, as a barque that in foul weather,
Tossed by two adverse winds together,
Is bruised, and beaten to and fro,
And knows not which to turn him to,   680
So fared the knight between two foes,
And knew not which of them t'oppose,
Till Orsin, charging with his lance
At Hudibras, by spiteful chance
Hit Cerdon such a bang as stunned   685
And laid him flat upon the ground.
At this the knight began to cheer up
And raising up himself on stirrup,
Cried out, '*Victoria!* Lie thou there,
And I shall straight despatch another   690
To bear thee company in death,
But first I'll halt awhile and breath.'
As well he might, for Orsin, grieved
At th'wound that Cerdon had received,
Ran to relieve him with his lore,   695
And cure the hurt he made before.

Meanwhile the knight had wheeled about
To breathe himself, and next find out
Th'advantage of the ground, where best
He might the ruffled foe infest.   700
This being resolved, he spurred his steed
To run at Orsin with full speed,
While he was busy in the care
Of Cerdon's wound, and unaware.
But he was quick, and had already   705
Unto the part applied remedy,
And, seeing th'enemy prepared,
Drew up and stood upon his guard.
Then like a warrior right expert
And skilful in the martial art,   710
The subtle knight straight made a halt,
And judged it best to stay th'assault

700 *infest*: attack.

Until he had relieved the squire,
And then (in order) to retire,
Or, as occasion should invite,   715
With forces joined renew the fight.
Ralpho, by this time disentranced,
Upon his bum himself advanced,
Though sorely bruised; his limbs all o'er
With ruthless bangs were stiff and sore.   720
Right fain he would have got upon
His feet again to get him gone,
When Hudibras to aid him came.

Quoth he (and called him by his name),
'Courage! The day at length is ours   725
And we once more as conquerours
Have both the field and honour won.
The foe is profligate and run—
I mean all such as can, for some
This hand hath sent to their long home,   730
And some lie sprawling on the ground
With many a gash and bloody wound.
Caesar himself could never say
He got two victories in a day
As I have done, that can say, "Twice I   735
In one day *Veni, vidi, vici*."
The foe's so numerous that we
Cannot so often *vincere*
As they *perire*, and yet enough
Be left to strike an afterblow.   740
Then lest they rally and once more
Put us to fight the business o'er,
Get up and mount thy steed. Despatch!
And let us both their motions watch.'

Quoth Ralph, 'I should not, if I were   745
In case for action, now be here;

---

728 *profligate*: overthrown.
730 *long home*: the grave; derived from Ecclesiastes 12:5.
736 'I came, I saw, I conquered'; words attributed to Julius Caesar at the end of
   his Pontic campaign (Suetonius, *Julius*, xxxvii. 2).
738 *vincere*: conquer.
739 *perire*: perish.

Nor have I turned my back or hanged
An arse, for fear of being banged.
It was for you I got these harms,
Adventuring to fetch off your arms.   750
The blows and drubs I have received
Have bruised my body and bereaved
My limbs of strength. Unless you stoop
And reach your hand to pull me up,
I shall lie here, and be a prey   755
To those who now are run away.'

'That shalt thou not', quoth Hudibras.
'We read the ancients held it was
More honourable far *servare*
Civem than slay an adversary.[n]   760
The one today we oft have done,
The other shall despatch anon.
And, though th'art of a different church,
I will not leave thee in the lurch.'

This said, he jogged his good steed nigher   765
And steered him gently toward the squier.
Then, bowing down his body, stretched
His hand out, and at Ralpho reached,
When Trulla, whom he did not mind,
Charged him like lightening behind.   770
She had been long in search about
Magnano's wound, to find it out,
But could find none, nor where the shot
That had so startled him was got.
But having found the worst was passed,   775
She fell to her own work at last:
The pillage of the prisoners,
Which in all feats of arms was hers.[n]
And now to plunder Ralph she flew,
When Hudibras his hard fate drew   780
To succour him; for as he bowed
To help him up, she laid a load
Of blows so heavy, and placed so well
On th'other side, that down he fell.

747–8 *hanged* | *An arse*: Cf. I. i. 450.

'Yield, scoundrel base,' quoth she, 'or die!   785
Thy life is mine and liberty.
But if thou think'st I took thee tardy,
And dar'st presume to be so hardy
To try thy fortune o'er afresh,
I'll waive my title to thy flesh,   790
Thy arms and baggage, now my right.
And if thou hast the heart to try't,
I'll lend thee back thyself awhile,
And once more for that carcass vile
Fight upon tick.' Quoth Hudibras,   795
'Thou offer'st nobly, valiant lass,
And I shall take thee at thy word.
First let me rise and take my sword.
That sword which has so oft this day
Through squadrons of my foes made way,   800
And some to other worlds despatched,
Now with a feeble spinster matched,
Will blush with blood ignoble stained,
By which no honour's to be gained.
But if thou'lt take m'advice in this,   805
Consider while thou may'st what 'tis
To interrupt a victor's course
B'opposing such a trivial force.
For if with conquest I come off
(And that I shall do sure enough),   810
Quarter thou canst not have nor grace,
By law of arms in such a case,
Both which I now do offer freely.'

'I scorn,' quoth she, 'thou coxcomb silly,'
(Clapping her hand upon her breech,   815
To show how much she prized his speech)
'Quarter or counsel from a foe.
If thou canst force me to it, do.
But lest it should again be said,
When I have once more won thy head,   820
I took thee napping, unprepared,
Arm, and betake thee to thy guard!'

This said, she to her tackle fell
And on the knight let fall a peal

Of blows so fierce, and pressed so home,   825
That he retired and followed 's bum.
'Stand to 't!' quoth she, 'Or yield to mercy.
It is not fighting arsy-versy
Shall serve thy turn.' This stirred his spleen
More than the danger he was in,   830
The blows he felt, or was to feel,
Although th'already made him reel.
Honour, despite, revenge and shame
At once unto his stomach came,
Which fired it so, he raised his arm   835
Above his head, and rained a storm
Of blows so terrible and thick
As if he meant to hash her quick.
But she upon her truncheon took them
And by oblique diversion broke them,   840
Waiting an opportunity
To pay all back with usury.
Which long she failed not of, for now
The knight with one dead-doing blow
Resolving to decide the fight,   845
And she with quick and cunning sleight
Avoiding it, the force and weight
He charged upon it was so great
As almost swayed him to the ground.
No sooner she th'advantage found   850
But in she flew, and seconding
With home-made thrust the heavy swing,
She laid him flat upon his side,
And mounting on his trunk astride,
Quoth she, 'I told thee what would come   855
Of all thy vapouring, base scum.
Say, will the law of arms allow
I may have grace and quarter now?
Or wilt thou rather break thy word
And stain thine honour than thy sword?   860
A man of war to damn his soul
In basely breaking his parole!
And when, before the fight, thou'dst vowed
To give no quarter in cold blood!

828 *arsy-versy*: back to front.
838 *quick*: alive.

Now thou hast got me for a Tartar,   865
To make m'against my will take quarter,
Why dost not put me to the sword,
But cowardly fly from thy word?'

Quoth Hudibras, 'The day's thine own.
Thou and thy stars have cast me down.   870
My laurels are transplanted now
And flourish on thy conquering brow.
My loss of honour's great enough:
Thou need'st not brand it with a scoff.
Sarcasmes may eclipse thine own   875
But cannot blur my lost renown.
I am not now in Fortune's power:
"He that is down can fall no lower".
The ancient heroes were illustrious
For being benigne and not blustrous   880
Against a vanquished foe. Their swords
Were sharp and trenchant, not their words;
And did in fight but cut work out
T'employ their courtesies about.'

Quoth she, 'Although thou hast deserved,   885
Base slubberdegullion, to be served
As thou didst vow to deal with me
If thou hadst got the victory,
Yet I had rather act a part
That suits my fame, than thy desert.   890
Thy arms, thy liberty, beside
All that's on th'outside of thy hide,
Are mine by military law,
Of which I will not bate one straw.
The rest, thy life and limbs, once more,   895
Though doubly forfeit, I restore.'

Quoth Hudibras, 'It is too late
For me to treat or stipulate.

---

865 '*To catch a Tartar*, instead of catching, to be catched in a trap' (B.E.,
   Dictionary . . . of the Canting Crew, 1699).
875 *Sarcasmes*: the spelling suggests this should be read as a trisyllable, as
   should 'benigne', l. 880 below.
878 A translation of the Latin proverb 'Qui iacet in terra non habet unde cadat.'

What thou command'st I must obey.
Yet those whom I expunged today, 900
Of thine own party, I let go,
And gave them life and freedom too,
Both dogs and bears upon their parole,
Whom I took prisoners in this quarrel.'

Quoth Trulla, 'Whether thou or they 905
Let one another run away
Concerns me not. But was't not thou
That gave Crowdero quarter too?
Crowdero whom, in irons bound,
Thou basely threw'st into Lob's pound, 910
Where still he lies, and with regret
His generous bowels rage and fret.
But now thy carcass shall redeem
And serve to be exchange for him.'

This said, the knight did straight submit 915
And laid his weapons at her feet.
Next he disrobed his gaberdine,
And with it did himself resign.
She took it and forthwith devesting
The mantle that she wore, said jesting, 920
'Take that, and wear it for my sake'.
Then threw it o'er his sturdy back.[n]
And as the French we conquered once,
Now give us laws for pantaloons,
The length of breeches and the gathers, 925
Port-canons, periwigs and feathers,
Just so the proud insulting lass
Arrayed and dighted Hudibras.

Meanwhile the other champions, yerst
In hurry of the fight dispersed, 930
Arrived when Trulla'd won the day
To share in th'honour and the prey,

900 *expunged*: vanquished.
910 *Lob's pound*: the stocks (colloquial).
912 *bowels*: heart.
926 *Port-canons*: ornamental rolls sewn round the legs of breeches.
929 *yerst*: formerly.

And out of Hudibras's hide
With vengeance to be satisfied,
Which now they were about to pour   935
Upon him in a wooden shower.
But Trulla thrust herself between,
And striding o'er his back again,
She brandished o'er her head his sword,
And vowed they should not break her word.   940
She'd given him quarter, and her blood
Or theirs should make that quarter good.
For she was bound by law of arms
To see him safe from further harms.
In dungeon deep Crowdero, cast   945
By Hudibras, as yet lay fast,
Where to the hard and ruthless stones
His great heart made perpetual moans.
Him she resolved that Hudibras
Should ransom, and supply his place.   950

This stopped their fury, and the basting
Which toward Hudibras was hasting.
They thought it was but just and right
That what she had achieved in fight
She should dispose of how she pleased: 955
Crowdero ought to be released,
Nor could that any way be done
So well as this she pitched upon;
For who a better could imagine?
This therefore they resolved t'engage in.   960
The knight and squier first they made
Rise from the ground where they were laid,
Then mounted both upon their horses,
But with their faces to their arses.
Orsin led Hudibras's beast   965
And Talgol that which Ralpho pressed,
Whom stout Magnano, valiant Cerdon
And Colon waited as a guard on,
All ushering Trulla in the rear
With th'arms of either prisoner.   970
In this proud order and array
They put themselves upon their way,

Striving to reach th'enchanted castle
Where stout Crowdero in durance lay still.
Thither with greater speed than shows   975
And triumphs over conquered foes
Do use t'allow, or than the bears
Or pageants borne before lord mayors
Are wont to use, they soon arrived,
In order soldierlike contrived,   980
Still marching in a warlike posture,
As fit for battle as for muster.
The knight and squire they first unhorse,
And bending 'gainst the fort their force,
They all advanced, and round about   985
Begirt the magical redoubt.
Magnan' led up in this adventure
And made way for the rest to enter.
For he was skilful in black art
No less than he that built the fort,   990
And with an iron mace laid flat
A breach, which straight all entered at,
And in the wooden dungeon found
Crowdero laid upon the ground.
Him they release from durance base,   995
Restored t'his fiddle and his case,
And liberty, his thirsty rage
With luscious vengeance to assuage.
For he no sooner was at large
But Trulla straight brought on her charge,   1000
And in the self-same limbo put
The knight and squire where he was shut;
Where, leaving them i'th' wretched hole,
Their bangs and durance to condole,
Confined and conjured into narrow   1005
Enchanted mansion, to know sorrow,
In the same order and array
Which they advanced, they marched away.

But Hudibras, who scorned to stoop
To fortune, or be said to droop,   1010
Cheered up himself with ends of verse
And sayings of philosophers.[n]

Quoth he, 'Th'one half of man, his mind,
Is *sui juris*, unconfined,
And cannot be laid by the heels,   1015
What e'er the other moiety feels.
'Tis not restraint or liberty
That makes men prisoners or free
But perturbations that possess
The mind or aequanimities.   1020
The whole world was not half so wide
To Alexander when he cried
Because he had but one to subdue,[n]
As was a paltry narrow tub to
Diogenes, who is not said   1025
(For ought that ever I could read)
To whine, put finger i'th' eye, and sob
Because he'd ne'er another tub.[n]
The ancients make two several kinds
Of prowess in heroic minds,   1030
The active and the passive valiant,[n]
Both which are *pari libra* gallant:
For both to give blows and to carry,
In fights are equinecessary;
But in defeats the passive stout   1035
Are always found to stand it out
Most desperately, and to outdo
The active, 'gainst a conquering foe.
Though we with blacks and blues are suggilled,
Or, as the vulgar say, are cudgelled,   1040
He that is valiant and dares fight,
Though drubbed, can lose no honour by't.
Honour's a lease for lives to come,
And cannot be extended from
The legal tenant; 'tis a chattel   1045
Not to be forfeited in battel.
If he that in the field is slain
Be in the bed of honour lain,

1014 *sui juris*: a law to itself; independent.
1015 *laid by the heels*: put in the stocks.
1019 *perturbations*: disturbances of the mind; a term used by the Stoics, as is 'aequanimities' in the next line.
1032 *pari libra*: in equal scale.
1039 *suggilled*: beaten black and blue.
1044 *extended*: a legal term: seized.

He that is beaten may be said
To lie in honour's truckle-bed.   1050
For as we see th'eclipsed sun
By mortals is more gazed upon,
Than when adorned with all his light
He shines in serene sky most bright,
So valour in a low estate   1055
Is most admired and wondered at.'

Quoth Ralph, 'How great I do not know
We may by being beaten grow;
But none that see how here we sit
Will judge us overgrown with wit.   1060
As gifted brethren, preaching by
A carnal hour-glass, do imply
Illumination can convey
Into them what they have to say
But not how much, so well enough   1065
Know you to charge, but not draw off.
For who without a cap and bauble,
Having subdued a bear and rabble,
And might with honour have come off,
Would put it to a second proof?   1070
A politic exploit, right fit
For Presbyterian zeal and wit!'

Quoth Hudibras, 'That cuckoo's tone,
Ralpho, thou always harp'st upon.
When thou at anything wouldst rail,   1075
Thou mak'st presbytery thy scale
To take the height on 't, and explain
To what degree it is profane.
Whats'ever will not with thy (what d'y' call?)
Thy "light" jump right thou call'st synodical;   1080
As if presbytery were a standard
To size whats'ever's to be slandered.
Dost not remember how this day
Thou to my beard wast bold to say

1050 *truckle-bed*: a small, low bed running on castors, usually pushed underneath a larger bed when not in use.
1061 *gifted brethren*: inspired Puritans.

That thou could'st prove bear-baiting equal   1085
With synods orthodox and legal?
Do if thou canst, for I deny 't,
And dare thee to 't with all thy "light".'

Quoth Ralpho, 'Truly that is no
Hard matter for a man to do   1090
That has but any guts in's brains,
And could believe it worth his pains.
But since you dare and urge me to it,
You'll find I've light enough to do it.

'Synods are mystical bear-gardens,   1095
Where elders, deputies, church-wardens
And other members of the court
Manage the Babylonish sport.
For prolocutor, scribe and bearward
Do differ only in a mere word.   1100
Both are but several synagogues
Of carnal men, and bears and dogs;
Both antichristian assemblies,
To mischief bent as far's in them lies;
Both stave and tail with fierce contests,   1105
The one with men, the other beasts.
The difference is, the one fights with
The tongue, the other with the teeth;
And that they bait but bears in this,
In th'other souls and consciences,   1110
Where saints themselves are brought to stake
For gospel-light and conscience sake,
Exposed to scribes and presbyters
Instead of mastiff dogs and curs,
Than whom they've less humanity,   1115
For these at souls of men will fly.
This to the prophet did appear
Who in a vision saw a bear,
Prefiguring the beastly rage
Of church rule in this latter age,   1120

1091 *guts in's brains*: proverbial: 'sense' (*ODEP* 341).
1105 *stave and tail*: Cf. I. ii. 163.
1117 *the prophet*: Daniel 7:5.

As is demonstrated at full
By him that baited the Pope's bull.
Bears naturally are beasts of prey
That live by rapine: so do they.
What are their orders, constitutions,   1125
Church-censures, curses, absolutions,
But several mystic chains they make
To tie poor Christians to the stake,
And then set heathen officers,
Instead of dogs, about their ears?   1130
For to prohibit and dispense,
To find out or to make offence,
Of hell and heaven to dispose,
To play with souls at fast and loose,
To set what characters they please,   1135
And mulcts on sin or godliness,
Reduce the church to gospel-order
By rapine, sacrilege and murder,
To make presbytery supreme
And kings themselves submit to them,   1140
And force all people, though against
Their consciences, to turn saints,
Must prove a pretty thriving trade
When saints monopolists are made.
When pious frauds and holy shifts   1145
Are "dispensations" and "gifts",
There godliness becomes mere ware
And every synod but a fair.

'Synods are whelps of th'Inquisition,
A mongrel breed of like pernicion,   1150
And, growing up, became the sires
Of scribes, commissioners and triers,[n]

1122 A learned divine in King James's time wrote a polemic work against the
Pope and gave it that unlucky nick-name of *The Pope's Bull Baited*.

1122 *him*: Henry Burton (see note to i. iii. 154), author of *The Baiting of the
Pope's Bull*, 1627.
1125 *constitutions*: decrees.
1126 *church-censures*: condemnations of spiritual offenders.
1129 *heathen*: secular.
1142 *turn saints*: become Presbyterians.
1146 *dispensations and gifts*: Puritan expressions for divine providence.

Whose business is by cunning sleight
To cast a figure for men's light;
To find in lines of beard and face   1155
The physiognomy of grace,
And by the sound and twang of nose,
If all be sound within disclose,
Free from a crack or flaw of sinning,
As men try pipkins by the ringing;   1160
By black caps underlaid with white
Give certain guess at inward light;
Which sergeants at the gospel wear
To make their spiritual calling clear;
The handkercher about the neck   1165
(Canonical crabat of Smeck,[n]
From whom the institution came
When church and state they set on flame,
And worn by them as badges then
Of spiritual warfaring men)   1170
Judge rightly if regeneration
Be of the newest cut in fashion.
Sure 'tis an orthodox opinion
That grace is founded in dominion.[n]
Great piety consists in pride;   1175
To rule is to be sanctified.
To domineer and to control
Both o'er the body and the soul
Is the most perfect discipline
Of church rule, and by right divine.   1180
Bel and the Dragon's chaplains were
More moderate than these by far;

1166 Smectymnuus was a club of parliamentary holders-forth, the characters
of whose names and talents were by themselves expressed in that senseless and
insignificant word. They wore handkerchers about their necks for a note of
distinction (as the officers of the parliament army then did), which afterwards
degenerated into carnal crabats.

1154 *cast a figure*: draw up a horoscope.
1157 *twang*: see I. i. 228 and note.
1161 *black caps*: the head-dress of Presbyterian ministers.
1163 Sergeants at law formerly wore a coif closely resembling the Presbyterian
minister's cap.
1166 *crabat*: cravat.
1181 *Bel and the Dragon*: the title of one of the books of the Apocrypha. It
describes how the priests of the idol Bel and their wives and children ate the
meat that was daily sacrificed to the god.

For they, poor knaves, were glad to cheat
To get their wives and children meat,
But these will not be fobbed off so: 1185
They must have wealth and power too,
Or else with blood and desolation
They'll tear it out o'th' heart o'th' nation.

'Sure these themselves from primitive
And heathen priesthood do derive 1190
When butchers were the only clerks,
Elders and presbyters of kirks,
Whose Directory was to kill,
And some believe it is so still.
The only difference is that then 1195
They slaughtered only beasts, now men.
For then to sacrifice a bullock,
Or now and then a child to Moloch,
They count a vile abomination,
But not to slaughter a whole nation. 1200
Presbytery does but translate
The Papacy to a Free State,
A Commonwealth of popery,
Where every village is a see
As well as Rome, and must maintain 1205
A tithe-pig metropolitan;
Where every presbyter and deacon
Commands the keys, for cheese and bacon,
And every hamlet's governed
By's holiness, the church's head, 1210
More haughty and severe in's place
Than Gregory and Boniface.[n]
Such church must, surely, be a monster
With many heads: for, if we conster

1193 *Directory*: an allusion to the *Directory for the Public Worship of God* with which, in 1644, the Presbyterians replaced the *Book of Common Prayer*.

1198 *Moloch*: the name of an idol worshipped by the Canaanites, to which children were sacrificed.

1206 *metropolitan*: archbishop. Ralpho here alludes to the fact that Presbyterian ministers received tithes.

1208 *the keys*: the 'keys of heaven and hell', the term used to describe the spiritual power of the clergy, through whom divine grace was transmitted.

1213 *monster*: the many-headed monster of Revelation 12. Puritan preachers frequently attempted to interpret the passage as a prophecy of contemporary political events.

1214 *conster*: construe, interpret.

What in th'Apocalypse we find,   1215
According to th'apostle's mind,
'Tis that the Whore of Babylon,
With many heads, did ride upon;
Which heads denote the sinful tribe
Of deacon, priest, lay-elder, scribe.   1220

'Lay-elder, Simeon to Levi,
Whose little finger is as heavy
As loins of patriarchs^n, prince-prelate,
And bishop-secular. This zealot
Is of a mongrel, diverse kind,   1225
Cleric before, and lay behind;
A lawless, linsey-woolsey brother,
Half of one order, half another;
A creature of amphibious nature,
On land a beast, a fish in water;   1230
That always preys on grace or sin;
A sheep without, a wolf within.
This fierce inquisitor has chief
Dominion over men's belief
And manners; can pronounce a saint   1235
Idolatrous or ignorant,
When superciliously he sifts
Through coarsest bolter others' gifts;
For all men live and judge amiss
Whose talents jump not just with his.   1240
He'll lay on gifts with hands, and place
On dullest noddle light and grace,
The manufacture of the kirk;
Those pastors are but th'handiwork
Of his mechanic paws, instilling   1245
Divinity in them by feeling,

1221 'Simeon and Levi are brethren; instruments of cruelty are in their habitations' (Genesis 49:5). The Levites were a special caste of priests.
1227 *lawless*: i.e. unlawful. The wearing of linsey-woolsey, a material woven from a mixture of flax and wool, was forbidden by Old Testament law (Deuteronomy 22:11).
1237 *superciliously*: dogmatically, dictatorially.
1240 *jump*: coincide.
1241 *gifts*: in the Biblical sense of 'the dispensations of God' (I Corinthians 12:1).

From whence they start up chosen vessels,
Made by contact, as men get measles.
So cardinals, they say, do grope
At th'other end the new-made pope.'[n]   1250

'Hold! Hold!' quoth Hudibras, ' "Soft fire",
They say, "does make sweet malt". Good squire,
Festina lente, not too fast;
For "Haste", the proverb says, "makes waste".
The quirks and cavils thou dost make   1255
Are false, and built upon mistake;
And I shall bring you, with your pack
Of fallacies, t'elenchi back,
And put your arguments in mood
And figure to be understood.   1260
I'll force you by right ratiocination
To leave your vitilitigation,
And make you keep to th'question close
And argue dialecticῶς.

'The question then, to state it first,   1265
Is which is better or which worst,
Synods or bears. Bears I avow
To be the worst, and synods thou.
But to make good th'assertion,
Thou say'st they're really all one.   1270
If so, not worst; for if they're *idem*,
Why then, "*Tantundem dat tantidem*".
For if they are the same, by course
Neither is better, neither worse.

1262 Vitilitigation is a word the knight was passionately in love with, and never
failed to use it upon all possible occasions, and therefore to omit it when it
fell in the way, had argued too great a neglect of his learning and parts, though
it means no more than a perverse humour of wrangling.

1247 *chosen vessels*: an allusion to Acts 9:15.
1251–2 The saying was proverbial (*ODEP* 750).
1253 *Festina lente*: 'hasten slowly', a Latin proverb.
1258 *elenchi*: logical refutation.
1259–60 Cf. i. i. 80 and note.
1264 *dialecticῶς*: logically.
1271 *idem*: the same.
1272 *Tantundem dat tantidem*: 'the same gives the same.'

But I deny they are the same,   1275
More than a maggot and I am.
That both are *animalia*
I grant, but not *rationalia*;
For though they do agree in kind,
Specific difference we find,   1280
And can no more make bears of these
Than prove my horse is Socrates.[n]

'That synods are bear-gardens too
Thou dost affirm; but I say "No",
And thus I prove it in a word: 1285
Whats'ever assembly's not empowered
To censure, curse, absolve and ordain
Can be no synod; but bear-garden
Has no such power; *ergo* 'tis none.
And so thy sophistry's o'erthrown.   1290

'But yet we are beside the question
Which thou didst raise the first contest on;
For that was "Whether bears are better
Than synod-men". I say "*Negatur*".
That bears are beasts, and synods men,   1295
Is held by all. They're better then.
For bears and dogs on four legs go,
As beasts, but synod-men on two.[n]
'Tis true they all have teeth and nails;
But prove that synod-men have tails;   1300
Or that a rugged, shaggy fur
Grows o'er the hide of presbyter;
Or that his snout and spacious ears
Do hold proportion with a bear's.
A bear's a savage beast, of all   1305
Most ugly and unnatural,
Whelped without form, until the dam
Have licked him into shape and frame;[n]

1277–8 An allusion to the definition of a man as 'a rational animal'.
1279–80 Hudibras argues that, although both belong to the same genus, they
    are of different species.
1289 *ergo*: therefore.
1294 *Negatur*: 'it is not so.'

But all thy light can ne'er evict
That ever synod-man was licked,   1310
Or brought to any other fashion
Than his own will and inclination.

'But thou dost further yet in this
Oppugn thyself and sense, that is,
Thou wouldst have presbyters to go   1315
For bears and dogs and bearwards too.
A strange chimera of beasts and men,
Made up of pieces heterogene,
Such as in nature never met
In eodem subjecto yet!   1320

'Thy other arguments are all
Supposures, hypothetical,
That do but beg, and we may choose
Either to grant them or refuse.
Much thou hast said which, I know when   1325
And where, thou stol'st from other men
(Whereby 'tis plain thy "light" and "gifts"
Are all but plagiary shifts),
And is the same that ranter said
That, arguing with me, broke my head,   1330
And tore a handful of my beard.
The self-same cavils then I heard,
When being in hot dispute about
This controversy, we fell out,
And what thou know'st I answered then   1335
Will serve to answer thee again.'

Quoth Ralpho, 'Nothing but th'abuse
Of human learning you produce;
Learning, that cobweb of the brain,
Profane, erroneous and vain;   1340
A trade of knowledge as replete
As others are with fraud and cheat;
An art t'encumber gifts and wit,
And render both for nothing fit;

1309 *evict*: evince; prove by argument.
1320 *In eodem subjecto*: 'in the same subject'.

Makes light unactive, dull and troubled,   1345
Like little David in Saul's doublet;[n]
A cheat that scholars put upon
Other men's reason and their own;
A fort of error, to ensconce
Absurdity and ignorance;   1350
That renders all the avenues
To truth impervious and abstruse,
By making plain things, in debate,
By art perplexed and intricate:
For nothing goes for sense or light   1355
That will not with old rules jump right;
As if rules were not in the schools
Derived from truth, but truth from rules.

'This pagan, heathenish invention
Is good for nothing but contention.   1360
For as in sword-and-buckler fight
All blows do on the target light,
So when men argue, the great'st part
O'th' contest falls on terms of art,
Until the fustian stuff be spent,   1365
And then they fall to th'argument.'

Quoth Hudibras, 'Friend Ralph, thou hast
Out-run the constable at last;
For thou art fallen on a new
Dispute, as senseless as untrue,   1370
But to the former opposite
And contrary as black to white;
Mere *disparata*, that concerning
Presbytery, this, human learning;
Two things s'averse, they never yet   1375
But in thy rambling fancy met.
But I shall take a fit occasion
T'evince thee by ratiocination
Some other time, in place more proper
Than this we're in; therefore let's stop here   1380
And rest our wearied bones awhile,
Already tired with other toil.

1356 *jump*: coincide.
1368 *Out-run the constable*: gone too far (a proverbial expression).
1373 *disparata*: 'essentially different things'.

Hudibras

The Second Part

CANTO I

THE ARGUMENT

The knight being clapped by th'heels in prison,
The last unhappy expedition,
Love brings his action on the case,
And lays it upon Hudibras.
How he receives the lady's visit,
And cunningly solicits his suit,
Which she defers; yet on parole
Redeems him from th'enchanted hole.

But now t'observe romantic method,
Let rusty steel awhile be sheathed;
And all those harsh and rugged sounds
Of bastinadoes, cuts and wounds
Exchanged to love's more gentle style,   5
To let our reader breathe awhile;
In which that we may be as brief as
Is possible, by way of preface.

Is't not enough to make one strange
That some men's fancies should ne'er change?   10
But make all people do and say
The same things still the self-same way?
Some writers make all ladies purloined,
And knights pursuing like a whirlwind;
Others make all their knights, in fits   15
Of jealousy to lose their wits,

1. The beginning of this second part may perhaps seem strange and abrupt to those who do not know that it was written of purpose in imitation of Virgil, who begins the fourth book of his *Aeneides* in the very same manner (*At regina gravi*, etc.). And this is enough to satisfy the curiosity of those who believe that invention and fancy ought to be measured (like cases in law) by precedents, or else they are in the power of the critic.

Argument 3 *action on the case*: 'writ against him' (a legal expression).
9 *strange*: wonder, be surprised.

Till drawing blood o'th' dames, like witches,
They're forthwith cured of their capriches.
Some always thrive in their amours
By pulling plasters off their sores;   20
As cripples do to get an alms,
Just so do they, and win their dames.
Some force whole regions, in despite
O' geography, to change their site,
Make former times shake hands with latter,   25
And that which was before come after.
But those that write in rhyme still make
The one verse for the other's sake:
For one for sense and one for rhyme
I think 's sufficient at one time.   30

But we forget in what sad plight
We lately left the captived knight
And pensive squire, both bruised in body
And conjured into safe custody.
Tired with dispute and speaking Latin,   35
As well as basting and bear-baiting,
And desperate of any course
To free himself by wit or force,
His only solace was, that now
His dog-bolt fortune was so low   40
That either it must quickly end
Or turn about again and mend;
In which he found th'event, no less
Than other times, beside his guess.

There is a tall, long-sided dame   45
(But wondrous light) ycleped Fame,[n]
That like a thin chameleon boards
Herself on air, and eats your words.

---

17 *like witches*: an allusion to the belief that someone held in the power of a
    witch could free himself by drawing her blood.
18 *capriches*: whims.
24–6 Cf. p. 260.
40 *dog-bolt*: wretched.
43 *event*: outcome.
47–8 There was a belief that the chameleon lived exclusively on air (Sir Thomas
    Browne, *Pseudodoxia Epidemica*, III. xxi).

Upon her shoulders wings she wears,
Like hanging sleeves, lined through with ears   50
And eyes and tongues, as poets list,
Made good by deep mythologist.
With these she through the welkin flies,
And sometimes carries truth, oft lies,
With letters hung, like eastern pigeons   55
And mercuries of furthest regions,
Diurnals writ for regulation
Of lying, to inform the nation,
And by their public use to bring down
The rate of whetstones in the kingdom.[n]   60
About her neck a packet-mail,
Fraught with advice, some fresh, some stale;
Of men that walked when they were dead,
And cows of monsters brought to bed;
Of hailstones big as pullet's eggs,   65
And puppies whelped with twice two legs;
A blazing star seen in the west
By six or seven men at least.
Two trumpets she does sound at once,
But both of clean contrary tones;   70
But whether both with the same wind,
Or one before and one behind,
We know not; only this can tell:
The one sounds vilely, th'other well.
And therefore vulgar authors name   75
Th'one good, the other evil fame.

This tattling gossip knew too well
What mischief Hudibras befell,
And straight the spiteful tidings bears
Of all to th'unkind widow's ears.[n]   80
Democritus ne'er laughed so loud
To see bawds carted through the crowd,

---

56 *mercuries*: newspapers.
61 *packet-mail*: mail packet.
62 *advice*: news.
81 *Democritus*: Greek philosopher (?460–?362 B.C.), popularly known as 'the
laughing philosopher'. This couplet is probably derived from Juvenal, *Satires*,
x. 33–7.

Or funerals with stately pomp
March slowly on in solemn dump
As she laughed out, until her back   85
As well as sides was like to crack.
She vowed she would go see the sight,
And visit the distressed knight,
To do the office of a neighbour
And be a gossip at his labour,   90
And from his wooden gaol, the stocks,
To set at large his fetterlocks,
And by exchange, parole or ransom
To free him from th'enchanted mansion.
This being resolved, she called for hood   95
And usher, implements abroad
Which ladies wear, beside a slender
Young waiting-damsel to attend her.
All which appearing, on she went
To find the knight in limbo pent,   100
And 'twas not long before she found
Him and his stout squire in the pound,
Both coupled in enchanted tether,
By further leg behind together;
For as he sat upon his rump,   105
His head like one in doleful dump
Between his knees, his hands applied
Unto his ears on either side,
And by him, in another hole,
Afflicted Ralpho, cheek by jowl.   110

She came upon him in his wooden
Magician's circle on the sudden,
As spirits do t'a conjurer
When in their dreadful shapes th'appear.
No sooner did the knight perceive her   115
But straight he fell into a fever,

84 *dump*: mournful music.
90 *gossip*: a familiar acquaintance; often used of a woman visiting a female
    friend who is in childbirth.
96 *usher*: a male attendant.
100 *limbo*: prison (colloquial).
104 *further leg behind*: i.e. their right hind legs.

Inflamed all over with disgrace
To be seen by her in such a place;
Which made him hang the head and scowl,
And wink and goggle like an owl.   120
He felt his brains begin to swim
When thus the dame accosted him:
'This place', quoth she, 'they say's enchanted
And with delinquent spirits haunted,
That here are tied in chains and scourged   125
Until their guilty crimes be purged.
Look! There are two of them appear
Like persons I have seen somewhere.
Some have mistaken blocks and posts
For spectres, apparitions, ghosts,   130
With saucer-eyes and horns, and some
Have heard the devil beat a drum,[n]
But if our eyes are not false glasses
That give a wrong account of faces,
That beard and I should be acquainted   135
Before 'twas conjured and enchanted;
For though it be disfigured somewhat
As if't had lately been in combat,
It did belong t'a worthy knight,
Howe'er this goblin is come by 't.'   140

When Hudibras the lady heard
To take kind notice of his beard,
And speak with such respect and honour
Both of the beard and the beard's owner,
He thought it best to set as good   145
A face upon it as he could,
And thus he spoke: 'Lady, your bright
And radiant eyes are in the right.
The beard's th'identic beard you knew,
The same numerically true;   150
Nor is it worn by fiend or elf
But its proprietor himself.'

---

124 *delinquent*: a term used by the Puritans to describe their political opponents.
   See note to I. i. 734, p. 291.
150 *numerically*: precisely.

'Oh heavens!' quoth she, 'Can that be true?
I do begin to fear 'tis you:
Not by your individual whiskers   155
But by your dialect and discourse,
That never spoke to man or beast
In notions vulgarly expressed.
But what malignant star, alas,
Has brought you both to this sad pass?'   160

Quoth he, 'The fortune of the war,
Which I am less afflicted for
Than to be seen with beard and face
By you in such a homely case.'

Quoth she, 'Those need not be ashamed   165
For being honourably maimed.
If he that is in battle conquered
Have any title to his own beard,
Though yours be sorely lugged and torn,
It does your visage more adorn   170
Than if 'twere pruned and starched and landered
And cut square by the Russian standard.
A torn beard's like a tattered ensign:
That's bravest which there are most rents in.
That petticoat about your shoulders   175
Does not so well become a soldier's,
And I'm afraid they are worse handled,
Although i'th' rear: your beard the van led.
And those uneasy bruises make
My heart for company to ache,   180
To see so worshipful a friend
I'th' pillory set at the wrong end.'

Quoth Hudibras, 'This thing called pain
Is (as the learned stoics maintain)
Not bad *simpliciter* nor good,   185
But merely as 'tis understood.[n]

164 *homely case*: humble predicament.
171 *landered*: laundered (spelling adopted for the sake of rhyme).
172 Square-cut beards were said to be worn generally by the Russians (Giles
Fletcher, *Of the Russe Common Wealth*, 1856, p. 146).
185 *simpliciter*: simply; inherently.

Sense is deceitful and may feign
As well in counterfeiting pain
As other gross phenomenas
In which it oft mistakes the case.   190
But since th'immortal intellect
(That's free from error and defect,
Whose objects still persist the same)
Is free from outward bruise or maim,
Which naught external can expose   195
To gross, material bangs or blows,
It follows we can ne'er be sure
Whether we pain or not endure,
And just so far are sore and grieved
As by the fancy is believed.   200

'Some have been wounded with conceit,
And died of mere opinion straight;
Others, though wounded sore, in reason
Felt no contusion nor discretion.
A Saxon duke[n] did grow so fat   205
That mice, as histories relate,
Eat grots and labyrinths to dwell in
His postic parts, without his feeling:
Then how is't possible a kick
Should e'er reach that way to the quick?'   210

Quoth she, 'I grant it is in vain
For one that's basted to feel pain,
Because the pangs his bones endure
Contribute nothing to the cure.
Yet honour hurt is wont to rage   215
With pain no medicine can assuage.'

Quoth he, 'That honour's very squeamish
That takes a basting for a blemish:

---

205 This history of the Duke of Saxony is not altogether so strange as that of a
bishop, his countryman, who was quite eaten up with rats and mice.[n]

---

201 *conceit*: imagination.
204 *discretion*: dissolution.
208 *postic*: posterior
211 *in vain*: useless.

For what's more honourable than scars,
Or skin to tatters rent in wars?   220
Some have been beaten till they know
What wood a cudgel's of by th'blow;
Some kicked until they can feel whether
A shoe be Spanish or neat's leather,
And yet have met, after long running,   225
With some whom they have taught that cunning.
The furthest way about, t'o'ercome,
In th'end does prove the nearest home.
By laws of learned duellists,
They that are bruised with wood or fists,   230
And think one beating may for once
Suffice, are cowards and poltroons;
But if they dare engage t'a second,
They're stout and gallant fellows reckoned.
Th'old Romans freedom did bestow;   235
Our princes worship, with a blow;
King Pyrrhus cured his splenetic
And testy courtiers with a kick;
The Negus, when some mighty lord
Or potentate's to be restored   240
And pardoned for some great offence
With which he's willing to dispense,
First has him laid upon his belly,
Then beaten back and side t'a jelly;
That done, he rises, humbly bows,   245
And gives thanks for the gracious blows,
Departs not meanly proud, and boasting
Of his magnificent rib-roasting.
The beaten soldier proves most manful
That, like his sword, endures the anvil,   250

---

237 Pyrrhus, King of Epirus, who, as Pliny says, had this occult quality in his
    toe. *Pollicis in dextro pede tactu lienosis medebatur.* L.7.C.ii.

227–8 Proverbial (*ODEP* 245).
235 An *alapa*, or blow on the face, was the formal token by which a Roman
    slave received his freedom.
236 *worship*: i.e. knighthood.
239 *Negus*: the ruler of Abyssinia. According to le Blanc (see I. ii. 282) he
    punished any nobleman found guilty of a crime in the way Butler describes
    (*The World Surveyed*, 1660, 190).
237 note: 'To touch the great toe of his right foot was a cure for inflammation
    of the spleen' (Pliny, *Natural History*, VII. ii. 155).

And justly's held more formidable
The more his valour's malleable;
But he that fears a bastinado
Will run away from his own shadow.
And though I'm now in durance fast,   255
By our own party basely cast,
Ransom, exchange, parole refused,
And worse than by the enemy used,
In close *catasta* shut, past hope
Of wit or valour to elope   260
(As beards, the nearer that they tend
To th'earth, still grow more reverend,
And cannons shoot the higher pitches
The lower we let down their breeches),
I'll make this low, dejected fate   265
Advance me to a greater height.'

Quoth she, 'You've almost made m'in love
With that which did my pity move.
Great wits and valours, like great states,
Do sometimes sink with their own weights;   270
Th'extremes of glory and of shame,
Like east and west, become the same;
No Indian prince has to his palace
More followers than a thief to th'gallows.
But if a beating seem so brave,   275
What glories must a whipping have?
Such great achievements cannot fail
To cast salt on a woman's tail.
For if I thought your natural talent
Of passive courage were so gallant,   280
As you strain hard to have it thought,
I could grow amorous and dote.'

When Hudibras this language heard,
He pricked up's ears and stroked his beard.

259 *Catasta* is but a pair of stocks in English, but heroical poetry must not admit
of any vulgar word (especially of paltry signification) and therefore some of
our modern authors are fain to import foreign words from abroad that were
never before heard of in our language.

259 *catasta*: the Latin word for the platform on which slaves were exposed for
sale.

Thought he, 'This is the lucky hour: 285
Wines work when vines are in the flower.ⁿ
This crisis then I'll set my rest on
And put her boldly to the question.'

'Madame, what you would seem to doubt,
Shall be to all the world made out: 290
How I've been drubbed and with what spirit
And magnanimity I bear it.
And if you doubt it to be true,
I'll stake myself down against you;
And if I fail in love or troth,   295
Be you the winner and take both.'

Quoth she, 'I've heard old cunning stagers
Say fools for arguments use wagers.
And though I praised your valour, yet
I did not mean to baulk your wit,   300
Which, if you have, you needs must know
What I have told you before now
And you b'experiment have proved:
I cannot love where I'm beloved.'

Quoth Hudibras, ' 'Tis a caprich   305
Beyond th'infliction of a witch;
So cheats to play with those still aim
That do not understand the game.
Love in your heart as idly burns
As fire in antique Roman urns   310
To warm the dead,ⁿ and vainly light
Those only that see nothing by 't.
Have you not power to entertain
And render love for love again,
As no man can draw in his breath   315
At once, and force out air beneath?
Or do you love yourself so much
To bear all rivals else a grutch?

287 *set my rest*: venture everything.
300 *baulk*: overlook.
309 *idly*: uselessly.
318 *grutch*: grudge.

What fate can lay a greater curse
Than you upon yourself would force? 320
For wedlock without love, some say,
Is but a lock without a key.
It is a kind of rape to marry
One that neglects or cares not for ye.
For what does make it ravishment 325
But being against the mind's consent?
A rape that is the more inhuman
For being acted by a woman.
Why are you fair, but to entice us
To love you, that you may despise us? 330
But though you cannot love, you say,
Out of your own fanatic way,
Why should you not, at least, allow
Those that love you to do so too?
For, as you fly me, and pursue 335
Love more averse, so I do you,
And am by your own doctrine taught
To practise what you call a fault.'

Quoth she, 'If what you say be true,
You must fly me as I do you, 340
But 'tis not what we do, but say,
In love and preaching that must sway.'

Quoth he, 'To bid me not to love
Is to forbid my pulse to move,
My beard to grow, my ears to prick up, 345
Or (when I'm in a fit) to hiccup.
Command me to piss out the moon,
And 'twill as easily be done.
Love's power's too great to be withstood
By feeble, human flesh and blood. 350
'Twas he that brought upon his knees
The hectoring kill-cow Hercules;
Reduced his leaguer lion's skin
T'a petticoat, and made him spin;

---

352 *kill-cow*: bully.
353 *leaguer*: a leaguer-coat was a military cloak. Hercules is often represented as wearing the skin of the Nemean lion.
353–6 An allusion to the servitude of Hercules to Omphale, Queen of Lydia.

Seized on his club and made it dwindle   355
T'a feeble distaff and a spindle.
'Twas he made emperors gallants
To their own sisters and their aunts;
Set popes and cardinals agog
To play with pages at leap-frog;   360
'Twas he that gave our senate purges
And fluxed the House of many a burgess;[n]
Made those that represent the nation
Submit, and suffer amputation,
And all the grandees o'th' Cabal   365
Adjourn to tubs at spring and fall.
He mounted synod-men and rod 'em
To Dirty Lane and Little Sodom;
Made 'em curvet like Spanish jennets,
And take the ring at Madame ——.   370
'Twas he that made Saint Francis do
More than the devil could tempt him to:
In cold and frosty weather, grow
Enamoured of a wife of snow,
And though she were of rigid temper,   375
With melting flames accost and tempt her;
Which after in enjoyment quenching,
He hung a garland on his engine.'[n]

Quoth she, 'If love have these effects,
Why is it not forbid our sex?   380
Why is't not damned and interdicted
For diabolical and wicked?

371 The ancient writers of the lives of saints were of the same sort of people
   who first writ of knight-errantry, and as in the one they rendered the brave
   actions of some very great persons ridiculous by their prodigious lies and
   sottish way of describing them, so they have abused the piety of some very
   devout persons by imposing such stories upon them, as this upon Saint
   Francis.

357–8 The Emperor Caligula committed incest with his sister (Suetonius,
   Caligula, xxiv).
366 *tubs*: sweating-tubs, used in the treatment of venereal disease.
368 Streets in the city of London notorious as centres of prostitution.
370 *the ring*: in horsemanship, a circle of metal, hung from a post, which the
   rider tried to carry off on his lance.
370 *Madame* ——: a certain Mrs. Bennett, described by Pepys as 'a famous
   strumpet' (*Diary*, 22 Sept. 1660).

And sung, as out of tune, against,
As Turk and Pope are by the saints?[n]
I find I've greater reason for it   385
Than I believ'd before, t'abhor it.'

Quoth Hudibras, 'These sad effects
Spring from your heathenish neglects
Of love's great power, which he returns
Upon yourselves with equal scorns,   390
And those who worthy lovers slight,
Plagues with preposterous appetite.
This made the beauteous Queen of Crete
To take a town bull for her sweet,
And from her greatness stoop so low   395
To be the rival of a cow;
Others to prostitute their great hearts
To be baboons' and monkeys' sweethearts;
Some with the devil himself in league grow,
By's representative, a negro.   400
'Twas this made vestal maids lovesick
And venture to be buried quick;
Some by their fathers and their brothers
To be made mistresses and mothers.
'Tis this that proudest dames enamours   405
On lackeys and *valets-des-chambres*;
Their haughty stomachs overcomes
And makes 'em stoop to dirty grooms,
To slight the world, and to disparage
Claps, issue, infamy and marriage.'   410

Quoth she, 'These judgements are severe,
Yet such as I should rather bear
Than trust men with their oaths, or prove
Their faith and secrecy in love.'

393 The history of Pasiphae is common enough, only this may be observed:
that though she brought the bull a son and heir, yet the husband was fain to
father it, as appears by the name, perhaps because the country being an island,
he was within the four seas[n] when the infant was begotten.

393 *Queen of Crete*: Pasiphae, who is said to have been enamoured of a bull
and given birth to the minotaur.
399 *devil*: proverbially thought to be black in colour (*ODEP* 63, 182).
402 *quick*: alive. Vestal virgins who broke their vow of continence were forced to
die of starvation while buried in a small room.

Says he, 'There is a weighty reason   415
For secrecy in love as treason.
Love is a burglarer, a felon,
That at the windore eye does steal in
To rob the heart, and with his prey
Steals out again a closer way,   420
Which whosoever can discover,
He's sure (as he deserves) to suffer.
Love is a fire that burns and sparkles
In men as naturally as in charcoals,
Which sooty chemists stop in holes   425
When out of wood they extract coals;[n]
So lovers should their passions choke
That though they burn, they may not smoke.
'Tis like that sturdy thief that stole
And dragged beasts backwards into's hole;   430
So love does lovers, and us men
Draws by the tails into his den,
That no impression may discover
And trace t'his cave the wary lover.
But if you doubt I should reveal   435
What you entrust me under seal,
I'll prove myself as close and virtuous
As your own secretary, Albertus.'

Quoth she, 'I grant you may be close
In hiding what your aims propose.   440
Love passions are like parables,
By which men still mean something else:
Though love be all the world's pretence,
Money's the mythologic sense,
The real substance of the shadow   445
Which all address and courtship's made to.'

438 Albertus Magnus was a Swedish bishop who wrote a very learned work,
  De Secretis Mulierum.

---

418 *windore*: window.
429 *thief*: the giant Cacus who stole oxen from Hercules. He dragged the animals
  into his cave backwards by their tails so that they left no footprints.
438 *Albertus*: Albertus Magnus (?1193–1280), Bishop of Ratisbon. Among the
  works formerly attributed to him is the *De Secretis Mulierum*, 1596.

Thought he, 'I understand your play,
And how to quit you your own way.
He that will win his dame must do
As love does when he bends his bow: 450
With one hand thrust the lady from,
And with the other pull her home.'
'I grant', quoth he, 'wealth is a great
Provocative to amorous heat.
It is all philtres and high diet   455
That makes love rampant and to fly out;
'Tis beauty always in the flower
That buds and blossoms at fourscore;
'Tis that by which the sun and moon
At their own weapons are out-done;   460
That makes knights errant fall in trances
And lay about 'em in romances;
'Tis virtue, wit and worth and all
That men divine and sacred call.
For what is worth in anything   465
But so much money as 'twill bring?
Or what but riches is there known
Which man can solely call his own;
In which no creature goes his half,
Unless it be to squint and laugh?   470
I do confess, with goods and land,
I'd have a wife at second hand,
And such you are. Nor is't your person
My stomach's set so sharp and fierce on,
But 'tis your better part, your riches,   475
That my enamoured heart bewitches.
Let me your fortune but possess,
And settle your person how you please,
Or make it o'er in trust to th'devil,
You'll find me reasonable and civil.'   480

.

---

470 Pliny in his *Natural History* affirms that *Uni animalium homini oculi de-pravantur, unde cognomina Strabonum et Paetorum*. Lib. 2.

---

469 *goes his half*: shares with him; resembles him.
470 note: 'Man is the only animal whose eyes are liable to distortion, which is the origin of the family names Squint-eye and Blinky' (Pliny, *Natural History*, trans. Rackham, 1940, iii. 527).

Quoth she, 'I like this plainness better
Than false mock-passion, speech or letter,
Or any feat of qualm or sowning
But hanging of yourself or drowning.
Your only way with me to break   485
Your mind is breaking of your neck.
For as when merchants break, o'erthrown
Like ninepins, they strike others down,
So that would break my heart, which done,
My tempting fortune is your own.   490
These are but trifles; every lover
Will damn himself over and over
And greater matters undertake
For a less worthy mistress' sake.
Yet they're the only ways to prove   495
Th'unfeigned realities of love.
For he that hangs, or beats out's brains,
The devil's in him if he feigns.'

Quoth Hudibras, 'This way's too rough
For mere experiment and proof.   500
It is no jesting, trivial matter
To swing in th'air or plunge in water,
And like a water-witch try love:
That's to destroy and not to prove,
As if a man should be dissected   505
To find what part is disaffected.
Your better way is to make over
In trust your fortune to your lover.
Trust is a trial: if it break,
'Tis not so desperate as a neck.   510
Beside, th'experiment's more certain:
Men venture necks to gain a fortune.
The soldier does it every day
(Eight to the week) for sixpence pay;

483 *sowning*: swooning.
485 *break your mind*: reveal your thoughts.
487 *break*: go bankrupt.
503 *water-witch*: a woman suspected of witchcraft who is subjected to the swim-
    ming test. If she did not sink she was believed to have revealed herself as a
    witch.

Your pettifoggers damn their souls   515
To share with knaves in cheating fools;
And merchants venturing through the main,
Slight pirates, rocks and horns for gain.
This is the way I advise you to:
Trust me and see what I will do.'   520

Quoth she, 'I should be loath to run
Myself all th'hazard and you none,
Which must be done, unless some deed
Of yours aforesaid do precede.
Give but yourself one gentle swing   525
For trial, and I'll cut the string;
Or give that reverend head a maul
Or two or three, against a wall,
To show you are a man of mettle
And I'll engage myself to settle.'   530

Quoth he, 'My head's not made of brass
As Friar Bacon's noddle was,
Nor like some Indian's skull, so tough
That authors say 'twas musket-proof,[n]
As it had need to be to enter   535
As yet on any new adventure.
You see what bangs it has endured,
That would, before new feats, be cured.
But if that's all you stand upon,
Here, strike me luck! It shall be done.'   540

Quoth she, 'The matter's not so far gone
As you suppose: two words t'a bargain.

532 The tradition of Friar Bacon and the brazen head is very commonly known
and, considering the times he lived in, is not much more strange than what
another great philosopher of his name has since delivered up, of a ring that,
being tied in a string, and held like a pendulum in the middle of a silver bowl,
will vibrate of itself, and tell exactly against the sides of the divining cup, the
same thing with 'Time is, Time was, etc.'[n]
533 American Indians, among whom the same authors affirm that there are others
whose skulls are so soft, to use their own words, *ut digito perforari possunt.*

---

532 See I. ii. 344 and note.
540 *strike me luck*: 'it's a bargain.'
542 Proverbial (*ODEP* 852).
533 note: 'that they could be perforated with the finger'.

That may be done, and time enough,
When you have given downright proof.
And yet 'tis no fantastic pike   545
I have to love, nor coy dislike;
'Tis no implicit, nice aversion
T'your conversation, mien or person,
But a just fear lest you should prove
False and perfidious in love.   550
For if I thought you could be true,
I could love twice as much as you.'

Quoth he 'My faith as adamantine
As chains of destiny I'll maintain;
True as Apollo ever spoke,   555
Or oracle from heart of oak.
And if you'll give my flame but vent,
Now in close hugger-mugger pent,
And shine upon me but benignly
With that one and that other pigsney,   560
The sun and day shall sooner part
Than love, or you, shake off my heart;
The sun, that shall no more dispense
His own, but your bright influence.
I'll carve your name on barks of trees,   565
With true-love's knots and flourishes,
That shall infuse eternal spring
And everlasting flourishing.
Drink every letter on 't in stum,[n]
And make it brisk champagne become.   570
Where e'er you tread your foot shall set
The primrose and the violet;
All spices, perfumes and sweet powders
Shall borrow from your breath their odours;

556 Jupiter's oracle in Epirus near the city of Dodona, *ubi nemus erat Jovi sacrum, quernum totum in quo Jovis Dodonaei templum fuisse narratur.*

---

545 *pike*: pique; animosity.
555 *Apollo*: i.e. through his oracle at Delphi.
556 The oracle delivered its messages through the rustling leaves of an oak tree (Herodotus, ii. 55).
560 *pigsney*: 'dear little eye', a term of endearment.
556 note: 'where there was a grove sacred to Jupiter, planted wholly with oaks, in which there is said to have been the temple of Jupiter at Dodona'.

Nature her charter shall renew   575
And take all lives of things from you;
The world depend upon your eye,
And when you frown upon it, die.
Only our loves shall still survive,
New worlds and natures to out-live,   580
And, like to heralds' moons, remain
All crescents, without change or wane.'

'Hold! Hold!' quoth she, 'No more of this!
Sir knight, you take your aim amiss.
For you will find it a hard chapter   585
To catch me with poetic rapture,
In which your mastery of art
Doth show itself, and not your heart;
Nor will you raise in mine combustion,
By dint of high heroic fustian.   590
She that with poetry is won
Is but a desk to write upon,
And what men say of her, they mean
No more than that on which they lean.
Some with Arabian spices strive   595
T'embalm her, cruelly alive;
Or season her, as French cooks use,
Their *hauts goûts*, *bouillis* or *ragoûts*;
Use her so barbarously ill,
To grind her lips upon a mill,   600
Until the facet doublet doth
Fit their rhymes rather than her mouth;
Her mouth compared t'an oyster's, with
A row of pearl in 't, 'stead of teeth;
Others make posies of her cheeks   605
Where red and whitest colours mix,
In which the lily and the rose
For Indian lake and ceruse goes.
The sun and moon, by her bright eyes
Eclipsed and darkened in the skies,   610

---

598 An *haut goût* is a highly seasoned dish; a *bouilli* is boiled or stewed meat; a
    ragoût is a highly seasoned stew.
601 *facet doublet*: a counterfeit jewel, ground down so that it has many facets or
    sides.
608 *Indian lake*: a red pigment used as a cosmetic.
608 *ceruse*: a cosmetic made from white lead.

Are but black patches that she wears,
Cut into suns and moons and stars,
By which astrologers, as well
As those in heaven above, can tell
What strange events they do foreshow   615
Unto her underworld below;
Her voice the music of the spheres,
So loud it deafens mortal ears,
As wise philosophers have thought,
And that's the cause we hear it not.   620
This has been done by some, who those
They adored in rhyme would kick in prose,
And in those ribbons would have hung
Of which melodiously they sung,
That have the hard fate to write best   625
Of those still that deserve it least.
It matters not how false or forced,
So the best things be said o'th' worst;
It goes for nothing when 'tis said
Only the arrow's drawn to th'head,   630
Whether it be a swan or goose
They level at; so shepherds use
To set the same mark on the hip
Both of their sound and rotten sheep.
For wits that carry low or wide   635
Must be aimed higher or beside
The mark, which else they ne'er come nigh
But when they take their aim awry.
But I do wonder you should choose
This way t'attack me with your muse,   640
As one cut out to pass your tricks on
With fulhams of poetic fiction.
I rather hoped I should no more
Hear from you o'th' gallanting score;
For hard dry-bastings use to prove   645
The readiest remedies in love,
Next a dry diet. But if those fail,
Yet this uneasy loop-hold gaol,

617–20 The range and volume of the music of the spheres was thought to be so
    great that human ears were unable to hear it.
642 *fulhams*: loaded dice.
645 *dry-bastings*: beatings.

In which you're hampered by the fetlock,
Cannot but put y'in mind of wedlock;   650
Wedlock, that's worse than any hole here,
If that may serve you for a cooler,
T'allay your mettle, all agog
Upon a wife, the heavier clog.
Nor rather thank your gentler fate   655
That, for a bruised or broken pate,
Has freed you from those knobs that grow
Much harder on the married brow.
But if no dread can cool your courage
From venturing on that dragon, marriage,   660
Yet give me quarter, and advance
To nobler aims your puissance.
Level at beauty and at wit:
The fairest mark is easiest hit.'

Quoth Hudibras, 'I'm beforehand   665
In that already, with your command;
For where does beauty and high wit
But in your constellation meet?'

Quoth she, 'What does a match imply
But likeness and equality?   670
I know you cannot think me fit
To be the yoke-fellow of your wit,
Nor take one of so mean deserts
To be the partner of your parts;
A grace which, if I could believe,   675
I've not the conscience to receive.'

'That conscience', quoth Hudibras,
'Is misinformed. I'll state the case:
A man may be a legal donor
Of anything whereof he's owner,   680
And may confer it where he lists,
I'th' judgement of all casuists.
Then wit and parts and valour may
Be alienated and made away
By those that are proprietors,   685
As I may give or sell my horse.'

Quoth she, 'I grant the case is true
And proper 'twixt your horse and you,
But whether I may take, as well
As you may give away, or sell?   690
Buyers you know are bid beware,
And worse than thieves receivers are.
How shall I answer hue and cry
For a roan gelding, twelve hands high,
All spurred and switched, a lock on's hoof,   695
A sorrel mane? Can I bring proof
Where, when, by whom, and what y'were sold for,
And in the open market tolled for?
Or, should I take you for a stray,
You must be kept a year and day[n]   700
Ere I can own you, here i'th' pound,
Where if you're sought you may be found,
And, in the meantime, I must pay
For all your provender and hay.'

Quoth he, 'It stands me much upon   705
T'enervate this objection,
And prove myself by topic clear
No gelding as you would infer.
Loss of virility's averred
To be the cause of loss of beard,   710
That does, like embryo in the womb,
Abortive on the chin become.
This first a woman did invent
In envy of man's ornament,
Semiramis of Babylon,   715
Who first of all cut men o'th' stone

715 Semiramis, Queen of Assyria, is said to be the first that invented eunuchs:
Semiramis teneros mares castravit omnium prima (Am. Marcel. L.xiv. p. 22).
Which is something strange in a lady of her constitution, who is said to have
received horses into her embraces as another queen did a bull. But that perhaps may be the reason why she after thought men not worth the while.

691–2 Both sayings are proverbial (*ODEP* 96 and 667).
695 *switched*: whipped.
698 *tolled for*: entered for sale in the toll-book of a cattle-market.
706 *enervate*: destroy the grounds of an argument.
707 *topic*: argument.
715 note: 'Semiramis was the first person of all to castrate young males' (Ammianus Marcellinus, XIV. vi. 17).

To mar their beards, and laid foundation
Of sow-geldering operation.
Look on this beard and tell me whether
Eunuchs wear such, or geldings either.   720
Next it appears I am no horse
That I can argue and discourse,
Have but two legs and ne'er a tail.'

Quoth she, 'That nothing will avail;
For some philosophers of late here   725
Write men have fower legs by nature,
And that 'tis custom makes them go
Erroneously upon but two;
As 'twas in Germany made good
B'a boy that lost himself in a wood,   730
And, growing down t'a man, was wont
With wolves upon all four to hunt.
As for your reasons drawn from tails,
We cannot say they're true or false
Till you explain yourself, and show   735
B'experiment 'tis so or no.'

Quoth he, 'If you'll join issue on't,
I'll give you satisfactory account,
So you will promise if you lose,
To settle all and be my spouse.'   740

'That never shall be done', quoth she,
'To one that wants a tail, by me.
For tails by nature sure were meant,
As well as beards, for ornament,
And, though the vulgar count them homely,   745
In man or beast they are so comely,
So *gentil*, *à la mode* and handsome,
I'll never marry man that wants one.
And till you can demonstrate plain
You have one equal to your mane,   750

725 Sir K. D. in his book *Of Bodies*, who has this story of the German boy, which he endeavours to make good by several natural reasons, by which those who have the dexterity to believe what they please may be fully satisfied of the probability of it.[n]

726 *fower*: four; a spelling adopted for the sake of the metre.

I'll be torn piecemeal by a horse
Ere I'll take you for better or worse.
The Prince of Cambay's daily food
Is asp and basilisk and toad,
Which makes him have so strong a breath,   755
Each night he stinks a queen to death;[n]
Yet I shall rather lie 'n his arms
Than yours, on any other terms.'

Quoth he, 'What nature can afford
I shall produce upon my word,   760
And if she ever gave that boon
To man, I'll prove that I have one—
I mean by postulate illation,
When you shall offer just occasion.
But since you've yet denied to give   765
My heart, your prisoner, a reprieve,
But made it sink down to my heel,
Let that at least your pity feel,
And for the sufferings of your martyr,
Give its poor entertainer quarter,   770
And by discharge or mainprize grant
Delivery from this base restraint.'

Quoth she, 'I grieve to see your leg
Stuck in a hole here like a peg,
And if I knew which way to do't   775
(Your honour safe), I'd let you out.
That dames by gaol-delivery
Of errant knights have seen set free,
When by enchantment they have been,
And sometimes for it too, laid in,   780
Is that which knights are bound to do
By order, oath and honour too.
For what are they renowned and famous else
But aiding of distressed damosels?
But for a lady no ways errant   785
To free a knight, we have no warrant

763 *illation*: inference from premises.
771 *mainprize*: obtaining the release of a prisoner by becoming surety for his
    appearance in court.
777 *gaol-delivery*: a pun on a legal term, meaning to clear a gaol of prisoners in
    order to bring them to trial.

In any authentical romance,
Or classic author yet of France.
And I'd be loath to have you break
An ancient custom for a freak,   790
Or innovation introduce
In place of things of antique use;
To free your heels by any course
That might b'unwholesome to your spurs;
Which if I should consent unto,   795
It is not in my power to do;
For 'tis a service must be done ye
With solemn previous ceremony,
Which always has been used t'untie
The charms of those who here do lie.   800
For as the ancients heretofore
To Honour's temple had no door
But that which thorough Virtue's lay,
So from this dungeon there's no way
To honoured freedom, but by passing   805
That other virtuous school of lashing,
Where knights are kept in narrow lists,
With wooden lockets 'bout their wrists,
In which they for a while are tenants,
And for their ladies suffer penance.   810
Whipping that's virtue's governess,
Tutress of arts and sciences;
That mends the gross mistakes of nature,
And puts new life into dull matter;
That lays foundation for renown,   815
And all the honours of the gown.
This suffered, they are set at large[n]
And freed with honourable discharge.
Then in their robes the penitentials
Are straight presented with credentials,   820
And in their way attended on
By magistrates of every town,
And, all respect and charges paid,
They're to their ancient seats conveyed.

801-3 The temple in Rome which had been dedicated to Honos was later enlarged and dedicated jointly to Honos and Virtus (Cicero, *De Natura Deorum*, II. xxiii).

Now if you'll venture for my sake   825
To try the toughness of your back,
And suffer, as the rest have done,
The laying of a whipping on
(And may you prosper in your suit,
As you with equal vigour do 't),   830
I here engage to be your bail,
And free you from unknightly gaol.
But since our sex's modesty
Will not allow I should be by,
Bring me on oath a fair account,   835
And honour too, when you have done't,
And I'll admit you to the place
You claim as due in my good grace.
If matrimony and hanging go
By destiny, why not whipping too?   840
What medicine else can cure the fits
Of lovers when they lose their wits?
Love is a boy by poets styled,
Then spare the rod and spill the child.
A Persian emperor whipped his grannum   845
The sea, his mother Venus came on,
And hence some reverend men approve
Of rosemary in making love.
As skilful coopers hoop their tubs
With Lydian and with Phrygian dubs,   850
Why may not whipping have as good
A grace, performed in time and mood,
With comely movement, and by art
Raise passion in a lady's heart?
It is an easier way to make   855
Love by, than that which many take.
Who would not rather suffer whipping
Than swallow toasts of bits of ribbin?

845 Xerxes who used to whip the seas and winds. *In corum atque eurum solitus
servire flagellis.* Juven. Sat. 10.

839–40 Proverbial (*ODEP* 513).
844 *spill*: spoil. The saying is proverbial (*ODEP* 759).
848 *rosemary*: thought to have grown near the sea because its Latin name, *ros
marinus*, means 'sea dew'.
858 *ribbin*: ribbon, a spelling adopted for the rhyme.
845 note: 'He used to lash with whips the west and east' (Juvenal, *Satires*, x.
180).

Make wicked verses, treats and faces,
And spell names over with beer glasses? 860
Be under vows to hang and die
Love's sacrifice, and all a lie?
With China oranges and tarts
And whining plays lay baits for hearts?
Bribe chambermaids with love and money 865
To break no roguish jests upon ye?
For lilies limned on cheeks, and roses
With painted perfumes, hazard noses?
Or, venturing to be brisk and wanton,
Do penance in a paper lantern? 870
All this you may compound for now
By suffering what I offer you,
Which is no more than has been done
By knights for ladies long agone.
Did not the great La Mancha do so 875
For the Infanta del Toboso?
Did not th'illustrious Bassa make
Himself a slave for miss's sake,
And with bull's pizzle for her love
Was tawed as gentle as a glove? 880
Was not young Florio sent, to cool
His love for Biancofiore, to school,
Where pedant made his pathic bum
For her sake suffer martyrdom?
Did not a certain lady whip 885
Of late her husband's own lordship,[n]
And, though a grandee of the House,

---

859 *treats*: entreaties.
860 *spell names*: i.e. drink a toast to each letter in a lady's name. Cf. ii. i. 569.
863 *China oranges*: common sweet oranges.
868 *hazard noses*: i.e. risk contracting syphilis which notoriously attacked the nose.
870 *paper lantern*: an allusion to a method of treating syphilis in which the patient's joints were wrapped in brown paper.
875–6 In *Don Quixote* it is not the hero but his squire, Sancho Panza who is advised to whip himself (ii. xxxv).
877 *Bassa*: the hero of Madeleine de Scudéry's romance *Ibrahim the Illustrious Bassa* who, as a result of his love for the princess, becomes the slave of Solyman the Magnificent.
879 *bull's pizzle*: the penis of a bull, dried and used as a whip.
881 *Florio*: the youthful lover of Biancofiore, whose story is told in Boccaccio's *Filocopo*. The boy's parents send him to school to distract his mind from Biancofiore.
883 *pathic*: passive; suffering.

Clawed him with fundamental blows?
Tied him stark naked to a bed-post
And firked his hide as if she'd rid post,   890
And after, in the sessions court
Where whipping's judged, had honour for't?
This swear you will perform, and then
I'll set you from th'enchanted den
And the magician's circle clear.'   895

Quoth he, 'I do profess and swear,
And will perform what you enjoin,
Or may I never see you mine.'

'Amen', quoth she, then turned about
And bid her squier let him out.   900
But ere an artist could be found
T'undo the charms another bound,
The sun grew low and left the skies,
Put down (some write) by ladies' eyes.
The moon pulled off her veil of light   905
That hides her face by day from sight
(Mysterious veil, of brightness made,
That's both her lustre and her shade),
And in the night as freely shone
As if her rays had been her own: 910
For darkness is the proper sphere
Where all false glories use t'appear.
The twinkling stars began to muster
And glitter with their borrowed lustre,
While sleep the wearied world relieved,   915
By counterfeiting death, revived.
Our votary thought it best t'adjourn
His whipping-penance till the morn,
And not to carry on a work
Of such importance in the dark   920
With erring haste, but rather stay
And do 't in th'open face of day,
And in the mean time go in quest
Of next retreat to take his rest.

890 *firked*: thrashed.
901 *artist*: craftsman; mechanic.
919 *carry on*: see I. i. 201 and note.

CANTO II

THE ARGUMENT

The knight and squire, in hot dispute,
Within an ace of falling out,
Are parted with a sudden fright
Of strange alarm and stranger sight,
With which adventuring to stickle,
They're sent away in nasty pickle.

'Tis strange how some men's tempers suit
(Like bawd and brandy) with dispute,
That for their own opinions stand fast
Only to have them clawed and canvast;
That keep their consciences in cases,   5
As fiddlers do their crowds and basses,
Ne'er to be used but when they're bent
To play a fit for argument;
Make true and false, unjust and just,
Of no use but to be discust;   10
Dispute and set a paradox
Like a strait boot upon the stocks,
And stretch it more unmercifully
Than Helmont, Montaigne, White or Tully.[n]
So th'ancient stoics in their porch   15
With fierce dispute maintained their church,
Beat out their brains in fight and study
To prove that virtue is a body,[n]

15 *In porticu* (*stoicorum schola Athenis*) *discipulorum seditionibus, mille quad-ringenti triginta cives interfecti sunt.* Diog. Laert. *in vita Zenonis*, p. 383. Those old virtuosos were better proficients in those exercises than the modern, who seldom improve higher than cuffing and kicking.

---

4 *clawed*: beaten. *canvast*: canvassed, knocked about; a spelling adopted for the rhyme.
6 *crowds*: fiddles.
8 *fit*: a strain of music.
12 *strait*: narrow, tight.
15 note: 'In the colonnade (at the school of the stoics in Athens) 1,430 citizens were killed in the riots of the students' (Diogenes Laertius, *Life of Zeno*, vi).

That *bonum* is an *animal*,[n]
Made good with stout polemic brawl,   20
In which some hundreds on the place
Were slain outright, and many a face
Retrenched of nose and eyes and beard
To maintain what their sect averred;
All which the knight and squire, in wrath,   25
Had like t'have suffered for their faith,
Each striving to make good his own,
As by the sequel shall be shown.

The sun had long since in the lap
Of Thetis taken out his nap,   30
And, like a lobster boiled, the morn
From black to red began to turn,
When Hudibras, whom thoughts and aching
'Twixt sleeping kept, all night, and waking,
Began to rub his drowsy eyes   35
And from his couch prepared to rise,
Resolving to despatch the deed
He vowed to do, with trusty speed.
But first with knocking loud and bawling,
He roused the squire, in truckle lolling,   40
And, after many circumstances
Which vulgar authors in romances
Do use to spend their time and wits on
To make impertinent description,
They got, with much ado, to horse,   45
And to the castle bent their course,
In which he to the dame before
To suffer whipping duty swore;
Where now arrived, and half unharnessed
To carry on the work in earnest,   50

---

19 *Bonum* is such a kind of animal as our modern virtuosi from Don Quixote
   will have windmills under sail to be. The same authors are of opinion that all
   ships are fishes while they are afloat but when they are run on ground or laid
   up in the dock, become ships again.

---

30 *Thetis*: the sea; a personification derived from the name of a sea-nymph.
44 *impertinent*: irrelevant.
50 See I. i. 201 and note.
19 note: Butler is presumably alluding to the ideas of Descartes and Hobbes.
   See note to I. ii. 56, 58, p. 292.

He stopped and paused upon the sudden,
And with a serious forehead plodding,
Sprung a new scruple in his head,
Which first he scratched, and after said,
'Whether it be direct infringing   55
An oath, if I should waive this swingeing,
And what I've sworn to bear, forbear,
And so b'equivocation swear,
Or whether 't be a lesser sin
To be forsworn than act the thing,   60
Are deep and subtle points which must,
T'inform my conscience, be discust;
In which to err a tittle may
To errors infinite make way,
And therefore I desire to know   65
Thy judgement ere we further go.'

Quoth Ralpho, 'Since you do enjoin 't,
I shall enlarge upon the point,
And, for my own part, do not doubt
Th'affirmative may be made out.   70
But first to state the case aright
For best advantage of our light.
And thus 'tis: whether 't be a sin
To claw and curry your own skin,
Greater or less than to forbear   75
And that you are forsworn, forswear.
But first o'th' first: the inward man
And outward, like a clan and clan,
Have always been at daggers drawing,
And one another clapperclawing;   80
Not that they really cuff or fence,
But in a spiritual, mystic sense,
Which to mistake, and make 'em squabble
In literal fray, 's abominable.
'Tis heathenish, in frequent use   85
With pagans and apostate Jews,
To offer sacrifice of Bridewells,
Like modern Indians to their idols

---

52 *plodding*: plotting; thinking hard.
74 *claw and curry*: beat and thrash.
87 *sacrifice of Bridewells*: i.e. whipping. The Bridewell was a house of correction in London where prisoners were frequently whipped.

And mongrel Christians of our times
That expiate less with greater crimes,   90
And call the foul abomination
"Contrition" and "mortification".
Is't not enough we're bruised and kicked
With sinful members of the wicked,
Our vessels, that are sanctified,   95
Profaned and curried, back and side,
But we must claw ourselves with shameful
And heathen stripes, by their example?
Which (were there nothing to forbid it)
Is impious because they did it.   100
This, therefore, may be justly reckoned
A heinous sin. Now to the second,
That saints may claim a dispensation
To swear and forswear on occasion;
I doubt not but it will appear   105
With pregnant light. The point is clear.
Oaths are but words, and words but wind,
Too feeble implements to bind
And hold with deeds proportion, so
As shadows to a substance do.   110
Then when they strive for place, 'tis fit
The weaker vessel should submit.
Although your church be opposite
To ours, as black friars are to white,
In rule and order, yet I grant   115
You are a reformado saint,
And what the saints do claim as due,
You may pretend a title to.
But saints whom oaths or vows oblige
Know little of their privilege,   120
Further, I mean, than carrying on
Some self-advantage of their own.
For if the dev'l to serve his turn
Can tell truth, why the saints should scorn,

---

95 *vessels*: a Puritan term for the body, as a receptacle for the soul.
107 *words but wind*: proverbial (*ODEP* 915).
112 An allusion to I Peter 3:7: 'giving honour unto the wife, as unto the weaker vessel'.
116 *reformado*: the name given to an officer who was left without a command, owing to the 'reforming' of his company.
123–4 Proverbial (*ODEP* 183).

When it serves theirs, to swear and lie,   125
I think there's little reason why,
Else h'has a greater power than they,
Which 'twere impiety to say.
We're not commanded to forbear
Indefinitely, at all to swear,   130
But to swear idly and in vain,
Without self-interest or gain.
For breaking of an oath and lying
Is but a kind of self-denying,
A saint-like virtue, and from hence   135
Some have broke oaths by providence,
Some to the glory of the Lord
Perjured themselves and broke their word,
And this the constant rule and practice
Of all our late apostles' acts is.   140
Was not the cause at first begun
With perjury, and carried on?
Was there an oath the godly took
But, in due time and place, they broke?
Did we not bring our oaths in first   145
Before our plate,[n] to have them burst
And cast in fitter models for
The present use of church and war?
Did not our worthies of the House,
Before they broke the peace, break vows?   150
And having freed us first from both
Th'Allegiance and Supremacy Oath,
Did they not next compel the nation
To take, and break, the Protestation?[n]
To swear, and after to recant   155
The Solemn League and Covenant?[n]
To take th'Engagement, and disclaim it,
Enforced by those who first did frame it?
Did they not swear at first to fight
For the King's safety and his right?   160
And after marched to find him out,
And charged him home with horse and foot?

131 *idly*: uselessly. An allusion to the third commandment, 'Thou shalt not take
the name of the Lord thy God in vain.'
160 See note to I. ii. 514, p. 294.

And yet still had the confidence
To swear it was in his defence?
Did they not swear to live and die   165
With Essex, and straight laid him by?[n]
If that were all, for some have swore
As false as they, if th'did no more.
Did they not swear to maintain law,
In which that swearing made a flaw?[n]   170
For protestant religion vow
That did that vowing disallow?
For privilege of parliament,
In which that swearing made a rent?
And since, of all the three, not one   175
Is left in being, 'tis well known.
Did they not swear, in express words,
To prop and back the House of Lords,
And after turned out the whole houseful
Of peers as dangerous and unuseful?[n]   180
So Cromwell, with deep oaths and vows,
Swore all the Commons out o'th' House,
Vowed that the redcoats would disband[n]—
Ay, marry would they, at their command!—
And trolled 'em on, and swore and swore,   185
Till th'army turned 'em out of door.[n]
This tells us plainly what they thought:
That oaths and swearing go for nought,
And that by them th'were only meant
To serve for an expedient.   190
What was the public faith found out for,
But to slur men of what they fought for?
The public faith, which everyone
Is bound t'observe, yet kept by none.
And if that go for nothing, why   195
Should private faith have such a tie?

'Oaths were not purposed, more than law,
To keep the good and just in awe,

185 *trolled*: enticed.
191 *public faith*: see note to i. ii. 557, p. 295.
192 *slur*: cheat.
197–8 'The law is not made for a righteous man, but for the lawless and dis-
    obedient, for the ungodly and for sinners' (I Timothy 1:9).

But to confine the bad and sinful,
Like moral cattle in a pinfold.   200
A saint's of th'heavenly realm a peer;
And as no peer is bound to swear
But on the gospel of his honour,
Of which he may dispose, as owner,
It follows, though the thing be forgery   205
And false, th'affirm, it is no perjury,
But a mere ceremony, and a breach
Of nothing but a form of speech,
And goes for no more when 'tis took
Than mere saluting of the book.   210
Suppose the scriptures are of force,
They're but commissions of course,
And saints have freedom to digress
And vary from 'em as they please,
Or misinterpret them, by private   215
Instructions, to all aims they drive at.
Then why should we ourselves abridge
And curtail our own privilege?
Quakers (that, like to lanterns, bear
Their light within 'em) will not swear.   220
Their gospel is an accidence
By which they construe conscience,
And hold no sin so deeply red
As that of breaking Priscian's head[n]
(The head and founder of their order,   225
That stirring hats held worse than murder).
These, thinking they're obliged to troth
In swearing, will not take an oath,
Like mules, who if they've not their will
To keep their own pace, stand stock still.   230
But they are weak, and little know
What free-born consciences may do.
'Tis the temptation of the devil
That makes all human actions evil:

202–3 'A peer sitting in judgement, gives not his verdict upon oath, like an ordinary juryman, but upon his honour' (Blackstone, *Commentaries on the Laws of England*, 1809, I. xii. 401).
220 *will not swear*: the Quakers refused to take oaths, in obedience to the Sermon on the Mount (Matthew 5:34–7).
226 The Quakers refused to remove their hats as a mark of respect.

For saints may do the same things by   235
The spirit, in sincerity,
Which other men are tempted to
And at the devil's instance do;
And yet the actions be contrary,
Just as the saints and wicked vary.   240
For as on land there is no beast
But in some fish at sea's expressed,[n]
So in the wicked there's no vice
Of which the saints have not a spice;
And yet that thing that's pious in   245
The one, in th'other is a sin.
Is't not ridiculous and nonsense
A saint should be a slave to conscience,
That ought to be above such fancies
As far as above ordinances?   250
She's of the wicked, as I guess
B'her looks, her language and her dress.
And though like constables we search
For false wares one another's church,
Yet all of us hold this for true: 255
No faith is to the wicked due;
For truth is precious and divine,
Too rich a pearl for carnal swine.'

Quoth Hudibras, 'All this is true,
Yet 'tis not fit that all men knew   260
Those mysteries and revelations;
And therefore topical evasions
Of subtle turns and shifts of sense
Serve best with th'wicked for pretence,
Such as the learned Jesuits use,   265
And Presbyterians, for excuse
Against the Protestants, when th'happen
To find their churches taken napping.
As thus: a breach of oath is duple
And either way admits a scruple,   270

---

250 *above ordinances*: i.e. above the law. Clarendon describes this phrase as
  'peculiar to that time' (*History of the Rebellion*, xvi. 88). Cf. p. 250.
256 Proverbial (*ODEP* 241).
262 *topical*: based on probability rather than demonstration.

And may be *ex parte* of the maker
More criminal than th'injured taker.
For he that strains too far a vow
Will break it like an o'er-bent bow;
And he that made and forced it, broke it,   275
Not he that for convenience took it.
A broken oath is, *quatenus* oath,
As sound t'all purposes of troth
As broken laws are ne'er the worse,
Nay, till they're broken, have no force.   280
What's justice to a man, or laws,
That never comes within their claws?
They have no power but to admonish,
Cannot control, coerce or punish
Until they're broken, and then touch   285
Those only that do make them such.
Beside, no engagement is allowed
By men in prison made, for good;
For when they're set at liberty,
They're from th'engagement too set free.   290
The rabbins write, when any Jew
Did make to God or man a vow
Which afterward he found untoward
And stubborn to be kept, or too hard,
Any three other Jews o'th' nation   295
Might free him from the obligation:
And have not two saints power to use
A greater privilege than three Jews?
The court of conscience, which in man
Should be supreme and sovereign,   300
Is't fit should be subordinate
To every petty court i'th' state,
And have less power than the lesser
To deal with perjury at pleasure?
Have its proceedings disallowed, or   305
Allowed at fancy of piepowder?

271 *ex parte*: 'on the side of'; a legal term.
277 *quatenus oath*: 'in so far as it is an oath'.
287–90 'If a man is under duress of imprisonment . . . he may allege this duress,
    and avoid the extorted bond' (Blackstone, I. i. 135–6).
306 *piepowder*: a summary court held at fairs and markets to deal with offences
    committed by itinerant dealers; from French *pied-poudreux*, 'dusty-footed'.

Tell all it does or does not know
For swearing *ex officio*?
Be forced t'impeach a broken hedge,
And pigs unringed at vis. frankpledge;   310
Discover thieves and bawds, recusants,
Priests, witches, eavesdroppers and nuisance;
Tell who did play at games unlawful
And who filled pots of ale but half full;
And have no power at all, nor shift,   315
To help itself at a dead lift?
Why should not conscience have vacation
As well as other courts o'th' nation?
Have equal power to adjourn
Appoint appearance and return,   320
And make as nice distinctions serve
To split a case? As those that carve,
Invoking cuckolds' names, hit joints,[n]
Why should not tricks as slight do points?
Is not th'High Court of Justice sworn   325
To just that law that serves their turn?
Make their own jealousies high treason
And fix 'em whomsoe'er they please on?
Cannot the learned counsel there
Make laws in any shape appear?   330
Mould 'em, as witches do their clay,
When they make pictures to destroy,[n]
And vex 'em into any form
That fits their purpose to do harm?
Rack 'em until they do confess,   335
Impeach of treason whom they please,
And most perfidiously condemn
Those that engaged their lives for them?
And yet do nothing in their own sense
But what they ought by oath and conscience?   340

308 *ex officio*: an oath which a man was bound to take on pain of imprisonment
    for contempt. He was also bound to answer any questions unless he wished
    silence to be taken as confession.
310 *vis. frankpledge*: a court held periodically for the production of members of
    a landowner's estate.
316 *at a dead lift*: in an extremity.
327 *jealousies*: suspicions.
333 *vex*: twist.

Can they not juggle, and with slight
Conveyance play with wrong and right,
And sell their blasts of wind as dear
As Lapland witches bottled air?
Will not fear, favour, bribe and grutch,   345
The same case several ways adjudge,
As seamen with the self-same gale
Will several different courses sail?
As when the sea breaks o'er its bounds
And overflows the level grounds,   350
Those banks and dams that, like a screen,
Did keep it out, now keep it in,
So when tyrannical usurpation
Invades the freedom of a nation,
The laws o'th' land, that were intended   355
To keep it out, are made defend it.
Does not in Chancery every man swear
What makes best for him, in his answer?
Is not the winding up witnesses
And nicking, more than half the business?   360
For witnesses like watches go
Just as they're set, too fast or slow,
And where in conscience they're strait-laced,
'Tis ten to one that side is cast.
Do not your juries give their verdict   365
As if they felt the cause, not heard it?
And as they please make matter of fact
Run all on one side, as they're packed?
Nature has made man's breast no windores
To publish what he does within doors,   370
Nor what dark secrets there inhabit,
Unless his own rash folly blab it.
If oaths can do a man no good
In his own business, why they should
In other matters do him hurt,   375
I think there's little reason for't.

342 *conveyance*: cunning; sleight of hand.
344 The witches of Lapland were popularly believed to sell winds to the merchants who traded there (Samuel Purchas, *Pilgrimes*, 1625, III. III. i. 444).
345 *grutch*: grudge.
360 *nicking*: probably used in the sense of 'resembling' with the suggestion that
witnesses are prepared in advance so that their evidence is consistent.
369 *windores*: windows (a normal seventeenth-century spelling).

He that imposes an oath, makes it,
Not he that for convenience takes it.
Then how can any man be said
To break an oath he never made?   380
These reasons may perhaps look oddly
To th'wicked, though they evince the godly;
But if they will not serve to clear
My honour, I am ne'er the near.
Honour is like that glassy bubble   385
That finds philosophers such trouble,[n]
Whose least part cracked, the whole does fly
And wits are cracked to find out why.'

Quoth Ralpho, 'Honour's but a word
To swear by only, in a lord;   390
In other men 'tis but a huff
To vapour with, instead of proof,
That like a wen looks big and swells,
Is senseless and just nothing else.'

'Let it', quoth he, 'be what it will,   395
It has the world's opinion still.
But, as men are not wise that run
The slightest hazard they may shun,
There may a medium be found out
To clear to all the world the doubt;   400
And that is, if a man may do 't
By proxy whipped, or substitute.'

'Though nice, and dark the point appear',
Quoth Ralph, 'it may hold up and clear.
That sinners may supply the place   405
Of suffering saints, is a plain case:
Justice gives sentence many times
On one man for another's crimes.
Our brethren of New England use
Choice malefactors to excuse,   410

382 *evince*: convince.
384 *ne'er the near*: no nearer my goal.
390 *in a lord*: see II. ii. 202 and note.
391 *huff*: boast.
392 *vapour*: brag.
404 *hold up*: clear up (generally applied to the weather).

And hang the guiltless in their stead,
Of whom the churches have less need,
As lately 't happened. In a town
There lived a cobbler, and but one,
That out of doctrine could cut use,   415
And mend men's lives as well as shoes.
This precious brother having slain
In times of peace an Indian
(Not out of malice, but mere zeal
Because he was an infidel),   420
The mighty Tottipottymoy
Sent to our elders an envoy,
Complaining sorely of the breach
Of league, held forth by brother Patch,
Against the articles in force   425
Between both churches, his and ours,
For which he craved the saints to render
Into his hands, or hang th'offender.
But they maturely having weighed
They had no more but him o'th' trade   430
(A man that served them in a double
Capacity, to teach and cobble),
Resolved to spare him; yet to do
The Indian Hogen Mogen too
Impartial justice, in his stead did   435
Hang an old weaver that was bed-rid.
Then wherefore may not you be skipped,
And in your place another whipped?
For all philosophers but the sceptic
Hold whipping may be sympathetic.'   440

'It is enough', quoth Hudibras.
'Thou hast resolved and cleared the case,
And canst in conscience not refuse
From thy own doctrine to raise use.
I know thou wilt not, for my sake,   445
Be tender-conscienced of thy back.

413 This history of the cobbler has been attested by persons of good credit who
were upon the place when it was done.

434 *Hogen Mogen*: chieftain; 'a popular corruption of the Dutch *Hoogmogend-
heiden*, "High Mightinesses", the title of the States-General' (*OED*).

Then strip thee of thy carnal jerkin
And give thy outward fellow a firking.
For when thy vessel is new hooped,
All leaks of sinning will be stopped.'   450

Quoth Ralpho, 'You mistake the matter.
For in all scruples of this nature,
No man includes himself, nor turns
The point upon his own concerns.
As no man of his own self catches   455
The itch, or amorous French aches,
So no man does himself convince
By his own doctrine of his sins,
And though all cry down self, none means
His own self in a literal sense.   460
Beside, it is not only foppish,
But vile, idolatrous and popish
For one man out of his own skin
To firk and whip another's sin,
As pedants out of schoolboys' breeches   465
Do claw and curry their own itches.
But in this case it is profane
And sinful too, because in vain;
For we must take our oaths upon it
You did the deed, when I have done it.'   470

Quoth Hudibras, 'That's answered soon.
Give us the whip, we'll lay it on.'

Quoth Ralpho, 'That we may swear true,
'Twere properer that I whipped you;
For when with your consent 'tis done,   475
The act is really your own.'

Quoth Hudibras, 'It is in vain,
I see, to argue 'gainst the grain,
Or, like the stars, incline men to
What they're averse themselves to do.   480

449 *hooped*: supplied with hoops, like a barrel; whipped (colloquial).
461 *foppish*: silly.
468 *in vain*: see note to II. ii. 131.

For when disputes are wearied out,
'Tis interest still resolves the doubt.
But since no reason can confute ye,
I'll try to force you to your duty
(For so it is, howe'er you mince it,   485
As e'er we part I shall evince it),
And curry, if you stand out, whether
You will or no, your stubborn leather.
Canst thou refuse to bear thy part
I'th' public work, base as thou art?   490
To higgle thus for a few blows,
To gain thy knight an opulent spouse?
Whose wealth his bowels yearn to purchase
Merely for th'interest of the churches,
And when he has it in his claws,   495
Will not be hidebound to the cause;
Nor shalt thou find him a curmudgeon
If thou despatch it without grudging.
If not, resolve before we go
That you and I must pull a crow.'   500

'You'd best,' quoth Ralpho, 'as the ancients
Say wisely, "have a care o'th' main chance",
And "look before you ere you leap",
For "as you sow you're like to reap".
And were y'as good as George-a-Green,   505
I shall make bold to turn again;
Nor am I doubtful of the issue
In a just quarrel, and mine is so.
Is't fitting for a man of honour
To whip the saints, like Bishop Bonner?[n]   510
A knight t'usurp the beadle's office,
For which you're like to raise brave trophies!
But I advise you, not for fear,
But for your own sake, to forbear,
And for the churches', which may chance   515
From hence to spring a variance,

---

485 *mince*: make light of; disparage.
500 *pull a crow*: settle the dispute.
504 Galatians 6:7.
505 *George-a-Green*: a hero of ballad and romance, one of whose exploits was
to fight a duel against Robin Hood.

And raise among themselves new scruples,
Whom common danger hardly couples.
Remember how in arms and politics
We still have worsted all your holy tricks,   520
Trepanned your party with intrigue,
And took your grandees down a peg;
New-modelled th'army,[n] and cashiered
All that to legion Smeck adhered;
Made a mere utensil o'your church,   525
And after left it in the lurch,
A scaffold to build up our own,
And when we'd done with 't, pulled it down;
O'er-reached your rabbins of the synod,
And snapped their canons with a "Why not?"   530
(Grave synod-men that were revered
For solid face and depth of beard);
Their classic model proved a maggot,
Their Directory an Indian pagod,
And drowned their discipline like a kitten,   535
On which they'd been so long a-sitting;[n]
Decried it as a holy cheat,
Grown out of date and obsolete,
And all the saints o'the first grass
As castling foals of Balaam's ass.'   540

At this the knight grew high in chafe
And, staring furiously on Ralph,
He trembled and looked pale with ire,
Like ashes first, then red as fire.
'Have I', quoth he, 'been ta'en in fight,   545
And for so many moons lain by't,
And when all other means did fail,
Have been exchanged for tubs of ale;

548 The knight was kept prisoner in Exeter and, after several exchanges proposed
but none accepted of, was at last released for a barrel of ale, as he often used
upon all occasions to declare.

---

524 *legion Smeck*: i.e. the Presbyterians. See I. iii. 1166 and note.
530 *snapped*: snapped at.
533 *maggot*: whim; fantastic notion.
534 *Directory*: i.e. the *Directory for Public Worship*. See note to I. iii. 1193.
Indian Pagod: pagan idol.
540 *castling*: abortive. The ass of the prophet Balaam had a vision of the Lord
(Numbers 22).

Not but they thought me worth a ransom
Much more considerable and handsome,   550
But for their own sakes, and for fear
They were not safe when I was there?
Now to be baffled by a scoundrel,
An upstart sect'ry and a mongrel,
Such as breed out of peccant humours   555
Of our own church, like wens or tumours,
And, like a maggot in a sore,
Would that which gave it life, devour.
It never shall be done or said!'

With that he seized upon his blade,   560
And Ralpho too, as quick and bold,
Upon his basket-hilt laid hold,
With equal readiness prepared
To draw and stand upon his guard,
When both were parted on the sudden   565
With hideous clamour and a loud one,
As if all sorts of noise had been
Contracted into one loud din;
Or that some member to be chosen
Had got the odds above a thousand,   570
And by the greatness of his noise
Proved fittest for his country's choice.
This strange surprisal put the knight
And wrathful squire into a fright,
And though they stood prepared with fatal,   575
Impetuous rancour to join battle,
Both thought it was their wisest course
To waive the fight and mount to horse,
And to secure, by swift retreating,
Themselves from danger of worse beating.   580
Yet neither of them would disparage,
By uttering of his mind, his courage;
Which made 'em stoutly keep their ground,
With horror and disdain wind-bound.
And now the cause of all their fear   585
By slow degrees approached so near
They might distinguish different noise
Of horns and pans and dogs and boys

584 *wind-bound*: held, like a ship, by contrary winds.

And kettle-drums, whose sullen dub
Sounds like the hooping of a tub.   590
But when the sight appeared in view
They found it was an antique show,[n]
A triumph that for pomp and state
Did proudest Romans emulate.
For as the aldermen of Rome   595
For foes at training overcome,
And not enlarging territory
(As some mistaken write in story),
Being mounted in their best array
Upon a car (and who but they?),   600
And followed with a world of tall lads
That merry ditties trolled and ballads,
Did ride with many a 'Good morrow',
Crying 'Hey for our town' through the borough,
So when this triumph drew so nigh   605
They might particulars descry,
They never saw two things so pat
In all respects as this and that.
First, he that led the cavalcate
Wore a sowgelder's flagellate,   610
On which he blew as strong a levet
As well-feed lawyer on his breviate,
When over one anothers' heads
They charge three ranks at once, like Swedes.[n]
Next pans and kettles of all keys,   615
From trebles down to double-bass,
And after them upon a nag
That might pass for a forehand stag,
A cornet rode, and on his staff
A smock displayed did proudly wave.   620
Then bagpipes of the loudest drones,
With snuffling, broken-winded tones,

596 *training*: military drill; hence, fighting.
597 A victorious Roman general was awarded an official triumph only if his
success had been won after serious fighting.
601 *tall*: bold, brave.
610 *flagellate*: flageolet. The sowgelder announced his arrival by blowing a
horn. Cf. I. ii. 537.
612 *breviate*: brief.
618 *forehand*: forehanded; well formed in the foreparts.
619 *cornet*: the officer who carried the colours in a troop of cavalry.
620 *displayed*: spread out (a term of heraldry).

Whose blasts of air in pockets shut
Sound filthier than from the gut,
And make a viler noise than swine   625
In windy weather when they whine.
Next one upon a pair of panniers
Full fraught with that which, for good manners,
Shall here be nameless, mixed with grains
Which he dispensed among the swains,   630
And busily upon the crowd
At random round about bestowed.
Then mounted on a horned horse,
One bore a gauntlet and gilt spurs,
Tied to the pommel of a long sword   635
He held reversed, the point turned downward.
Next after, on a raw-boned steed,
The conqueror's standard-bearer rid,
And bore aloft before the champion
A petticoat displayed and rampant;   640
Near whom the Amazon triumphant
Bestrid her beast, and on the rump on 't
Sat face to tail, and bum to bum
The warrior whilom overcome,
Armed with a spindle and a distaff   645
Which, as he rode, she made him twist off,
And when he loitered, o'er her shoulder
Chastised the reformado soldier.
Before the dame, and round about,
Marched whifflers and staffiers on foot,   650
With lacqueys, grooms, valets and pages,
In fit and proper equipages,
Of whom some torches bore, some links,
Before the proud virago minx,
That was both madam and a don,   655
Like Nero's Sporus or Pope Joan;
And at fit periods the whole rout
Set up their throats with clamorous shout.

650 *whifflers*: attendants employed to clear the way for a procession. *Staffiers*:
footmen.
656 *Sporus*: the boy whom Nero took as a wife (Suetonius, *Nero*, xxviii). *Pope
Joan*: a fictitious female pope who was said to have disguised herself as a man.

The knight, transported, and the squire
Put up their weapons and their ire,   660
And Hudibras, who used to ponder
On such sights with judicious wonder,
Could hold no longer to impart
His animadversions for his heart.

Quoth he, 'In all my life till now   665
I ne'er saw so profane a show.
It is a paganish invention
Which heathen writers often mention,
And he that made it had read Goodwin
(I warrant him) and understood him,   670
With all the Grecian Speeds and Stows
That best describe these ancient shows,
And has observed all fit decorums
We find described by old historians.
For as a Roman conqueror   675
That put an end to foreign war,
Entering the town in triumph for it,
Bore a slave with him in his chariot,
So this insulting female brave
Carries behind her here a slave;   680
And as the ancients long ago,
When they in field defied the foe,
Hung out their mantles *della guer*,
So her proud standard-bearer here
Waves on his spear in dreadful manner   685
A Tyrian petticoat for a banner.

678   ——*Et sibi consul*
    Ne placeat, curru servus portatur eodem Juven. Sat. 10.
683 *Tunica coccinea solebat pridie quam dimicandum esset, supra praetorium
    poni quasi admonitio et indicium futurae pugnae.* Lipsius in Tacit. p. 56.

664 *for his heart*: 'for the life of him'.
669 *Goodwin*: Thomas Godwin, author of works on Roman antiquities.
671 *Speeds and Stows*: John Speed and John Stow were both seventeenth-
    century writers of history. Speed was also a cartographer.
678 note: 'And so that the consul may not fancy himself too much, the slave rides
    in the same chariot' (Juvenal, *Satires*, x. 41–2).
683 note: 'The scarlet tunic used to be spread out on the day before a battle
    above the general's tent as a warning and a signal of fighting to come' (Justus
    Lipsius, *Ad Annales Cornelii Taciti Liber Commentarius*, 1585, p. 55).

> Next links and torches, heretofore
> Still borne before the emperor;
> And as in antique triumphs eggs
> Were borne for mystical intrigues,   690
> There's one in truncheon like a ladle,
> That carries eggs too, fresh or adle,
> And still at random as he goes,
> Among the rabble-rout bestows.'
>
> Quoth Ralpho, 'You mistake the matter;   695
> For all th'antiquity you smatter
> Is but a riding used of course
> When the grey mare's the better horse;
> When o'er the breeches greedy women
> Fight to extend their vast dominion,   700
> And in the cause impatient Grizel
> Has drubbed her husband with bull's pizzle,
> And brought him under covert-baron,
> To turn her vassal with a murrain;
> When wives their sexes shift, like hares,   705
> And ride their husbands like nightmares,
> And they, in mortal battle vanquished,
> Are of their charter disenfranchised,
> And by the right of war like gills
> Condemned to distaff, horns and wheels.   710
> For when men by their wives are cowed,
> Their horns, of course, are understood.'

687 That the Roman emperors were wont to have torches borne before them by day in public appears by Herodian in Pertinace. Lip. in Tacit. p. 16.

689–90 Eggs were carried in procession at the ceremonial games held by the Greeks in honour of Ceres.

692 *adle*: addled (altered for the sake of the rhyme).

698 A proverb (*ODEP* 338).

701 *Grisel*: see note to I. ii. 772.

702 *bull's pizzle*: see note to II. i. 879.

703 *covert-baron*: i.e. made him act the wife. A married woman, under the protection of her husband, is said to be under covert-baron.

705 Hares were popularly supposed to change their sex annually (Sir Thomas Browne, *Pseudodoxia Epidemica*, III. xvii).

706 *nightmares*: succubae.

709 *gills*: wenches.

687 note: Butler's sources are Herodianus, Basle, 1535, p. 95, and the edition of Lipsius's commentary on Tacitus noted above.

Quoth Hudibras, 'Thou still giv'st sentence
Impertinently and against sense.
'Tis not the least disparagement   715
To be defeated by th'event;
Nor to be beaten by main force,
That does not make a man the worse,
Although his shoulders with batoon
Be clawed and cudgelled to some tune.   720
A tailor's prentice has no hard
Measure that's banged with a true yard.
But to turn tail or run away,
And without blows give up the day,
Or to surrender ere the assault,   725
That's no man's fortune but his fault,
And renders men of honour less
Than all th'adversity of success;
And only unto such this show
Of horns and petticoats is due.   730
There is a lesser profanation,
Like that the Romans called "ovation".
For as ovation was allowed
For conquest purchased without blood,
So men decree those lesser shows   735
For victory gotten without blows,
By dint of hard, sharp words, which some
Give battle with and overcome.
These, mounted in a chair curule,
Which moderns call a cucking-stool,   740
March proudly to the river's side
And o'er the waves in triumph ride,
Like dukes of Venice, who are said
The Adriatic Sea to wed,[n]
And have a gentler wife than those   745
For whom the state decrees those shows.
But both are heathenish, and come
From th'whores of Babylon and Rome,

714 *impertinently*: irrelevantly.
719 *batoon*: baton.
720 *to some tune*: considerably.
733–4 A Roman general who had won a victory after little fighting was awarded
 an ovation, as a lesser form of triumph.

And by the saints should be withstood
As antichristian and lewd,   750
And we as such should now contribute
Our utmost strugglings to prohibit.'

This said, they both advanced, and rode
A dog-trot through the bawling crowd
T'attack the leader, and still pressed   755
Till they approached him breast to breast.
Then Hudibras with face and hand
Made signs for silence, which obtained,
'What means', quoth he, 'this devil's procession,
With men of orthodox profession?   760
'Tis ethnic and idolatrous,
From heathenism derived to us.
Does not the whore of Babylon ride
Upon her horned beast astride,
Like this proud dame, who either is   765
A type of her, or she of this?
Are things of superstitious function
Fit to be used in gospel sunshine?
It is an antichristian opera,
Much used in midnight times of popery,   770
A running after self-inventions
Of wicked and profane intentions,
To scandalize that sex for scolding,
To whom the saints are so beholding:
Women that were our first apostles,   775
Without whose aid we'd all been lost else;
Women that left no stone unturned
In which the cause might be concerned;
Brought in their children's spoons and whistles
To purchase swords, carbines and pistols,   780
Their husbands, cullies, and sweethearts,
To take the saints' and churches' parts;
Drew several gifted brethren in
That for the bishops would have been,

761 *ethnic*: pagan.
763–4 Revelation 17:3.
766 *type*: representation; symbol.
771 An allusion to Psalm 106:38.
779–80 An allusion to the time when Parliament appealed for money and plate
   to maintain the army. See also I. ii. 561–76.
781 *cullies*: dupes, gulls.

And fixed 'em constant to the party   785
With motives powerful and hearty;
Their husbands robbed and made hard shifts
T'administer unto their gifts
All they could rap and run and pilfer,
To scraps and ends of gold and silver;   790
Rubbed down the teachers, tired and spent
With holding forth for parliament;
Pampered and edified their zeal
With marrow puddings many a meal;
Enabled them, with store of meat,   795
On controverted points to eat,
And crammed 'em till their guts did ache
With caudle, custard and plum cake.
What have they done, or what left undone,
That might advance the cause at London?   800
Marched rank and file with drum and ensign
T'entrench the city, for defence in;
Raised rampires with their own soft hands,
To put the enemy to stands;
From ladies down to oyster-wenches   805
Laboured like pioneers in trenches;
Fell to their pickaxes and tools,
And helped the men to dig like moles?
Have not the handmaids of the city
Chosen of their members a committee   810
For raising of a common purse,
Out of their wages to raise horse?
And do they not as triers sit
To judge what officers are fit?
Have they —— ?' At that an egg, let fly,   815
Hit him directly o'er the eye
And, running down his cheek, besmeared
With orange-tawny slime his beard;
But beard and slime being of one hue,
The wound the less appeared in view.   820

789 *rap and run*: snatch and steal.
792 *holding forth*: preaching.
793 *edified*: built up.
796 'To eat those kinds of food which might be forbidden'. Cf. I. i. 225–8.
798 *caudle*: a warm drink made of gruel and spices, formerly given to invalids.
813 *triers*: see note to I. iii. 1152, p. 297.

Then he that on the panniers rode
Let fly on th'other side a load,
And quickly charged again, gave fully
In Ralpho's face another volley.
The knight was startled with the smell   825
And for his sword began to feel,
And Ralpho, smothered with the stink,
Grasped his; when one that bore a link
O'th' sudden clapped his flaming cudgel,
Like linstock to the horse's touch-hole;   830
And straight another with his flambeaux
Gave Ralpho's o'er the eyes a damned blow.
The beasts began to kick and fling,
And forced the rout to make a ring,
Through which they quickly broke their way   835
And brought them off from further fray,
And, though disordered in retreat,
Each of them stoutly kept his seat;
For quitting both their swords and reins,
They grasped with all their strength the manes;   840
And to avoid the foe's pursuit,
With spurring put their cattle to't,
And till all four were out of wind
And danger too, ne'er looked behind.

After they'd paused awhile, supplying   845
Their spirits, spent with fight and flying,
And Hudibras recruited force
Of lungs, for action or discourse,
Quoth he, 'That man is sure to lose
That fouls his hands with dirty foes: 850
For where no honour's to be gained,
'Tis thrown away in being maintained.
'Twas ill for us we had to do
With so dishonourable a foe;
For though the law of arms does bar   855
The use of venomed shot in war,
Yet by the nauseous smell and noisome,
Their case-shot savours strong of poison,

---

858 *case-shot*: a collection of small projectiles, enclosed in a case and fired from
a cannon.

And doubtless have been chewed with teeth
Of some that had a stinking breath;   860
Else when we put it to the push,
They had not giv'n us such a brush.
But as those poltroons that fling dirt
Do but defile but cannot hurt,
So all the honour they have won,   865
Or we have lost, is much at one.
'Twas well we made so resolute
A brave retreat, without pursuit;
For if we had not, we had sped
Much worse, to be in triumph led,   870
Than which the ancients held no state
Of man's life more unfortunate.
But if this bold adventure e'er
Do chance to reach the widow's ear,
It may, being destined to assert   875
Her sex's honour, reach her heart.
And as such homely treats, they say,
Portend good fortune, so this may.
Vespasian, being daubed with dirt,
Was destined to the empire for 't,   880
And, from a scavenger, did come
To be a mighty prince in Rome.
And why may not this foul address
Presage in love the same success?
Then let us straight, to cleanse our wounds,   885
Advance in quest of nearest ponds,
And after, as we first designed,
Swear I've performed what she enjoined.'

---

879 *C. Caesar succensens, propter curam verrendis viis non adhibitam, luto iussit oppleri, congesto per milites in praetextae sinum.* Sueton. in Vespas. Ca. 5.

---

861 *the push*: the test.

877–8 An allusion to the proverb 'Shitten luck is good luck' (*ODEP* 724).

879–82 When Vespasian was aedile, Caligula became angry with him for neglecting his duty to keep the streets clean, and ordered him to be covered with mud.

879 note: 'Caius Caesar, enraged that attention was not paid to cleaning the streets, ordered him to be covered with mud, which was piled up by the soldiers in the fold of his toga' (Suetonius, *Vespasian*, v. iii).

CANTO III

Doubtless the pleasure is as great
Of being cheated as to cheat;
As lookers-on feel most delight
That least perceive a juggler's sleight,
And still the less they understand,   5
The more th'admire his sleight of hand.
Some with a noise and greasy light
Are snapped, as men catch larks by night;[n]
Ensnared and hampered by the soul,
As nooses by the legs catch fowl.   10
Some with a medicine and receipt
Are drawn to nibble at the bait,
And though it be a two-foot trout,
'Tis with a single hair pulled out.
Others believe no voice t'an organ   15
So sweet as lawyer's in a bar-gown,
Until, with subtle cobweb-cheats,
They're catched in subtle law, like nets,
In which, when once they are embrangled,
The more they stir the more they're tangled,   20
And while their purses can dispute
There's no end of th'immortal suit.
Others still gape t'anticipate
The cabinet designs of fate,

Argument 3 *Rosicrucian*: see note to I. i. 539, p. 291.

Apply to wizards to foresee   25
What shall, and what shall never be,
And, as those vultures do forebode,
Believe events prove bad or good;
A flam more senseless than the roguery
Of old aruspicy and augury,   30
That out of garbages of cattle
Presaged th'events of truce or battle;
From flight of birds or chickens pecking
Success of great'st attempts would reckon;[n]
Though cheats, yet more intelligible   35
Than those that with the stars do fribble.

This Hudibras by proof found true,
As in due time and place we'll show.
For he, with beard and face made clean,
Being mounted on his steed again   40
(And Ralpho got a-cock-horse too
Upon his beast with much ado),
Advanced on for the widow's house,
T'acquit himself and pay his vows,
When various thoughts began to bustle   45
And with his inward man to justle.
He thought what danger might accrue
If she should find he swore untrue;
Or if his squire or he should fail,
And not be punctual in their tale,   50
It might at once the ruin prove
Both of his honour, faith and love.
But if he should forbear to go,
She might conclude he'd broke his vow,
And that he durst not now for shame   55
Appear in court to try his claim.
This was the penn'orth of his thought,
To pass time and uneasy trot.

30 *aruspicy*: divination by the inspection of entrails, formerly practised by
   Roman augurs.
46 *justle*: jostle.
50 *be punctual*: coincide exactly.

Quoth he, 'In all my past adventures
I ne'er was set so on the tenters,   60
Or taken tardy with dilemma
That, every way I turn, does hem me,
And with inextricable doubt
Besets my puzzled wits about.
For though the dame has been my bail   65
To free me from enchanted gaol,
Yet, as a dog committed close
For some offence, by chance breaks loose
And quits his clog, but all in vain
He still draws after him his chain,   70
So though my ankle she has quitted,
My heart continues still committed,
And like a bailed and mainprized lover,
Although at large, I am bound over.
And when I shall appear in court   75
To plead my cause and answer for 't,
Unless the judge do partial prove,
What will become of me and love?
For if in our account we vary,
Or but in circumstance miscarry,   80
Or if she put me to strict proof,
And make me pull my doublet off
To show by evident record,
Writ on my skin, I've kept my word,
How can I e'er expect to have her,   85
Having demurred unto her favour?
But faith and love and honour lost,
Shall be reduced t'a knight o'th' post.
Beside, that stripping may prevent
What I'm to prove by argument,   90
And justify I have a tail,
And that way too my proof may fail.
O, that I could enucleate
And solve the problems of my fate!

60 *on the tenters*: on tenterhooks.
61 *taken tardy*: caught unawares.
73 *mainprized*: see note to II. i. 771.
83 *evident record*: written evidence.
88 *knight o'th' post*: professional perjurer.

Or find by necromantic art   95
How far the destinies take my part.
For if I were not more than certain
To win and wear her, and her fortune,
I'd go no further in this courtship,
To hazard soul, estate and worship.   100
For though an oath obliges not
Where anything is to be got,
As thou hast proved, yet 'tis profane
And sinful when men swear in vain.'

Quoth Ralph, 'Not far from hence doth dwell   105
A cunning man, hight Sidrophel,
That deals in destiny's dark counsels,
And sage opinions of the moon sells,
To whom all people far and near
On deep importances repair.   110
When brass and pewter hap to stray,
And linen slinks out of the way;
When geese and pullen are seduced,
And sows of sucking pigs are chewsed;
When cattle feel indisposition,   115
And need th'opinion of physician;
When murrain reigns in hogs or sheep,
And chickens languish of the pip;
When yeast and outward means do fail
And have no power to work on ale;   120
When butter does refuse to come,
And love proves cross and humoursome,
To him with questions and with urine
They for discovery flock, or curing.'

Quoth Hudibras, 'This Sidrophel   125
I've heard of, and should like it well,
If thou canst prove the saints have freedom
To go to sorcerers when they need 'em.'[n]

Says Ralpho, 'There's no doubt of that.
Those principles I quoted late   130

98 *win and wear*: possess and enjoy (*ODEP* 892).
104 *in vain*: see note to II. ii. 131.
106 *Sidrophel*: the name, derived from Latin and Greek, means 'star lover'.
113 *pullen*: poultry.   114 *chewsed*: tricked.

> Prove that the godly may allege
> For anything their privilege,
> And to the devil himself may go,
> If they have motives thereunto.
> For as there is a war between   135
> The devil and them, it is no sin
> If they, by subtle stratagem,
> Make use of him as he does them.
> Has not this present parliament
> A ledger to the devil sent,   140
> Fully empowered to treat about
> Finding revolted witches out?[n]
> And has not he within a year
> Hanged three score of 'em in one shire?
> Some only for not being drowned,   145
> And some for sitting above ground[n]
> Whole days and nights upon their breeches,
> And feeling pain, were hanged for witches;
> And some for putting knavish tricks
> Upon green geese and turkey chicks   150
> Or pigs that suddenly deceased
> Of griefs unnatural, as he guessed;
> Who after proved himself a witch
> And made a rod for his own breech.[n]
> Did not the devil appear to Martin   155
> Luther in Germany for certain,
> And would have gulled him with a trick,
> But Mart. was too, too politick?[n]
> Did he not help the Dutch to purge,
> At Antwerp, their cathedral church?   160

140 The witchfinder in Suffolk, who in the Presbyterian times had a commission to discover witches, of whom, right or wrong, he caused sixty to be hanged within the compass of one year, and among the rest an old minister who had been a painful preacher for many years.
160 In the beginning of the civil wars of Flanders, the common people of Antwerp, in a tumult, broke open the cathedral church to demolish images and shrines, and did so much mischief in a small time that Strada writes there were several devils seen very busy among them, otherwise it had been impossible.

---

140 *ledger*: agent, commissioner.
145 See note to II. i. 503.
150 *green geese*: goslings.
160 note *Strada*: Famianus Strada, in whose *De Bello Belgico* (I. v. 154), published in Rome in 1640, Butler found this information.

Sing catches to the saints at Mascon,[n]
And tell them all they came to ask him?
Appear in divers shapes to Kelly?[n]
And speak i'th' nun of Loudun's belly?[n]
Meet with the parliament's committee   165
At Woodstock, on a personal treaty?
At Sarum take a cavalier,
I'th' cause's service, prisoner,
As Withers, in immortal rhyme,
Has registered to after time?   170
Do not our great reformers use
This Sidrophel to forebode news?[n]
To write of victories next year,
And castles taken yet in th'air?
Of battles fought at sea, and ships   175
Sunk two years hence, the last eclipse?
A total overthrow given the King
In Cornwall, horse and foot, next spring?
And has not he point-blank foretold
Whats'e'er the close committee would?   180
Made Mars and Saturn for the cause,
The moon for fundamental laws?
The Ram and Bull and Goat declare
Against the Book of Common Prayer?

---

161 This devil of Mascon delivered all his oracles, like his forefathers, in verse, which he sung to tunes. He made several lampoons upon the Huguenots, and foretold them many things which afterwards came to pass, as may be seen in his memoirs, written in French.

163 The history of Dr. Dee and the devil, published by Mer. Casaubon (Isaac Fil.), Prebend of Canterbury, has a large account of all those passages, in which the style of the true and false angels appears to be penned by one and the same person.

164 The nun of Loudun, in France, and all her tricks have been seen by many persons of quality of this nation yet living, who have made very good observations upon the French book written upon that occasion.

166 A committee of the Long Parliament, sitting in the King's house in Woodstock park, were terrified with several apparitions, the particulars whereof were then the news of the whole nation.

170 Withers has a long story in doggerel of a soldier of the King's army who, being a prisoner at Salisbury, and drinking a health to the devil upon his knees, was carried away by him through a single pane of glass.

---

169 *Withers*: See note to I. i. 640. I have been unable to trace the poem to which Butler alludes.

182 *fundamental laws*: see note to I. i. 755, p. 291.

184 *Common Prayer*: the Presbyterians replaced the *Book of Common Prayer* with their own *Directory for Public Worship*.

The Scorpion take the Protestation,   185
And Bear engage for reformation?
Made all the royal stars recant,
Compound, and take the Covenant?'

Quoth Hudibras, 'The case is clear:
The saints may 'mploy a conjurer,   190
As thou hast proved it by their practice.
No argument like matter of fact is,
And we are best of all led to
Men's principles, by what they do.
Then let us straight advance in quest   195
Of this profound gymnosophist,
And as the Fates and he advise,
Pursue or waive this enterprise.'

This said, he turned about his steed
And forthwith on th'adventure rid.   200
Where leave we him and Ralph awhile
And to the conjurer turn our style,
To let the reader understand
What's useful to him beforehand.

He had been long towards mathematics,   205
Optics, philosophy and statics,
Magic, horoscopy, astrology,
And was old dog at physiology.
But, as a dog that turns the spit
Bestirs himself, and plies his feet   210
To climb the wheel, but all in vain,
His own weight brings him down again,
And still he's in the self-same place
Where at his setting out he was,
So in the circle of the arts   215
Did he advance his natural parts,
Till falling back still, for retreat,
He fell to juggle, cant and cheat.
For, as those fowls that live in water
Are never wet, he did but smatter.   220

185 *Protestation*: see note to I. i. 755, pp. 291–2.
188 *Covenant*: see note to I. i. 730, p. 291.

What e'er he laboured to appear,
His understanding still was clear.
Yet none a deeper knowledge boasted,
Since old Hodge Bacon and Bob Grosted.
Th'intelligible world he knew,   225
And all men dream on 't, to be true:[n]
That in this world there's not a wart
That has not there a counterpart,
Nor can there on the face of ground
An individual beard be found   230
That has not, in that foreign nation,
A fellow of the self-same fashion,
So cut, so coloured and so curled
As those are in th'inferior world.
He'd read Dee's prefaces before   235
The devil and Euclid o'er and o'er,
And all th'intrigues 'twixt him and Kelly,
Lescus and th'Emperor, would tell ye,[n]
But with the moon was more familiar
Than e'er was almanack well-willer;   240
Her secrets understood so clear
That some believed he had been there;
Knew when she was in fittest mood
For cutting corns or letting blood;
When for anointing scabs or itches,   245
Or to the bum applying leeches;
When sows and bitches may be spayed,
And in what sign best cider's made;
Whether the wane be, or increase,
Best to set garlic or sow pease;   250

---

224 Roger Bacon, commonly called Friar Bacon, lived in the reign of our Edward
I and, for some little skill he had in the mathematics, was by the rabble ac-
counted a conjurer, and had the sottish story of the brazen head fathered
upon him by the ignorant monks of those days. Robert Grosthead was Bishop
of Lincoln in the reign of Henry III. He was a learned man for those times
and, for that reason, suspected by the clergy to be a conjurer, for which crime
being degraded by Pope Innocent IV, and summoned to appear at Rome, he
appealed to the tribunal of Christ, which our lawyers say is illegal, if not a
praemunire, for offering to sue in a foreign court.

240 *almanack well-willer*: a person well-disposed to astrology.
224 note: For the legend of Bacon and the brazen head, see note to I. ii. 344.
Grosseteste was several times engaged in controversy with Innocent IV but not
on charges of practising alchemy.

Who first found out the man i'th' moon
That to the ancients was unknown;
How many dukes and earls and peers
Are in the planetary spheres;
Their airy empire and command,   255
Their several strengths by sea and land;
What factions th'have and what they drive at
In public vogue, and what in private;
With what designs and interests
Each party manages contests.   260
He made an instrument to know
If the moon shine at full or no,
That would as soon as e'er she shone, straight
Whether 'twere day or night demonstrate;
Tell what her diameter t'an inch is,   265
And prove she is not made of green cheese.
It would demonstrate that the man in
The moon's a Sea Mediterranean,
And that it is no dog nor bitch
That stands behind him at his breech,   270
But a huge Caspian Sea or lake,
With arms which men for legs mistake;
How large a gulf his tail composes,
And what a goodly bay his nose is;
How many German leagues by th'scale   275
Cape Snout's from Promontory Tail.
He made a planetary gin
Which rats would run their own heads in,
And come of purpose to be taken,
Without th'expense of cheese or bacon.   280
With lute strings he would counterfeit
Maggots, that crawl on dish of meat;
Quote moles and spots, on any place
O'th' body, by the index-face;
Detect lost maidenheads by sneezing,   285
Or breaking wind of dames, or pissing;
Cure warts and corns with application
Of medicines to th'imagination;

267–76 Butler here satirizes the naming of lunar features after terrestrial mountains and seas by the German astronomer Hevelius. His description of the
  moon was first published in 1647.

Fright agues into dogs, and scare
With rhymes the tooth ache and catarrh;   290
Chase evil spirits away by dint
Of sickle, horseshoe, hollow flint;
Spit fire out of a walnut shell,
Which made the Roman slaves rebel,[n]
And fire a mine in China, here,   295
With sympathetic gunpowder.
He knew whatsoever's to be known,
But much more than he knew would own:
What medicine 'twas that Paracelsus
Could make a man with, as he tells us;[n]   300
What figured slates are best to make,
On watery surface, duck or drake;
What bowling-stones, in running race
Upon a board, have swiftest pace;
Whether a pulse beat in the black   305
List of a dappled louse's back;[n]
If systole or diastole move
Quickest when he's in wrath or love;
When two of them do run a race,
Whether they gallop, trot or pace;   310
How many scores a flea will jump
Of his own length from head to rump,
Which Socrates and Chaerephon
In vain assayed so long agone;
Whether his snout a perfect nose is,   315
And not an elephant's proboscis;
How many different specieses
Of maggots breed in rotten cheese,
And which are next of kin to those
Engendered in a chandler's nose,   320
Or those not seen, but understood,
That live in vinegar and wood.

A paltry wretch he had, half-starved,
That him in place of zany served,

---

313 Aristophanes, in his comedy of *The Clouds*, brings in Socrates and Chaerephon, measuring the leap of a flea from the one's beard to the other's.

---

306 *list*: stripe.
313 note: See Aristophanes, *Clouds*, 143–53.

Hight Whachum,[n] bred to dash and draw,   325
Not wine, but more unwholesome law;
To make 'twixt words and lines huge gaps,
Wide as meridians in maps;
To squander paper, and spare ink,
Or cheat men of their words, some think.   330
From this, by merited degrees,
He to more high advancement rise,
To be an under-conjurer,
Or journeyman astrologer.
His business was to pump and wheedle,   335
And men with their own keys unriddle;
To make them to themselves give answers,
For which they pay the necromancers;
To fetch and carry intelligence
Of whom and what and where and whence,   340
And all discoveries disperse
Among th'whole pack of conjurers;
What cutpurses have left with them
For the right owners to redeem;
And what they dare not vent, find out,   345
To gain themselves and th'art repute;
Draw figures, schemes and horoscopes
Of Newgate, Bridewell, brokers' shops,
Of thieves ascendant in the cart,
And find out all by rules of art: 350
Which way a serving-man, that's run
With clothes or money away, is gone;
Who picked a fob at holding-forth,
And where a watch, for half the worth,
May be redeemed; or stolen plate   355
Restored at conscionable rate.
Beside all this, he served his master
In quality of poetaster,
And rhymes appropriate could make
To every month in th'almanac;   360
When terms begin and end could tell,
With their returns, in doggerel;[n]

325 *dash and draw*: write speedily and draw up.
353 *holding-forth*: sermon (a Puritan expression).
356 *conscionable*: equitable.

When the Exchequer opes and shuts,
And sowgelder with safety cuts;
When men may eat and drink their fill,   365
And when be temperate, if they will;
When use, and when abstain from vice,
Figs, grapes, phlebotomy and spice.
And as in prisons mean rogues beat
Hemp for the service of the great,   370
So Whachum beat his dirty brains
T'advance his master's fame and gains,
And, like the devil's oracles,
Put into doggerel rhymes his spells,
Which over every month's blank page   375
In th'almanac, strange bilks presage.
He would an elegy compose
On maggots squeezed out of his nose;
In lyric numbers write an ode on
His mistress, eating a black pudden,   380
And when imprisoned air escaped her,
It puffed him with poetic rapture.
His sonnets charmed th'attentive crowd,
By wide-mouthed mortal trolled aloud,
That, circled with his long-eared guests,   385
Like Orpheus looked among the beasts.
A carman's horse could not pass by
But stood tied up to poetry;
No porter's burden passed along
But served for burden to his song;   390
Each window like a pill'ry appears,
With heads thrust through, nailed by the ears;
All trades run in as to the sight
Of monsters, or their dear delight
The gallow-tree, when cutting purse   395
Breeds business for heroic verse,
Which none does hear but would have hung
T'have been the theme of such a song.

363 *Exchequer*: one of the four central courts at Westminster.
369–70 Petty offenders were made to beat hemp which might subsequently be
    used in the hangman's rope.
373 The oracle at Delphi delivered its pronouncements in hexameters.
376 *bilks*: deceptions.
386 Orpheus was said to have had the power to tame wild beasts with his music.

Those two together long had lived
In mansion prudently contrived,   400
Where neither tree nor house could bar
The free detection of a star,
And nigh an ancient obelisk
Was raised by him, found out by Fisk,
On which was written, not in words   405
But hieroglyphic mute of birds,
Many rare, pithy saws concerning
The worth of astrologic learning.
From top of this there hung a rope
To which he fastened telescope,   410
The spectacles with which the stars
He reads in smallest characters.
It happened as a boy one night
Did fly his tercel of a kite,
The strangest long-winged hawk that flies,   415
That, like a bird of paradise
Or herald's martlet, has no legs,[n]
Nor hatches young ones, nor lays eggs.
His train was six yards long, milk-white,
At th'end of which there hung a light,   420
Enclosed in lantern made of paper,
That far off like a star did appear.
This, Sidrophel by chance espied,
And with amazement staring wide,
'Bless us!' quoth he, 'What dreadful wonder   425
Is that appears in heaven yonder?
A comet, and without a beard?
Or star that ne'er before appeared?
I'm certain 'tis not in the scroll
Of all those beasts and fish and fowl   430
With which, like Indian plantations,
The learned stock the constellations;

---

404 This Fisk was a late famous astrologer who flourished about the time of
Subtle and Face, and was equally celebrated by Ben Jonson.

---

404 *Fisk*: Nicholas Fisk who, according to the astrologer Lilly, practised astrology in London in about 1633 (*History of his Life and Times*, 1715, pp. 29–31).
406 *mute*: excrement.
404 note: Fisk is not actually 'celebrated' by Ben Jonson but mentioned only
once in his plays (*Devil is an Ass*, I. ii. 3). Subtle and Face are two of the principle characters in Jonson's *The Alchemist*.

Nor those that drawn for signs have bin
To th'houses where the planets inn.
It must be supernaturall,   435
Unless it be that cannon-ball
That, shot in th'air, point-blank, upright,
Was borne to that prodigious height,
That learn'd philosophers maintain
It ne'er came backwards down again,   440
But in the airy region yet
Hangs like the body of Mahomet.
For if it be above the shade
That by the earth's round bulk is made,
'Tis probable it may from far   445
Appear no bullet but a star.'

This said, he to his engine flew,
Placed near at hand in open view,
And raised it till it levelled right
Against the glow-worm tail of kite.   450
Then, peeping through, 'Bless us!' quoth he.
'It is a planet now I see,
And if I err not, by his proper
Figure, that's like tobacco-stopper,
It should be Saturn. Yes, 'tis clear   455
'Tis Saturn. But what makes he there?
He's got between the dragon's tail
And further leg behind o'th' whale.
Pray heaven divert the fatal omen,
For 'tis a prodigy not common,   460
And can no less than the world's end
Or nature's funeral portend.'

436 This experiment was tried by some foreign virtuosos who planted a piece
of ordnance point-blank against the zenith, and having fired it, the bullet
never rebounded back again, which made them all conclude that it sticks in
the mark. But Descartes was of opinion that it does but hang in the air.[n]

434 *inn*: lodge.
442 Mahomet's coffin was said to have hung in mid-air in its temple in Mecca,
held up by lodestones.
454 *tobacco-stopper*: an implement for pressing down tobacco in a pipe. The
planet Saturn was represented in astrological books by a sign shaped like a
tobacco-stopper.
457 *dragon's tail*: 'the descending node of the moon's orbit with the ecliptic'
(*OED*).
458 *whale*: the constellation *Cetus*. See also note to II. i. 104.

With that, he fell again to pry
Through perspective more wistfully,
When, by mischance, the fatal string   465
That kept the towering fowl on wing,
Breaking, down fell the star. 'Well shot!'
Quoth Whachum, who right wisely thought
He'd levelled at a star and hit it.
But Sidrophel, more subtle-witted,   470
Cried out, 'What horrible and fearful
Portent is this to see a star fall!
It threatens nature, and the doom
Will not be long before it come.
When stars do fall 'tis plain enough   475
The Day of Judgement's not far off,
As lately 'twas revealed to Sedgwick,
And some of us find out by magic.
Then, since the time we have to live
In this world's shortened, let us strive   480
To make our best advantage of it
And pay our losses with our profit.'

This feat fell out not long before
The knight, upon the forenamed score,
In quest of Sidrophel advancing,   485
Was now in prospect of the mansion;
Whom he discovering, turned his glass,
And found far off 'twas Hudibras.

'Whachum,' quoth he, 'look yonder. Some
To try, or use our art, are come.   490
The one's the learned knight. Seek out
And pump 'em what they come about.'
Whachum advanced with all submissness
T'accost 'em, but much more their business.

477 This Sedgwick had many persons (and some of quality) that believed in him,
and prepared to keep the Day of Judgement with him, but were disappointed;
for which the false prophet was afterwards called by the name of Doomsday
Sedgwick.[n]

---

464 *wistfully*: intently.
483 *feat*: event.
494 *accost*: (i) approach; (ii) discover.

He held the stirrup while the knight   495
From leathern bare-bones did alight,
And, taking from his hand the bridle,
Approached, the dark squire to unriddle.
He gave him first the time o'th' day
And welcomed him, as he might say,   500
And asked him whence they came, and whither
Their business lay. Quoth Ralpho, 'Hither.'
'Did you not lose ——?' Quoth Ralpho, 'Nay.'
Quoth Whachum, 'Sir, I meant your way.
Your knight ——'. Quoth Ralpho, 'is a lover,   505
And pains intolerable doth suffer;
For lovers' hearts are not their own hearts,
Nor lights nor lungs, and so forth downwards.'
'What time ——? Quoth Ralpho, 'Sir, too long.
Three years it off and on has hung.'   510
Quoth he, 'I meant what time o'th' day 'tis.'
Quoth Ralpho, 'Between seven and eight 'tis.'
'Why then,' quoth Wachum, 'my small art
Tells me the dame has a hard heart,
Or great estate.' Quoth Ralph, 'A jointer,   515
Which makes him have so hot a mind t'her.'

Meanwhile the knight was making water
Before he fell upon the matter;
Which having done, the wizard steps in
To give him suitable reception,   520
But kept his business at a bay
Till Whachum put him in the way;
Who having now by Ralpho's light
Expounded th'errand of the knight
And what he came to know, drew near   525
To whisper in the conjurer's ear;
Which he prevented thus: 'What was't',
Quoth he, 'that I was saying last
Before these gentlemen arrived?'
Quoth Whachum, 'Venus you retrived   530

498 *dark*: unknown.
515 *jointer*: jointress.
530 *retrived*: discovered. The spelling is altered to fit the rhyme.
530–6 Whachum conveys to Sidrophel, by means of astrological terms, the in-
    formation he has discovered about Hudibras. Venus and Mars signify the
    widow and the knight.

In opposition with Mars,
And no benigne, friendly stars
T'allay th'effect.' Quoth wizard, 'So!
In Virgo?' 'Ha!' quoth Whachum, 'No.'
'Has Saturn nothing to do in it?'   535
'One tenth of's circle to a minute.'
' 'Tis well', quoth he. 'Sir, you'll excuse
This rudeness I am forced to use.
It is a scheme and face of heaven,
As th'aspects are disposed this even,   540
I was contemplating upon
When you arrived. But now I've done.'

Quoth Hudibras, 'If I appear
Unseasonable in coming here
At such a time, to interrupt   545
Your speculations, which I hoped
Assistance from, and come to use,
'Tis fit that I ask your excuse.'

'By no means, sir', quoth Sidrophel.
'The stars your coming did foretell.   550
I did expect you here, and know
Before you speak, your business too.'

Quoth Hudibras, 'Make that appear,
And I shall credit whatsoe'er
You tell me after, on your word,   555
Howe'er unlikely or absurd.'

'You are in love, sir, with a widow',
Quoth he, 'that does not greatly heed you,
And for three years has rid your wit
And passion without drawing bit.   560
And now your business is to know
If you shall carry her or no.'

Quoth Hudibras, 'You're in the right.
But how the devil you come by 't

532 *benigne*: pronounced as a trisyllable.
536 One-tenth of Saturn's circle is three years. The planet takes thirty years to
   revolve round the sun.

I can't imagine; for the stars,   565
I'm sure, can tell no more than a horse,
Nor can their aspects (though you pore
Your eyes out on 'em) tell you more
Than th'oracle of sieve and shears,
That turns as certain as the spheres.   570
But if the devil's of your counsel,
Much may be done, my noble donzel,
And 'tis on his account I come
To know from you my fatal doom.'

Quoth Sidrophel, 'If you suppose,   575
Sir Knight, that I am one of those,
I might suspect and take th'alarm
Your business is but to inform.
But if it be, 'tis ne'er the near:
You have a wrong sow by the ear.   580
For I assure you, for my part
I only deal by rules of art
Such as are lawful, and judge by
Conclusions of astrology;
But for the devil, know nothing by him   585
But only this, that I defy him.'

Quoth he, 'Whatever others deem ye,
I understand your metonymy,
Your words of second-hand intention
When things by wrongful names you mention,   590
The mystic sense of all your terms,
That are, indeed, but magic charms
To raise the devil, and mean one thing,
And that is downright conjuring,
And in itself's more warrantable   595
Than cheat or canting to a rabble,
Or putting tricks upon the moon
Which by confederacy are done.

569 *sieve and shears*: see note to I. ii. 348, p. 294.
572 *donzel*: gentleman (Italian *donzello*).
579 *ne'er the near*: 'no nearer to your purpose' (*ODEP* 211).
580 Proverbial (*ODEP* 756).

Your ancient conjurers were wont
To make her from her sphere dismount,   600
And to their incantations stoop.
They scorned to pore through telescope,
Or idly play at bo-peep with her
To find out cloudy or fair weather,
Which every almanac can tell,   605
Perhaps as learnedly and well
As you yourself. Then, friend, I doubt
You go the furthest way about.
Your modern Indian magician
Makes but a hole in th'earth to piss in,[n]   610
And straight resolves all questions by 't,
And seldom fails to be i'th' right.
The Rosicrucian way's more sure:
To bring the devil to the lure,
Each of 'em has a sev'ral gin   615
To catch intelligences in.
Some by the nose with fumes trepan 'em,
As Dunstan did the devil's grannum,
Others with characters and words
Catch 'em as men in nets do birds,   620
And some with symbols, signs and tricks,
Engraved in planetary nicks,
With their own influences will fetch 'em
Down from their orbs, arrest and catch 'em;
Make 'em depose and answer to   625
All questions ere they let them go.
Bumbastus kept a devil's bird
Shut in the pommel of his sword,

609 This compendious new way of magic is affirmed by Monsieur Le Blanc, in
his *Travels*, to be used in the East Indies.
627 Paracelsus is said to have kept a small devil prisoner in the pommel of his
sword, which was the reason, perhaps, why he was so valiant in his drink.
Howsoever it was to better purpose than Hannibal carried poison in his, to

599–601 The witches of Thessaly were celebrated for their power to charm the
moon down from the sky (Plutarch, *De Defectu Oraculorum*, xiii. 417).
613 *Rosicrucian*: see note to I. i. 539, p. 291.
616 *intelligences*: see note to I. i. 528, p. 290.
618 Saint Dunstan was said to have been tempted by the Devil in the shape of a
beautiful woman whom the saint repulsed by gripping her nose with hot
pincers.
622 *planetary nicks*: at critical moments of planetary influence.
627 *Bumbastus*: the German philosopher and alchemist Paracelsus, whose
original name was Theophrastus Bombast von Hohenheim.

That taught him all the cunning pranks
Of past and future mountebanks.   630
Kelly did all his feats upon
The devil's looking-glass, a stone,
Where playing with him at bo-peep,
He solved all problems ne'er so deep.
Agrippa kept a Stygian pug   635
I'th' garb and habit of a dog,
That was his tutor,[n] and the cur
Read to th'occult philosopher,
And taught him subtly to maintain
All other sciences are vain.'   640

To this quoth Sidrophello, 'Sir,
Agrippa was no conjurer,
Nor Paracelsus, no nor Behmen,
Nor was the dog a cacodemon,
But a true dog that would show tricks   645
For th'Emperor, and leap o'er sticks;
Would fetch and carry, was more civil
Than other dogs, but yet no devil;
And whatsoe'er he's said to do,
He went the self-same way we go.   650
As for the Rosy Cross philosophers,
Whom you will have to be but sorcerers,
What they pretend to is no more
Than Trismegistus did before,
Pythagoras, old Zoroaster,   655
And Apollonius their master,[n]

---

despatch himself if he should happen to be surprised in any great extremity.
For the sword would have done the feat alone much better and more soldierlike, and it was below the honour of so great a commander to go out of the
world like a rat.
635 Cornelius Agrippa had a dog that was suspected to be a spirit, for some
tricks he was wont to do beyond the capacity of a dog, as it was thought. But
the author of *Magia Adamica* has taken a great deal of pains to vindicate both
the doctor and the dog from that aspersion, in which he has shown a very great
respect and kindness for them both.

---

631 *Kelly*: Edward Kelly, the assistant to the alchemist John Dee, who claimed
   to foretell the future by gazing into a crystal. See note to II. iii. 237, p. 301.
635 *Agrippa*: see note to II. iii. 163, p. 301.
640 An allusion to Cornelius Agrippa's *De Incertitudine et Vanitate Scientiarum*,
   1530 ('*Of the Uncertainty and Vanity of the Sciences*').
64 *Behmen*: the philosopher Jacob Boehme. See note to I. i. 536, p. 291.

To whom they do confess they owe
All that they do and all they know.'

Quoth Hudibras, 'Alas, what is't to us
Whether 'twere said by Trismegistus,   660
If it be nonsense, false or mystic,
Or not intelligible, or sophistic.
'Tis not antiquity nor author
That makes truth truth, although time's daughter.
'Twas he that put her in the pit   665
Before he pulled her out of it,
And as he eats his sons, just so
He feeds upon his daughters too.
Nor does it follow, 'cause a herald
Can make a gentleman, scarce a year old,   670
To be descended of a race
Of ancient kings, in a small space,
That we should all opinion hold
Authentic that we can make old.'

Quoth Sidrophel, 'It is no part   675
Of prudence to cry down an art,
And what you may perform, deny
Because you understand not why
(As Averroes played but a mean trick
To damn our whole art for eccentric),   680
For who knows all that knowledge contains?
Men dwell not on the tops of mountains
But on their sides, or rising's seat:
So 'tis with knowledge's vast height.
Do not the histories of all ages   685
Relate miraculous presages

---

679 *Averroes astronomiam propter excentricos contempsit.* Phil. Melanchthon
in Elem. Phys. p. 781.

---

664 This is an allusion to the proverb that 'Truth is the daughter of time' (*ODEP*
844).
665 An allusion to the proverb 'Truth lies at the bottom of a pit' (*ODEP*
844).
667 An allusion to the proverb 'Time devours all things' (*ODEP* 823).
679 note: 'Averroes despised astronomy for being eccentric' (Melanchthon,
Initia Doctrinae Physicae, Wittenberg, 1581, pp. 88–9). Averroes was the
twelfth-century Arabian philosopher who lived in Spain.

Of strange turns in the world's affairs,
Foreseen b'astrologers, soothsayers,
Chaldeans, learn'd genethliacs,
And some that have writ almanacs?   690
The Median Emperor dreamt his daughter
Had pissed all Asia under water,
And that a vine, sprung from her hanches,
O'erspread his empire with its branches.[n]
And did not soothsayers expound it,   695
As after by th'event he found it?
When Caesar in the senate fell,
Did not the sun eclipsed foretell,
And, in resentment of his slaughter,
Looked pale for almost a year after?   700
Augustus, having b'oversight
Put on his left shoe 'fore the right,
Had like to have been slain that day
By soldiers mutining for pay.
Are there not myriads of this sort,   705
Which stories of all times report?
It is not ominous in all countries
When crows and ravens croak upon trees?
The Roman senate, when within
The city walls an owl was seen,   710

691 Astyages, King of Media, had this dream of his daughter Mandane, and the
interpretation from the magi, wherefore he married her to a Persian of mean
quality, by whom she had Cyrus, who conquered all Asia and translated the
empire from the Medes to the Persians. Herodot. L. 2.
697 *Fiunt aliquando prodigiosi et longiores solis defectus, quales occiso Caesare
Dictatore et antoniano bello, totius anni pallore continuo.* Plin.
701 *Divus Augustus laevum sibi prodidit calceum praepostere indutum quo die
seditione militum prope afflictus est.* Idem Lib. 2.
709 *Romani L. Crasso et C. Mario Coss. bubone viso, urbem lustrabant.*

---

689 *Chaldeans*: astrologers. Astrological divination was originally developed by
the Babylonians. A 'genethliac' is an astrologer who draws up nativities or
horoscopes.
697 note: 'Portentous and protracted eclipses of the sun occur, such as the one
after the murder of Caesar the dictator and during the Antonine War, which
caused almost a whole year's continuous gloom' (Pliny, *Natural History*,
II. xxx. 30).
701 note: 'The divine Augustus put abroad a story that on the day on which
he was almost overthrown by the army, he had put his left boot on the wrong
foot' (Pliny, *Natural Histroy*, II. vii. 5).
709 note: 'In the consulship of Mucius Crassus and Caius Marius, when an
eagle-owl had appeared, the Romans purified the city' (Pliny, *Natural History*,
x. xii. 17).

Did cause their clergy with lustrations
(Our synod calls "humiliations")
The round-faced prodigy t'avert
From doing town or country hurt.
And if an owl have so much power,   715
Why should not planets have much more?
That in a region far above
Inferior fowls of the air move,
And should see further, and foreknow
More than their augury below,   720
Though that once served the polity
Of mighty states to govern by;
And this is that we take in hand
By powerful art to understand;
Which how we have performed, all ages   725
Can speak th'events of our presages.
Have we not lately in the moon
Found a New World, to th'old unknown?
Discovered sea and land Columbus
And Magellan could never compass?   730
Made mountains with our tubes appear,
And cattle grazing on 'em there?'

Quoth Hudibras, 'You lie so ope
That I, without a telescope,
Can find your tricks out, and descry   735
Where you tell truth and where you lie.
For Anaxagoras, long agon,
Saw hills, as well as you, i'th' moon,
And held the sun was but a piece
Of red-hot iron as big as Greece;   740

---

737 *Anaxagoras affirmabat solem candens ferrum esse, et Peloponneso majorem;*
lunam habitacula in se habere, et colles et valles. Fertur dixisse caelum omne ex
lapidibus esse compositum; damnatus et in exilium pulsus est quod impie, solem
candentem laminam esse dixisset. Diogen. Laert. in Anaxag. p. 11. 13.

---

712 *humiliations*: days of prayer and fasting. Parliament used to set aside such
  days for the nation to acknowledge its errors and seek the guidance of God.
737 note: 'Anaxagoras declared the sun to be a mass of red-hot metal and to be
  larger than the Peloponnesus; he declared that there were dwellings on the
  moon and hills and ravines. He declared the whole firmament to be made of
  stones; he was condemned on a charge of impiety because he declared the
  sun to be a mass of red-hot metal' (Diogenes Laertius, *Anaxagoras*, ii. 8–12).

Believed the heavens were made of stone
Because the sun had voided one,
And, rather than he would recant
Th'opinion, suffered banishment.

'But what, alas, is it to us   745
Whether in the moon men thus, or thus
Do eat their porridge, cut their corns,
Or whether they have tails or horns?
What trade from thence can you advance
But what we nearer have from France?   750
What can our travellers bring home
That is not to be learnt at Rome?
What politics or strange opinions
That are not in our own dominions?
What science can be brought from thence   755
In which we do not here commence?
What revelations or religions
That are not in our native regions?
Are sweating lanterns or screen-fans
Made better there than th'are in France?   760
Or do they teach to sing and play
O'th' guitar there a newer way?
Can they make plays there that shall fit
The public humour, with less wit?
Write wittier dances, quainter shows,   765
Or fight with more ingenious blows?
Or does the man i'th' moon look big
And wear a huger periwig,
Show in his gait or face more tricks
Than our own native lunatics?   770
But if w'outdo him here at home,
What good of your design can come?
As wind in th'hypochondries pent
Is but a blast if downward sent,
But if it upwards chance to fly   775
Becomes new light and prophecy,

---

759 *sweating lanterns*: the 'tubs' in which patients were treated for venereal
disease by sweating. 'Screen fans' were used by ladies sitting near a fire to
protect their faces from the heat.
773 *hypochondries*: abdomen.

So when your speculations tend
Above their just and useful end,
Although they promise strange and great
Discoveries of things far-fet, 780
They are but idle dreams and fancies,
And savour strongly of the ganzas.
Tell me but what's the natural cause
Why on a sign no painter draws
The full moon ever, but the half. 785
Resolve that with your Jacob's staff;
Or why wolves raise a hubbub at her,
And dogs howl when she shines in water;
And I shall freely give my vote
You may know something more remote.' 790

At this deep Sidrophel looked wise,
And staring round, with owl-like eyes,
He put his face into a posture
Of sapience, and began to bluster.
For having three times shook his head 795
To stir his wit up, thus he said:

'Art has no mortal enemies
Next ignorance, but owls and geese;
Those consecrated geese in orders
That to the Capitol were warders, 800
And being then upon patrol,
With noise alone beat off the Gaul;[n]
Or those Athenian sceptic owls
That will not credit their own souls,
Or any science understand 805
Beyond the reach of eye or hand,

780 *fet*: a dialect form of 'fetched'.
782 *ganzas*: an allusion to Bishop Godwin's romance *The Man in the Moon, or a Discourse of a Voyage thither*, 1638. The narrator is carried up to the moon by certain birds called ganzas.
786 *Jacob's staff*: an instrument formerly used for measuring the altitude of the sun.
787 Cf. the proverb 'The wolf barks in vain at the moon' (*ODEP* 194).
788 Cf. the proverb 'The moon does not heed the barking of dogs' (*ODEP* 541).
797 'Art has no enemy but ignorance' was a proverbial saying (*ODEP* 19).
803 *sceptic owls*: i.e. the Greek sceptics who argued that sense-impressions were often contradictory and held that no knowledge was certain. 'Owl' was a colloquialism for a fool.

But measuring all things by their own
Knowledge, hold nothing's to be known.
Those wholesale critics that in coffee-
Houses cry down all philosophy,   810
And will not know upon what ground
In nature we our doctrine found,
Although with pregnant evidence
We can demonstrate it to sense;
As I just now have done to you,   815
Foretelling what you came to know.
Were the stars only made to light
Robbers and burglarers by night?
To wait on drunkards, thieves, gold-finders,
And lovers solacing behind doors?   820
Or giving one another pledges
Of matrimony under hedges?
Or witches simpling, and on gibbets
Cutting from malefactors snippets?
Or from the pillory tips of ears   825
Of rebel saints and perjurers?
Only to stand by and look on
But not know what is said or done?
Is there a constellation there
That was not born and bred up here?   830
And therefore cannot be to learn
In any inferior concern.
Were they not, during all their lives,
Most of 'em pirates, whores and thieves?
And is it like they have not still   835
In their old practices some skill?
Is there a planet that by birth
Does not derive its house from earth?
And therefore probably must know
What is, and hath been, done below?   840
Who made the Balance, or whence came
The Bull, the Lion and the Ram?

823 *simpling*: collecting 'simples', or herbs.
823–4 Portions of the bodies of malefactors were thought to be used by witches
   in spells and medicines.
825–6 Convicted perjurers were punished by standing in the pillory and having
   their ears cut. Cf. I. iii. 152–4.
841 *Balance*: the constellation *Libra* or the Scales.

Did not we here the Argo rig;
Make Berenice's Periwig?
Whose livery does the Coachman wear?   845
Or who made Cassiopeia's chair?
And therefore, as they came from hence,
With us may hold intelligence.
Plato denied the world can be
Governed without geometry   850
(For money being the common scale
Of things by measure, weight and tale,
In all th'affairs of church and state
'Tis both the balance and the weight),
Then much less can it be without   855
Divine astrology made out,
That puts the other down in worth
As far as heaven's above earth.'

'These reasons,' quoth the knight, 'I grant
Are something more significant   860
Than any that the learned use
Upon this subject to produce;
And yet they're far from satisfactory
T'establish and keep up your factory.
The Egyptians say the sun has twice   865
Shifted his setting and his rise;
Twice has he risen in the west,
As many times set in the east;
But whether that be true or no,
The devil any of you know.   870

865 *Ægyptii decem millia annorum et amplius recensent; et observatum est in hoc tanto spatio, bis mutata esse loca ortuum et occasuum solis; ita ut sol bis ortus sit ubi nunc occidit, et bis descenderit ubi nunc oritur.* Phil. Melanct. Lib. I. p. 60.

844 *Berenice's Periwig*: the constellation *Coma Berenices* or Berenice's Hair.
845 *Coachman*: part of the Plough, otherwise known as Charles's Wain.
849–50 Plutarch ascribes to Plato the remark that 'God always plays the geometer' (*Symposiacs*, VIII. ii. i).
864 *factory*: the act of making; 'business'.
865 note: 'The Egyptians have surveyed for ten thousand years; and it has been observed in this long period that the places of the sun's rising and setting have twice changed; consequently the sun has twice risen where it now sets, and twice set where it now rises' (Melanchthon, *Initia Doctrinae Physicae*, Wittenberg, 1581, p. 72).

Some hold the heavens, like a top,
Are kept by circulation up,
And 'twere not for their wheeling round,
They'd instantly fall to the ground,
As sage Empedocles of old,   875
And from him modern authors hold.
Plato believed the sun and moon
Below all other planets run;
Some Mercury, some Venus seat
Above the sun himself in height;   880
The learned Scaliger complained
'Gainst what Copernicus maintained,
That, in twelve hundred years and odd,
The sun had left his ancient road,
And nearer to the earth is come   885
'Bove fifty thousand miles from home;
Swore 'twas a most notorious flam,
And he that had so little shame
To vent such fopperies abroad,
Deserved to have his rump well clawed;   890
Which Monsieur Bodin hearing, swore
That he deserved the rod much more,
That durst upon a truth give doom;
He knew less than the Pope of Rome.

871 *Causa quare caelum non cadit, secundum Empedoclem, est velocitas sui motus.*
Comment in L. 2. Aristot. *De Caelo.*

877 *Plato solem et lunam caeteris planetis inferiores esse putavit.* G. Cunnin. in
Cosmogr. L. I. p. 11.

881 *Copernicus in libris revolutionum, deinde Reinholdus, post etiam Stadius,
mathematici nobiles, perspicuis demonstrationibus docuerunt solis apsida terris
esse propiorem quam Ptolomaei aetate duodecim partibus, id est uno ac triginta
terrae semidiametris.* Jo. Bod. Met. Hist. p. 455.

---

881 *Scaliger*: Julius Caesar Scaliger (1484–1558), Italian philosopher and
scientist.

890 *clawed*: thrashed.

891 *Bodin*: Jean Bodin (1530–96), French political philosopher.

871 note: 'The reason why the sky does not fall, according to Empedocles, is the
swiftness of its own motion.' See Aristotle, *De Caelo*, ii. 13. 295ᵃ.

877 note: 'Plato thought that the sun and moon were lower than the other
planets.' See William Cunningham, *The Cosmographical Glasse*, 1559, i. 11.

881 note: 'Copernicus in the books *About the Motion of the Heavenly Bodies*,
then Reinhold, and afterwards Stadius, well-known mathematicians, showed
with clear demonstrations that the apsis of the sun was nearer to the earth
than it was in the age of Ptolomy by twelve degrees, that is, thirty-one semi-
diameters of the earth' (Bodin, *Method for the Easy Comprehension of History*,
trans. Reynolds, New York, 1945, p. 318).

Cardan believed great states depend   895
Upon the tip o'th' Bear's tail's end;
That as she whisked it towards the sun,
Strowed mighty empires up and down;
Which others say must needs be false
Because your true bears have no tails.   900
Some say the zodiac constellations
Have long since changed their antique stations
Above a sign, and prove the same
In Taurus now, once in the Ram;
Affirm the trigons chopped and changed,   905
The watery with the fiery ranged.
Then how can their effects still hold
To be the same they were of old?
This, though the art were true, would make
Our modern soothsayers mistake,   910
And is one cause they tell more lies
In figures and nativities
Than th'old Chaldean conjurers
In so many hundred thousand years;
Beside their nonsense in translating,   915
For want of accidence and Latin;
Like *idus* and *calendae* englished
The quarter-days by skilful linguist.[n]
And yet, with canting, sleight and cheat,
'Twill serve their turn to do the feat;   920
Make fools believe in their foreseeing
Of things, before they are in being;

---

895 *Putat Cardanus ab extrema cauda Helices seu Majoris Ursae omne magnum
imperium pendere.* Idem p. 325.
913 *Chaldaei jactant se quadingenta septuaginta annorum millia in periclitandis
experiundisque puerorum animis posuisse.* Cicero.

---

895 *Cardan*: Girolamo Cardan (1501–76), Italian mathematician and astrologer.
905 *trigons*: the sets of three signs of the zodiac. The twelve signs were divided
  into four sets of three, each set corresponding to one of the four elements of
  earth, air, fire, and water.
913 *Chaldean*: see note to II. iii. 689.
895 note: 'Cardan believes that every great empire depends upon the tail star of
  Helice, or the Great Bear' (Bodin, p. 232).
913 note: 'The Babylonians boast that they spent four hundred and seventy
  thousand years in testing children and putting them to the trial' (Cicero, *De
  Divinatione*, II. xlvi. 97).

To swallow gudgeons ere they're catched,
And count their chickens ere they're hatched;
Make them the constellations prompt,   925
And give 'em back their own accompt;
But still the best to him that gives
The best price for 't, or best believes.
Some towns and cities, some for brevity
Have cast the versal world's nativity,   930
And make the infant stars confess,
Like fools or children, what they please.
Some calculate the hidden fates
Of monkeys, puppy-dogs and cats;
Some running nags, and fighting cocks;   935
Some love, trade, lawsuits and the pox.
Some take a measure of the lives
Of fathers, mothers, husbands, wives,
Make opposition, trine and quartile
Tell who is barren and who fertile,   940
As if the planet's first aspect
The tender infant did infect
In soul and body, and instil
All future good and future ill,
Which, in their dark fatalities lurking,   945
At destined periods fall a-working,
And break out, like the hidden seeds
Of long diseases, into deeds;
In friendships, enmities and strife,
And all th'emergencies of life.   950
No sooner does he peep into
The world but he has done his do,
Catched all diseases, took all physic,
That cures or kills a man that is sick;
Married his punctual dose of wives,   955
Is cuckolded and breaks or thrives.
There's but the twinkling of a star
Between a man of peace and war,

---

923 *swallow gudgeons*: a proverbial expression meaning 'to be tricked' (*ODEP* 791).

939 These are astrological terms for the relative positions between planets. An opposition is 180 degrees, a trine is 120 degrees, and a quartile 90 degrees. Cf. p. 253.

956 *breaks*: goes bankrupt.

A thief and justice, fool and knave,
A huffing officer and a slave,   960
A crafty lawyer and pick pocket,
A great philosopher and a blockhead,
A formal preacher and a player,
A learn'd physician and man slayer;
As if men from the stars did suck   965
Old age, diseases and ill luck,
Wit, folly, honour, virtue, vice,
Trade, travel, women, claps and dice,
And draw with the first air they breathe,
Battle and murder, sudden death.   970
Are not these fine commodities
To be imported from the skies?
And vended here among the rabble
For staple goods and warrantable?
Like money by the Druids borrowed,   975
In th'other world to be restored.'

Quoth Sidrophel, 'To let you know
You wrong the arts and artists too;
Since arguments are lost on those
That do our principles oppose,   980
I will (although I've don 't before)
Demonstrate to your sense once more,
And draw a figure that shall tell you
What you perhaps forget befell you,
By way of horary inspection,   985
Which some account our worst erection.'
With that, he circles draws and squares,
With ciphers, astral characters;
Then looks 'em o'er to understand 'em,
Although set down hab-nab at random.   990

975 *Druidae pecuniam mutuo accipiebant in posteriore vitae redituri.* Patricius
Tom. 2. p. 97.

---

985 *horary inspection*: inspecting a figure of the heavens, erected for the moment
   at which the question is asked.
990 *hab-nab*: hit or miss.
975 note: 'The Druids used to accept money reciprocally intending to repay it
   in the next life' (Franciscus Patricius, *De Institutione Reipublicae*, Strasbourg,
   1594, ii. vii. 97).

Quoth he, 'This scheme of th'heavens set
Discovers how in fight you met
At Kingston with a maypole idol,[n]
And that y'were banged both back and side well,
And though you overcame the bear,   995
The dogs beat you at Brentford fair,
Where sturdy butchers broke your noddle
And handled you like a fopdoodle.'

Quoth Hudibras, 'I now perceive
You are no conjurer, by your leave.   1000
That paltry story is untrue,
And forged to cheat such gulls as you.'

'Not true?' quoth he, 'Howe'er you vapour,
I can what I affirm make appear.
Whachum shall justify t'your face,   1005
And prove he was upon the place.
He played the saltimbanco's part,
Transformed t'a Frenchman by my art.[n]
He stole your cloak and picked your pocket,
Chewsed and chaldesed ye like a blockhead.   1010
And what you lost I can produce,
If you deny it, here i'th' house.'

Quoth Hudibras, 'I do believe
That argument's demonstrative.
Ralpho, bear witness and go and fetch us   1015
A constable to seize the wretches.
For though they're both false knaves and cheats,
Imposters, jugglers, counterfeits,

1001 There was a notorious idiot, that is here described by the name
and character of Whachum, who counterfeited a Second Part of *Hudibras*,
as untowardly as Captain Po, who could not write himself and yet made a
shift to stand on the pillory for forging other men's hands, as his fellow
Whachum no doubt deserved; in whose abominable doggerel this story
of Hudibras and a French mountebank at Brentford fair is as properly
described.

---

998 *fopdoodle*: fool.
1010 *Chewsed*: tricked. *Chaldesed* is a word coined by Butler, presumably from
'Chaldean', the name given by the Romans to astrologers.

I'll make 'em serve for perpendiculars,
As true as e'er were used by bricklayers.   1020
They're guilty by their own confessions
Of felony, and at the sessions,
Upon the bench I will so handle 'em
That the vibration of this pendulum
Shall make all tailors' yards of one   1025
Unanimous opinion;
A thing he long has vapoured of,
But now shall make it out by proof.'

Quoth Sidrophel, 'I do not doubt
To find friends that will bear me out.   1030
Nor have I hazarded my art
And neck so long on the state's part,
To be exposed in th'end to suffer
By such a braggadocio huffer.'

'Huffer?' quoth Hudibras, 'This sword   1035
Shall down thy false throat cram that word.
Ralpho, make haste, and call an officer
To apprehend this stygian sophister.
Meanwhile I'll hold 'em at a bay
Lest he and Whachum run away.'   1040

But Sidrophel, who from th'aspect
Of Hudibras did now erect
A figure worse portending far
Than that of most malignant star,
Believed it now the fittest moment   1045
To shun the danger that might come on 't,

1024 The device of the vibration of a pendulum was intended to settle a certain
measure of ells and yards etc. (that should have its foundation in nature) all
the world over. For by swinging a weight at the end of a string, and calculating,
by the motion of the sun or any star, how long the vibration would last, in
proportion to the length of the string and weight of the pendulum, they thought
to reduce it back again, and from any part of time compute the exact length of
any string that must necessarily vibrate in so much space of time. So that if a
man should ask in China for a quarter of an hour of satin or taffeta, they
would know perfectly what is meant, and all mankind learn a new way to
measure things no more by the yard, foot, or inch, but by the hour, quarter,
and minute.[n]

1034 *huffer*: boaster.

While Hudibras was all alone,
And he and Whachum two to one.
This being resolved, he spied by chance
Behind the door an iron lance   1050
That many a sturdy limb had gored,
And legs and loins and shoulders bored.
He snatched it up and made a pass
To make his way through Hudibras.
Whachum had got a fier-fork   1055
With which he vowed to do his work,
But Hudibras was well prepared
And stoutly stood upon his guard.
He put by Sidrophello's thrust,
And in, right manfully, he rushed.   1060
The weapon from his gripe he wrung,
And laid him on the earth along.
Whachum his sea coal prong threw by,
And basely turned his back to fly,
But Hudibras gave him a twitch   1065
As quick as lightning in the breech,
Just in the place where honour's lodged,
As wise philosophers have judged,
Because a kick in that part more
Hurts honour than deep wounds before.   1070

Quoth Hudibras, 'The stars determine
You are my prisoners, base vermin.
Could they not tell you so, as well
As what I came to know, foretell?
By this, what cheats you are we find,   1075
That in your own concerns are blind.
Your lives are now at my dispose,
To be redeemed by fine or blows.
But who his honour would defile,
To take or sell two lives so vile?   1080
I'll give you quarter, but your pillage,
The conquering warrior's crop and tillage,
Which with his sword he reaps and ploughs,
That mine, the law of arms allows.'

This said in haste, in haste he fell   1085
To rummaging of Sidrophel.

First he expounded both his pockets,
And found a watch with rings and lockets
Which had been left with him, t'erect
A figure for, and so detect;   1090
A copper plate, with almanacs
Engraved upon 't, with other knacks
Of Booker's, Lilly's, Sarah Jimmer's,
And blank schemes to discover nimmers,
A moon-dial, with Napier's Bones,   1095
And several constellation stones,
Engraved in planetary hours,
That over mortals had strange powers
To make 'em thrive in law or trade,
And stab or poison to evade,   1100
In wit or wisdom to improve,
And be victorious in love.
Whachum had neither cross nor pile:
His plunder was not worth the while;
All which the conqueror did discompt   1105
To pay for curing of his rump.

But Sidrophel, as full of tricks
As Rota men of politics,
Straight cast about to over-reach
Th'unwary conqueror with a fetch,   1110
And make him glad at least to quit
His victory, and fly the pit,

1087 *expounded*: exposed to view.
1093 John Booker (1601–67) was an astrologer and author of almanacs; William
    Lilly (1602–81) was probably the best-known astrologer of his time; Sarah
    Jinner was the author of almanacs and predictions in the middle of the seven-
    teenth century.
1094 *nimmers*: thieves.
1095 *Napier's Bones*: an early aid to multiplication and division, consisting of
    strips of bone marked out with digits. They were named after their inventor,
    John Napier (1550–1617).
1096 *constellation stones*: precious stones thought to bear the influence of par-
    ticular constellations. They were often engraved with the sign of their con-
    stellation and were used as antidotes against poisons.
1103 *cross nor pile*: 'head nor tail'; money.
1108 *Rota men*: members of the Rota, a club founded by James Harrington
    (1611–77) for the discussion of political theories.

Before the secular prince of darkness
Arrived to seize upon his carcass.
And, as a fox, with hot pursuit   1115
Chased through a warren, cast about
To save his credit, and among
Dead vermin on a gallows hung;
And while the dogs ran underneath,
Escaped by counterfeiting death,   1120
Not out of cunning, but a train
Of atoms jostling in his brain,
As learn'd philosophers give out,[n]
So Sidrophello cast about,
And fell to 's wonted trade again,   1125
To feign himself in earnest slain.
First stretched out one leg, then another,
And seeming in his breast to smother
A broken sigh, quoth he, 'Where am I?
Alive or dead? Or which way came I   1130
Through so immense a space so soon?
But now I thought myself in th'moon,
And that a monster with huge whiskers,
More formidable than a Switzer's,
My body through and through had drilled,   1135
And Whachum by my side had killed;
Had cross-examined both our hose,
And plundered all we had to lose.
Look, there he is! I see him now,
And feel the place I am run through;   1140
And there lies Whachum by my side,
Stone dead and in his own blood dyed.
Oh! Oh!' With that he fetched a groan
And fell again into a swoon,
Shut both his eyes and stopped his breath,   1145
And, to the life, out-acted death,
That Hudibras, to all appearing,
Believed him to be dead as herring.

1113 As the devil is the spiritual prince of darkness, so is the constable the
secular, who governs in the night with as great authority as his colleague, but
far more imperiously.

1134 *Switzer*: Swiss mercenary troops were notorious for their ferocity and
brutality.
1148 *dead as herring*: proverbial (*ODEP* 170).

He held it now no longer safe
To tarry the return of Ralph,   1150
But rather leave him in the lurch.
Thought he, 'He has abused our church,
Refused to give himself one firk
To carry on the public work;
Despised our synod men like dirt,   1155
And made their discipline his sport;
Divulged the secrets of their classes,
And their conventions proved high places;
Disparaged their tithe pigs as pagan,
And set at naught their cheese and bacon;   1160
Railed at their Covenant, and jeered
Their reverend persons to my beard;
For all which scandals to be quit
At once, this juncture falls out fit.
I'll make him henceforth to beware,   1165
And tempt my fury if he dare.
He must, at least, hold up his hand,
By twelve freeholders to be scanned,
Who, by their skill in palmistry,
Will quickly read his destiny,   1170
And make him glad to read his lesson,
Or take a turn for 't at the session,
Unless his light and gifts prove truer
Than ever yet they did, I'm sure.
For if he 'scape with whipping now,   1175
'Tis more than he can hope to do;
And that will disengage my conscience
Of th'obligation, in his own sense.
I'll make him now by force abide
What he by gentle means denied,   1180

1153 *give himself one firk*: stir himself in the slightest.
1156 *discipline*: government.
1158 *high places*: seats of idolatry. The high places mentioned in the Old Testa-
    ment were the hills on which religious sacrifices were carried out. 'Conven-
    tions' is used in the sense of 'assemblies'.
1161 *Covenant*: see note to I. i. 730, p. 291.
1168 *twelve freeholders*: the 'twelve free and lawful men' who formed the jury
    in a court of law.
1171 *read his lesson*: i.e. claim benefit of clergy. All accused men who could
    demonstrate their ability to read were exempted from sentence for their first
    conviction.
1179 *abide*: endure; put up with.

To give my honour satisfaction,
And right the brethren in the action.'

This being resolved, with equal speed
And conduct he approached his steed,
And with activity unwont,   1185
Assayed the lofty beast to mount;
Which once achieved, he spurred his palfrey,
To get from th'enemy and Ralph free;
Left danger, fears, and foes behind,
And beat, at least three lengths, the wind.   1190

The Elephant in the Moon[n]

A learn'd society of late,
The glory of a foreign state,
Agreed upon a summer's night
To search the moon by her own light
To take an inventory of all   5
Her real estate and personal,
And make an accurate survey
Of all her lands, and how they lay,
As true as that of Ireland, where
The sly surveyors stole a shire;[n]   10
T'observe her country how 'twas planted,
With what sh'abounded most or wanted,
And make the properest observations
For settling of new plantations,
If the society should incline   15
T'attempt so glorious a design.
   This was the purpose of their meeting,
For which they chose a time as fitting,
When at the full her radiant light
And influence too were at their height.   20
And now the lofty tube, the scale
With which they heaven itself assail,
Was mounted full against the moon,
And all stood ready to fall on,
Impatient who should have the honour   25
To plant an ensign first upon her.
   When one who for his deep belief
Was virtuoso then in chief,
Approved the most profound and wise
To solve impossibilities,   30

---

21 *tube*: telescope; also cannon (introducing the military metaphor). *scale*:
   ladder.
28 *virtuoso*: one who has a general interest in the arts and sciences, or who pur-
   sues some particular investigations. Butler exploits the unfavourable sense:
   dilettante or trifler.

Advancing gravely to apply
To th'optic glass his judging eye,
Cried 'Strange!'—then reinforced his sight
Against the moon with all his might,
And bent his penetrating brow   35
As if he meant to gaze her through.
When all the rest began t'admire,
And like a train from him took fire,
Surprized with wonder beforehand
At what they did not understand,   40
Cried out, impatient to know what
The matter was they wondered at.
   Quoth he, 'Th'inhabitants o'th' moon!
Who when the sun shines hot at noon
Do live in cellars underground   45
Of eight miles deep and eighty round^n
(In which at once they fortify
Against the sun and th'enemy),
Which they count towns and cities there
Because their people's civiler   50
Than those rude peasants that are found
To live upon the upper ground,
Called Privolvans, with whom they are
Perpetually in open war.
And now both armies, highly 'nraged,   55
Are in a bloody fight engaged,
And many fall on both sides slain,
As by the glass 'tis clear and plain.
Look quickly then, that everyone
May see the fight before 'tis done.'   60
   With that a great philosopher,
Admired and famous far and near
As one of singular invention
But universal comprehension,
Applied one eye and half a nose   65
Unto the optic engine close.
For he had lately undertook
To prove, and publish in a book,

---

37 *admire*: express astonishment.
53 *Privolvans*: the name given by Kepler to the dwellers on the far side of the
   moon; so called because they are deprived (*privati*) of the sight of the revolving earth (*volva*).

That men whose natural eyes are out
May by more powerful art be brought   70
To see with th'empty holes as plain
As if their eyes were in again,
And (if they chanced to fail of those)
To make an optic of a nose,[n]
As clearly 't may by those that wear   75
But spectacles be made appear,
By which both senses' being united
Does render them much better sighted.
This great man, having fixed both sights
To view the formidable fights,   80
Observed his best, and then cried out,
'The battle's desperately fought:
The gallant Subvolvani rally,
And from their trenches make a sally
Upon the stubborn enemy,   85
Who now begin to rout and fly.
    'These silly, ranting Privolvans
Have every summer their campaigns,
And muster like the warlike sons
Of Rawhead and of Bloody-Bones,   90
As numerous as soland-geese
I'th' islands of the Orcades,
Courageously to make a stand
And face their neighbours hand to hand
Until the longed-for winter's come,   95
And then return in triumph home
To spend the rest o'th' year in lies
And vapouring of their victories.
    'From th'old Arcadians they're believed
To be, before the moon, derived;   100
And when her orb was new-created
To people her were thence translated.
For as th'Arcadians were reputed
Of all the Grecians the most stupid,

---

83 *Subvolvani*: the name given by Kepler to the dwellers on the near side of
the moon; so called because they are 'below' the revolving earth.
86 *rout*: break into rout.
90 *Rawhead . . . Bloody-Bones*: fictitious monsters, used to frighten children.
91 *soland-geese*: gannets. They frequent the 'Orcades' or Orkneys.

Whom nothing in the world could bring   105
To civil life but fiddling,
They still retain the antique course
And custom of their ancestors,
And always sing and fiddle to
Things of the greatest weight they do.'[n]   110
  While thus the learn'd man entertains
Th' assembly with the Privolvans,
Another of as great renown
And solid judgment in the moon,
That understood her various soils[n]   115
And which produced best gennet-moyles,
And in the register of fame
Had entered his long-living name,
After he had pored long and hard
In th'engine, gave a start and stared.   120
  Quoth he, 'A stranger sight appears
Than e'er was seen in all the spheres,
A wonder more unparalleled
Than ever mortal tube beheld.
An elephant from one of those   125
Two mighty armies is broke loose,
And with the horror of the fight
Appears amazed and in a fright.
Look quickly, lest the sight of us
Should cause the startled beast t'imboss.   130
  'It is a large one, far more great
Than e'er was bred in Afric yet;
From which we boldly may infer
The moon is much the fruitfuller.
And since the mighty Pyrrhus brought   135
Those living castles first, 'tis thought,
Against the Romans in the field,
It may an argument be held
(Arcadia being but a piece,
As his dominions were, of Greece)   140
To prove what this illustrious person
Has made so noble a discourse on,

116 *gennet-moyles*: a variety of cider apple.
130 *imboss*: plunge into a wood, hide itself.
135 *Pyrrhus*: king of Epirus, who gave the Romans their first experience of
  elephants in his campaigns of 281–279 B.C.
141 *illustrious person*: the previous speaker.

And amply satisfied us all
O'th' Privolvans' original.[n]
   'That elephants are in the moon,   145
Though we had now discovered none,
Is easily made manifest,
Since from the greatest to the least
All other stars and constellations
Have cattle of all sorts of nations,   150
And heaven, like a Tartar's horde,
With great and numerous droves is stored;
And if the moon produce by nature
A people of so vast a stature,
'Tis consequent she should bring forth   155
Far greater beasts too than the earth
(As by the best accounts appears
Of all our great'st discoverers),
And that those monstrous creatures there
Are not such rarities as here.'   160
   Meanwhile the rest had had a sight
Of all particulars o'th' fight,
And every man with equal care
Perused of th'elephant his share,
Proud of his interest in the glory   165
Of so miraculous a story,
When one who for his excellence
In heightening words and shadowing sense
And magnifying all he writ
With curious microscopic wit,   170
Was magnified himself no less
In home and foreign colleges,
Began, transported with the twang
Of his own *trillo*, thus t'harangue:
   'Most excellent and virtuous friends,   175
This great discovery makes amends
For all our unsuccessful pains
And lost expense of time and brains.

---

150 *nations*: kinds; as here the Ram, the Bull, the Lion, etc.
154 *so vast a stature*: see l. 46 above, and end-note.
168 *heightening*: making a colour more luminous; opposite of shadowing.
174 *trillo*: elegantly tremulous sounds, a trill.
175 *virtuous*: virtuoso-like; but here not excluding 'full of virtue'.

For by this sole phenomenon
We've gotten ground upon the moon,   180
And gained a pass, to hold dispute
With all the planets that stand out,
To carry this most virtuous war
Home to the door of every star,
And plant th'artillery of our tubes   185
Against their proudest magnitudes,
To stretch our victories beyond
Th'extent of planetary ground,
And fix our engines and our ensigns
Upon the fixed stars' vast dimensions   190
(Which Archimede so long ago
Durst not presume to wish to do),
And prove if they are other suns,
As some have held opinions,[n]
Or windows in th'empyreum   195
From whence those bright effluvias come
Like flames of fire (as others guess)
That shine i'th' mouths of furnaces.[n]
'Nor is this all we have achieved,
But more: henceforth to be believed,   200
And have no more our best designs,
Because they're ours, believed ill signs.
T'out-throw, and stretch, and to enlarge
Shall now no more be laid t'our charge;
Nor shall our ablest virtuosos   205
Prove arguments for coffee-houses;
Nor those devices that are laid
Too truly on us, nor those made,
Hereafter gain belief among
Our strictest judges, right or wrong.   210
Nor shall our past misfortunes more
Be charged upon the ancient score:
No more our making old dogs young[n]
Make men suspect us still i'th' wrong;

189 *engines*: instruments of war; their telescopes.
190 The eighth Ptolemaic sphere, that of the fixed stars, encompassed the seven
planetary spheres, and would therefore be of vast dimensions.
191–2 Archimedes offered only to apply his engine (a lever) to the earth.
203 *out-throw*: throw beyond something; here beyond just limits, exaggerate.
206 *arguments*: themes.

Nor new-invented chariots draw   215
The boys to course us without law;
Nor putting pigs t'a bitch to nurse,
To turn 'em into mongrel curs,
Make them suspect our skulls are brittle
And hold too much wit or too little;   220
Nor shall our speculations whether
An elder-stick will save the leather
Of schoolboys' breeches from the rod[n]
Make all we do appear as odd.
This one discovery's enough   225
To take all former scandals off.
    'But since the world's incredulous
Of all our scrutinies, and us,
And with a prejudice prevents
Our best and worst experiments   230
(As if th'were destined to miscarry,
In consort tried or solitary),
And since it is uncertain when
Such wonders will occur again,
Let us as cautiously contrive   235
To draw an exact narrative
Of what we every one can swear
Our eyes themselves have seen appear,
That when we publish the account
We all may take our oaths upon 't.'   240
    This said, they all with one consent
Agreed to draw up th'instrument
And, for the general satisfaction,
To print it in the next *Transaction*.
But whilst the chiefs were drawing up   245
This strange memoir o'th' telescope,
One, peeping in the tube by chance,
Beheld the elephant advance,
And from the west side of the moon
To th'east was in a moment gone.   250
This being related gave a stop
To what the rest were drawing up;

---

216 *course us without law*: (i) persecute us without mercy; (ii) race against us
   without handicap. 'Law' was time or distance allowed a hunted animal by way
   of fair start.
229 *prevents*: debars.

And every man, amazed anew
How it could possibly be true
That any beast should run a race   255
So monstrous in so short a space,
Resolved, howe'er, to make it good—
At least, as possible as he could—
And rather his own eyes condemn
Than question what he'd seen with them.   260
    While all were thus resolved, a man
Of great renown there, thus began:
' 'Tis strange, I grant. But who can say
What cannot be, what can, and may—
Especially at so hugely vast   265
A distance as this wonder's placed,
Where the least error of the sight
May show things false, but never right?
Nor can we try them, so far off,
By any sublunary proof;   270
For who can say that nature there
Has the same laws she goes by here?
Nor is it like she has infused
In every species there produced
The same efforts she does confer   275
Upon the same productions here,
Since those with us of several nations
Have such prodigious variations,
And she affects so much to use
Variety in all she does.   280
Hence may b'inferred that, though I grant
We've seen i'th' moon an elephant,
That elephant may differ so
From those upon the earth below
Both in his bulk and force and speed,   285
As being of a different breed,
That, though our own are but slow-paced,
Theirs there may fly, or run as fast,
And yet be elephants no less
Than those of Indian pedigrees.'   290
    This said, another of great worth,
Famed for his learned works put forth,

275 *efforts*: powers, properties.

Looked wise, then said, 'All this is true,
And learnedly observed by you.
But there's another reason for 't,   295
That falls but very little short
Of mathematic demonstration
Upon an accurate calculation,
And that is: As the earth and moon
Do both move contrary upon   300
Their axes, the rapidity
Of both their motions cannot be
But so prodigiously fast
That vaster spaces may be passed
In less time than the beast has gone,   305
Though he'd no motion of his own;
Which we can take no measure of,
As you have cleared by learned proof.
This granted, we may boldly thence
Lay claim t'a nobler inference,   310
And make this great phenomenon
(Were there no other) serve alone
To clear the grand hypothesis
O'th' motion of the earth from this.'
   With this they all were satisfied,   315
As men are wont o'th' biased side,
Applauded the profound dispute,
And grew more gay and resolute
By having overcome all doubt
Than if it never had fall'n out,   320
And to complete their narrative
Agreed t'insert this strange retrieve.
   But while they were diverted all
With wording the memorial,
The footboys for diversion too,   325
As having nothing else to do,
Seeing the telescope at leisure,
Turned virtuosos for their pleasure,
Began to gaze upon the moon
As those they waited on had done,   330
With monkeys' ingenuity
That love to practise what they see.

322 *retrieve*: the second discovery and flight of a bird that has already been
sprung; here used figuratively.

When one, whose turn it was to peep,
Saw something in the engine creep,
And, viewing well, discovered more   335
Than all the learn'd had done before.
Quoth he, 'A little thing is slunk
Into the long star-gazing trunk,
And now is gotten down so nigh
I have him just against mine eye.'   340
    This being overheard by one
Who was not so far overgrown
In any virtuous speculation
To judge by mere imagination,
Immediately he made a guess   345
At solving all appearances
(A way far more significant
Than all their hints of th'elephant),
And found upon a second view
His own hypothesis most true;   350
For he had scarce applied his eye
To th'engine but immediately
He found a mouse was gotten in
The hollow tube and, shut between
The two glass windows in restraint,   355
Was swelled into an elephant,
And proved the virtuous occasion
Of all this learned dissertation.
And as a mountain heretofore
Was great with child, they say, and bore   360
A silly mouse, this mouse as strange
Brought forth a mountain in exchange.
    Meanwhile the rest in consultation
Had penned the wonderful narration,
And set their hands and seals and wit   365
T'attest the truth of what they'd writ,
When this accurst phenomenon
Confounded all they'd said or done.
For 'twas no sooner hinted at
But th'all were in a tumult straight,   370

338 *trunk*: tube.
359–61 Horace, *Ars Poetica*, 139 ('Parturient montes, nascetur ridiculus mus':
   'The mountains will be in labour, and a funny little mouse be born').

More furiously enraged by far
Than those that in the moon made war,
To find so admirable a hint,
When they had all agreed t'have seen 't
And were engaged to make it out,   375
Obstructed with a paltry doubt.
   When one whose task was to determine
And solve th'appearances of vermin,
Who'd made profound discoveries
In frogs and toads and rats and mice   380
(Though not so curious, 'tis true,
As many a wise rat-catcher knew),
After he had with signs made way
For something great he had to say,
At last prevailed:[n] 'This disquisition   385
Is half of it in my discission;
For though the elephant as beast
Belongs of right to all the rest,
The mouse, being but a vermin, none
Has title to but I alone;   390
And therefore hope I may be heard
In my own province with regard.
   'It is no wonder we're cried down
And made the talk of all the town,
That rants and swears for all our great   395
Attempts we have done nothing yet,
If every one have leave to doubt,
When some great secret's half made out,
And, 'cause perhaps it is not true,
Obstruct and ruin all we do.   400
And no great act was ever done,
Nor ever can, with truth alone,
If nothing else but truth w'allow,
'Tis no great matter what we do.
For truth is too reserved and nice   405
T'appear in mixed societies,
Delights in solitary abodes,
And never shows herself in crowds,

---

373 *hint*: something that may be laid hold of; thus both a suggestion and an
   opportunity.
381 *curious*: skilful.
386 *discission*: division by cutting into something; punning with 'decision'.

A sullen little thing below
All matters of pretence and show,   410
That deal in novelty and change,
Not of things true, but rare and strange,
To treat the world with what is fit
And proper to its natural wit—
The world, that never sets esteem   415
On what things are, but what they seem,
And if they be not strange and new,
They're ne'er the better for being true.
      'For what has mankind gained by knowing
His little truth but his undoing,   420
Which wisely was by nature hidden,
And only for his good forbidden?[n]
And therefore with great prudence does
The world still strive to keep it close;
For if all secret truths were known,   425
Who would not be once more undone?
For truth has always danger in 't,
And here perhaps may cross some hint
We have already agreed upon,
And vainly frustrate all we've done,   430
Only to make new work for Stubbs
And all the academic clubs.
      'How much then ought we have a care
That no man know above his share,
Nor dare to understand henceforth   435
More than his contribution's worth,
That those who've purchased of the College
A share or half a share of knowledge
And brought in none, but spent repute,
Should not b'admitted to dispute,   440
Nor any man pretend to know
More than his dividend comes to!
For partners have been always known
To cheat their public interest prone;
And if we do not look to ours,   445
'Tis sure to run the selfsame course.'

431 *Stubbs*: Henry Stubbe (1632–76), the physician who published attacks
    (1670–1) on the Royal Society apologists Thomas Sprat and Joseph Glanvill.
432 *clubs*: cliques.
436 *contribution*: a shilling per week from each member of the Society.
444 to be prone to satisfy personal interests at the expense of the partnership's.

This said, the whole assembly allowed
The doctrine to be right and good,
And from the truth of what they'd heard
Resolved: to give truth no regard,   450
But what was for their turn to vouch,
And either find or make it such;
That 'twas more noble to create
Things like truth out of strong conceit
Than with vexatious pains and doubt   455
To find, or think t'have found, her out.
    This being resolved, they one by one
Reviewed the tube, the mouse, and moon;
But still the narrower they pried,
The more they were unsatisfied,   460
In no one thing they saw agreeing,
As if they'd several faiths of seeing.
Some swore upon a second view
That all they'd seen before was true,
And that they never would recant   465
One syllable of th'elephant;
Avowed his snout could be no mouse's,
But a true elephant's proboscis.
Others began to doubt and waver,
Uncertain which o'th' two to favour,   470
And knew not whether to espouse
The cause of th'elephant or mouse.
Some held no way so orthodox
To try it as the ballot-box,
And like the nations patriots   475
To find or make the truth by votes.
Others conceived it much more fit
T'unmount the tube and open it,
And for their private satisfaction
To re-examine the transaction,   480
And after explicate the rest
As they should find cause for the best.
    To this, as th'only expedient,
The whole assembly gave consent.

---

454 *conceit*: imagination.
462 *faiths*: i.e. religious faiths.
481 *explicate*: extricate (from their difficulties).

But e'er the tube was half let down,   485
It cleared the first phenomenon;
For at the end prodigious swarms
Of flies and gnats, like men in arms,
Had all passed muster by mischance
Both for the Sub- and Privolvans.   490
This being discovered put them all
Into a fresh and fiercer brawl,
Ashamed that men so grave and wise
Should be chaldesed by gnats and flies,
And take the feeble insects' swarms   495
For mighty troops of men-at-arms—
As vain as those who, when the moon
Bright in a crystal river shone,
Threw casting-nets as subtly at her
To catch and pull her out o'th' water.[n]   500
But when they had unscrewed the glass
To find out where th'impostor was,
And saw the mouse that by mishap
Had made the telescope a trap,
Amazed, confounded, and afflicted   505
To be so openly convicted,
Immediately they get them gone
With this discovery alone:
    That those who greedily pursue
Things wonderful instead of true,   510
That in their speculations choose
To make discoveries strange news,[n]
And natural history a gazette
Of tales stupendous and far-fet,
Hold no truth worthy to be known   515
That is not huge and overgrown,
And explicate appearances
Not as they are, but as they please,
In vain strive nature to suborn,
And for their pains are paid with scorn.   520

---

486 *cleared*: clarified.
494 *chaldesed*: see *Hudibras*, II. iii. 1010.
514 *far-fet*: far-fetched.

Satire upon the Royal Society[n]

A learned man, whom once a week
A hundred virtuosos seek
And like an oracle apply to
T'ask questions and admire and lie to,
Who entertained them all of course   5
(As men take wives for better or worse),
And passed them all for men of parts,
Though some but sceptics in their hearts;
For when they're cast into a lump,
Their talents equally must jump,   10
As metals mixed, the rich and base,
Do both at equal values pass.
   With these the ordinary debate
Was after news and things of state:
Which way the dreadful comet went   15
In sixty-four, and what it meant;[n]
What nations yet are to bewail
The operation of its tail,
Or whether France or Holland yet
Or Germany be in its debt;   20
What wars and plagues in Christendom
Have happened since, and what to come;
What kings are dead, how many queens
And princesses are poisoned since,
And who shall next of all by turn   25
Make courts wear black and tradesmen mourn;
What parties next of foot or horse
Will rout, or routed be, of course;
What German marches and retreats
Will furnish the next month's gazettes;   30
What pestilent contagion next,
And what part of the world, infects;
What dreadful meteor, and where,
Shall in the heavens next appear,
And when again shall lay embargo   35

Upon the admiral, the good ship *Argo*.
　Why currents turn in seas of ice
Some thrice a day and some but twice,
And why the tides at night and noon
Court, like Caligula, the moon;[n]   40
What is the natural cause why fish,
That always drink, do never piss,
Or whether in their home, the deep,
By day or night they ever sleep;
If grass be green or snow be white   45
But only as they take the light;[n]
Whether possessions of the devil
Or mere temptations do most evil;
What is't that makes all fountains still
Within the earth to run uphill,   50
But on the outside down again,
As if th'attempt had been in vain;[n]
Or what's the strange magnetic cause
The steel or loadstone's drawn, or draws
The star the needle which the stone   55
Has only been but touched upon—
Whether the North Star's influence
With both does hold intelligence
(For red-hot iron, held tow'rds the Pole,
Turns of itself to 't when 'tis cool),[n]   60
Or whether male and female screws
In th'iron and stone th'effect produce;
What makes the body of the sun,
That such a rapid course does run,
To draw no tail behind through th'air   65
As comets do when they appear,
Which other planets cannot do,
Because they do not burn, but glow;
Whether the moon be sea or land
Or charcoal or a quenched firebrand,   70
Or if the dark holes that appear
Are only pores, not cities, there;

---

36 *admiral*: flagship. The 'Argo' is a southern constellation.
40 *Caligula*: Roman emperor A.D. 37–41. His immoral proposals to the moon
　are noted by Suetonius (*Caligula*, xxii).
63–8 See p. 271 below.
68 *glow*: probably 'are only illuminated by the sun' (p. 271); reflect.

Whether the atmosphere turn round,
Or keep a just pace with the ground,
Or loiter lazily behind   75
And clog the air with gusts of wind;
Or whether crescents in the wane
(For so an author has it plain)
Do burn quite out, or wear away
Their snuffs upon the edge of day;[n]   80
Whether the sea increase, or waste,
And, if it do, how long 'twill last;
Or, if the sun approaches near
The earth, how soon it will be there.
    These were their learned speculations;   85
And all their constant occupations
To measure wind, and weigh the air,[n]
And turn a circle to a square;
To make a powder of the sun,
By which all doctors should b'undone;   90
To find the North-west Passage out,
Although the farthest way about;
If chemists from a rose's ashes
Can raise the rose itself in glasses;[n]
Whether the line of incidence   95
Rise from the object or the sense;[n]
To stew th'elixir in a bath
Of hope, credulity, and faith;
To explicate by subtle hints
The grain of diamonds and flints;   100
And in the braying of an ass
Find out the treble and the bass;
If mares neigh alto, and a cow
A double diapason low.

81–2 See pp. 270–1 below.
89–90 *To make . . . b'undone* to capture that essence in sunbeams which would
    prove the elixir or universal cure.
104 'The organ at Exeter Cathedral, constructed by John Loosemore, possessed
    a remarkable feature in its Double Open Diapason, which contained the
    largest pipes made until this time in England' (Grove, *Dictionary of Music and
    Musicians*, 1954, s.v. 'Organ. History. The Restoration Organs').

Satire upon Our Ridiculous Imitation of the French[n]

Who would not rather get him gone
Beyond th'intolerablest zone,
Or steer his passage through those seas
That burn in flames or those that freeze,
Than see one nation go to school   5
And learn of another, like a fool?
   To study all its tricks and fashions
With epidemic affectations,
And dare to wear no mode or dress
But what they in their wisdom please,   10
As monkeys are by being taught
To put on gloves and stockings caught;
Submit to all that they devise,
As if it wore their liveries;
Make ready and dress th'imagination   15
Not with the clothes, but with the fashion,
And change it (to fulfil the curse
Of Adam's Fall) for new, though worse:
To make their breeches fall or rise
From middle legs to middle thighs,   20
The tropics between which the hose
Move always as the fashion goes;
Sometimes wear hats like pyramids
And sometimes flat like pipkin's lids,
With broad brims sometimes like umbrellas   25
And sometimes narrow as Punchinello's;
In coldest weather go unbraced,
And close in hot as if th'were laced;

8 *epidemic*: 'prevalent among a people or a community at a special time, and produced by some special causes not generally present in the affected locality' (*OED*), as opposed to endemic.
10 *they*: the French.
11–12 The clothes, which they have picked up and put on, hindering their escape.
17 *the curse*: Genesis 3:7; *Paradise Lost*, ix. 1073–4, 1091–115.
20 *legs*: calves.

Sometimes with sleeves and bodies wide,
And sometimes straiter than a hide;   30
Wear perukes, and with false grey hairs
Disguise the true ones and their years
That, when they're modish with the young,
The old may seem so in the throng.
   And as some pupils have been known   35
In time to put their tutors down,
So ours are often found t'have got
More tricks than ever they were taught.
With sly intrigues and artifices
Usurp their poxes and their vices: 40
With garnitures upon their shoes
Make good their claim to gouty toes;
By sudden starts and shrugs and groans
Pretend to aches in their bones,
To scabs and botches, and lay trains   45
To prove their running of the reins;
And lest they should seem destitute
Of any mange that's in repute,
And be behindhand with the mode,
Will swear to crystalline and node,   50
And, that they may not lose their right,
Make it appear how they came by 't.
   Disdain the country where th'were born,
As bastards their own mothers scorn,
And that which brought them forth condemn   55
(As it deserves) for bearing them;
Admire whate'er they find abroad,
But nothing here, though e'er so good;
Be natives wheresoe'er they come,
And only foreigners at home,   60
To which th'appear so far estranged
As if they'd been i'th' cradle changed,
Or—from beyond the seas conveyed
By witches—not born here but laid,
Or by outlandish fathers were   65
Begotten on their mothers here,

---

44 *aches*: pronounced āch'ês.
45 *botches*: boils, ulcers.
46 *running of the reins*: discharge from diseased kidneys; gonorrhoea.
50 *crystalline and node*: venereal pustules and tumours.

And therefore justly slight that nation
Where they've so mongrel a relation,
And seek out other climates where
They may degenerate less than here—   70
As woodcocks, when their plumes are grown,
Borne on the wind's wings and their own,
Forsake the countries where they're hatched,
And seek out others, to be catched.
 So they more naturally may please   75
And humour their own geniuses,
Apply to all things which they see
With their own fancies best agree;
No matter how ridiculous,
'Tis all one if it be in use;   80
For nothing can be bad or good
But as 'tis in or out of mode,
And as the nations are that use it,
All ought to practise or refuse it;
T'observe their postures, move and stand   85
As they give out the word o'command,
To learn the dullest of their whims
And how to wear their very limbs,
To turn and manage every part
Like puppets by their rules of art,   90
To shrug discreetly, act, and tread,
And politicly shake the head,
Until the ignorant (that guess
At all things by th'appearances)
To see how art and nature strive   95
Believe them really alive,
And that they're very men, not things
That move by puppet-work and springs;
When truly all their feats have been
As well performed by motion-men,   100
And the worst drolls of Punchinellos
Were much th'ingeniouser fellows;

69–70 See p. 283.
71 *woodcocks*: commonly applied to persons easily duped.
80 *in use*: in fashion.
83 'and according as the nations using it are in or out of mode'.
100 *motion-men*: puppets.

For when they're perfect in their lesson,
Th'hypothesis grows out of season,
And, all their labour lost, they're fain   105
To learn new and begin again.
   To talk eternally and loud,
And all together in a crowd,
No matter what, for in the noise
No man minds what another says;   110
T'assume a confidence beyond
Mankind for solid and profound,
And still the less and less they know,
The greater dose of that allow;
Decry all things; for to be wise   115
Is not to know, but to despise,
And deep, judicious confidence
Has still the odds of wit and sense,
And can pretend a title to
Far greater things than they can do;   120
T'adorn their English with French scraps,
And give their very language claps;
To *jernie* rightly, and renounce
I'th' pure and most approved of tones;
And, while they idly think t'enrich,   125
Adulterate their native speech;
For though to smatter ends of Greek
Or Latin be the rhetoric
Of pedants counted, and vainglorious,
To smatter French is meritorious,   130
And to forget their mother tongue,
Or purposely to speak it wrong,
A hopeful sign of parts, and wit,
And that th'improve and benefit—
As those that have been taught amiss   135
In liberal arts and sciences
Must all they'd learnt before in vain
Forget quite, and begin again.

112 *for solid*: for (being of) sound scholarship.
114 *that*: i.e. 'confidence'.
123 *jernie*: This fashionable oath was a corruption of *je renie Dieu* (I renounce
  God).

To the Happy Memory
of the most Renowned Duval.
A Pindaric Ode[n]

I

'Tis true to compliment the dead
Is as impertinent and vain
As 'twas of old to call them back again,
   Or like the Tartars give them wives
   With settlements for after-lives;[n]   5
For all that can be done or said,
Though e'er so noble, great, and good,
By them is neither heard nor understood.
   All our fine sleights and tricks of art
First to create and then adore desert,   10
   And those romances which we frame
   To raise ourselves not them a name,
In vain are stuffed with ranting flatteries
And such as, if they knew, they would despise.
For as those times 'the golden age' we call   15
In which there was no gold in use at all,
   So we plant glory and renown
   Where it was ne'er deserved nor known,
   But to worse purpose many times
   To flourish o'er nefarious crimes,   20
And cheat the world, that never seems to mind
How good or bad men die, but what they leave behind.

II

And yet the brave Duval, whose name
Can never be worn out by fame;
That lived and died to leave behind   25
A great example to mankind;
That fell a public sacrifice,
From ruin to preserve those few
Who, though born false, may be made true,
And teach the world to be more just and wise;   30

---

12 See 'A Small Poet', below, p. 259.
15–16 Gold was not mined until the iron age (Ovid, *Metamorphoses*, i. 138–42).
21–2 Cf. 'Elephant', ll. 415–18.

Ought not like vulgar ashes rest
Unmentioned in his silent chest,
Not for his own, but public, interest.
He, like a pious man, some years before
    Th'arrival of his fatal hour,   35
    Made every day he had to live
To his last minute a preparative;
    Taught the wild Arabs on the road
    To act in a more *gentee* mode,
Take prizes more obligingly than those   40
    Who never had been bred *filous*,
And how to hang in a more graceful fashion
Than e'er was known before to the dull English nation.

III

In France, the staple of new modes,
Where garbs and miens are current goods,   45
That serves the ruder northern nations
With methods of address and treat,
Prescribes new garnitures and fashions,
    And how to drink and how to eat
No out-of-fashion wine or meat,   50
    To understand cravats and plumes,
And the most modish from the old perfumes,
    To know the age and pedigrees
    Of points of Flanders or Venice,
Cast their nativities, and to a day   55
Foretell how long they'll hold and when decay,
    T'affect the purest negligences
        In gestures, gaits, and miens,
    And speak by repartee-routines
Out of the most authentic of romances,   60

32 *chest*: coffin.
37 *preparative*: preparation.
38 'An Highwayman / Is a wild Arab, that lives by robbing of small caravans . . .' (*Characters*).
39 *gentee*: a modish new borrowing of Fr. *gentil* (cf. gentle, genteel, jaunty).
40 *prizes*: booty, plunder. *obligingly*: courteously, but also obligatorily.
41 *filous*: (French) thieves.
44 *staple*: 'a town or country which is the principal market or entrepôt for some particular class of merchandise' (*OED*).
47 *address*: courteous approach, courtship. *treat*: treating or entertaining guests.
54 *Flanders and Venice*: i.e. lace from . . .
57 *negligences*: modes of fashionably careless indifference.

And to demonstrate with substantial reason
What ribands all the year are in or out of season,

IV

In this great academy of mankind
 He had his birth and education,
Where all men are s'ingeniously inclined   65
 They understand by imitation,
Improve untaught before they are aware,
As if they sucked their breeding from the air
 That naturally does dispense
To all a deep and solid confidence,   70
 A virtue of that precious use
 That he whom bounteous heaven endues
But with a moderate share of it
Can want no worth, abilities, or wit.
 In all the deep hermetic arts   75
 (For so of late the learned call
 All tricks, if strange and mystical)
 He had improved his natural parts,
 And with his magic rod could sound
 Where hidden treasure might be found.   80
He, like a lord o'th' manor, seized upon
 Whatever happened in his way,
  As lawful weft and stray,
And after by the custom kept it as his own.

V

From these first rudiments he grew   85
To nobler feats, and tried his force
Upon whole troops of foot and horse,
Whom he as bravely did subdue;
Declared all caravans that go
Upon the king's highway the foe;   90
Made many desperate attacks
Upon itinerant brigades
Of all professions, ranks, and trades,
On carriers' loads and pedlars' packs;

---

65 *s'ingeniously inclined*: endowed with such genius and talents.
70–4 See 'Imitation of the French', ll. 111–20.
75 *hermetic arts*: see *Hudibras*, I. i. 523–72 and end-notes
79–80 Duval's pistol as a type of divining rod (and magic wand).

Made 'em lay down their arms and yield,   95
And, to the smallest piece, restore
All that by cheating they had gained before,
And after plundered all the baggage of the field.
In every bold affair of war
He had the chief command and led them on;   100
For no man is judged fit to have the care
Of others' lives until he's made it known
How much he does despise and scorn his own.

VI

Whole provinces 'twixt sun and sun
Have by his conquering sword been won,   105
And mighty sums of money laid
For ransom upon every man,
And hostages delivered till 'twas paid.
Th'excise and chimney publican,[n]
The Jew forestaller and enhancer,   110
To him for all their crimes did answer.
He vanquished the most fierce and fell
Of all his foes, the constable,
And oft had beat his quarters up
And routed him and all his troop.   115
He took the dreadful lawyer's fees,
That in his own allowed highway
Does feats of arms as great as his,
And when th'encounter in it wins the day
(Safe in his garrison, the court,   120
Where meaner criminals are sentenced for 't).
To this stern foe he oft gave quarter,
But as the Scotchman did t'a Tartar,
That he in time to come
Might in return from him receive his fatal doom.[n]   125

VII

He would have starved this mighty town
And brought its haughty spirit down,

---

83 *weft*: waif; 'a piece of property which is found ownerless and which, if un-
claimed within a fixed period after due notice given, falls to the lord of the
manor' (*OED*).
104 *'twixt sun and sun*: between sunrise and sunset.
121 *meaner criminals*: i.e. than the lawyer.
122–5 See *Hudibras*, I. iii. 865–6.

Have cut it off from all relief,
And like a wise and valiant chief
   Made many a fierce assault   130
Upon all ammunition carts
And those that bring up cheese or malt
Or bacon from remoter parts.
No convoy e'er so strong with food
Durst venture on the desperate road.   135
He made th'undaunted waggoner obey,
And the fierce higgler contribution pay;
   The savage butcher and stout drover
Durst not to him their feeble troops discover;
   And if he had but kept the field,   140
   In time had made the city yield;
For great towns, like to crocodiles, are found
I'th' belly aptest to receive a mortal wound.[n]

VIII

But when the fatal hour arrived
   In which his stars began to frown,   145
   And had in close cabals contrived
To pull him from his height of glory down,
   And he, by numerous foes opprest,
   Was in th'enchanted dungeon cast,
      Secured with mighty guards,   150
   Lest he by force or stratagem
Might prove too cunning for their chains and
      them,
And break through all their locks and bolts and
      wards,
   Had both his legs by charms committed
      To one another's charge   155
   That neither might be set at large,
And all their fury and revenge outwitted,
   As jewels of high value are
   Kept under locks with greater care
      Than those of meaner rates,   160
So he was in stone walls, and chains, and iron grates.

---

137 *higgler*: an itinerant dealer, trading country produce for town wares.
146 *cabals*: secret meetings.

IX

Thither came ladies from all parts
To offer up close prisoners their hearts,
  Which he received as tribute due,
And made them yield up love and honour too,   165
  But in more brave heroic ways
  Than e'er were practised yet in plays;
For those two spiteful foes,[n] who never meet
  But full of hot contests and piques
  About punctilios and mere tricks,   170
Did all their quarrels to his doom submit,
  And (far more generous and free)
In contemplation only of him did agree,
  Both fully satisfied—the one
  With those fresh laurels he had won   175
  And all the brave renowned feats
    He had performed in arms,
The other with his person and his charms.
  For just as larks are catched in nets
  By gazing on a piece of glass,   180
So, while the ladies viewed his brighter eyes
  And smoother polished face,
Their gentle hearts, alas! were taken by surprise.

X

Never did bold knight, to relieve
Distressed dames, such dreadful feats achieve   185
  As feeble damsels for his sake
  Would have been proud to undertake,
  And, bravely ambitious to redeem
    The world's loss and their own,
Strove who should have the honour to lay down   190
    And change a life with him;
  But finding all their hopes in vain
  To move his fixed, determined fate,
  Their life itself began to hate,
  As if it were an infamy   195
  To live when he was doomed to die,[n]
    Made loud appeals and moans
  To less hard-hearted grates and stones,

170 *tricks*: illusions, shams.

Came swelled in sighs and drowned in tears
To yield themselves his fellow sufferers,   200
And followed him like prisoners of war
Chained to the lofty wheels of his triumphant car.

201–2 *And followed* . . . *car* i.e. they followed the cart which carried condemned
men from Newgate to Tyburn.

Repartees between Cat and Puss
at a Caterwauling
in the Modern Heroic Way[n]

It was about the middle age of night,
When half the earth stood in the other's light,
And sleep, death's brother, yet a friend to life,
Gave wearied nature a restorative,
When Puss, wrapped warm in his own native furs,   5
Dreamt fondly of as soft and warm amours,
Of making gallantry in gutter-tiles
And sporting on delightful fagot-piles,
Of bolting out of bushes in the dark
As ladies use at midnight in the Park,   10
Or seeking in tall garrets an alcove
For assignations in th'affairs of love.
At once his passion was both false and true,
And the more false the more in earnest grew.
He fancied that he heard those amorous charms   15
That used to summon him to soft alarms,
To which he always brought an equal flame
To fight a rival or to court a dame;
And as in dreams love's raptures are more taking
Than all their actual enjoyments waking,   20
His amorous passion grew to that extreme
His dream itself awaked him from his dream.
Thought he, 'What place is this? Or whither art
Thou vanished from me, mistress of my heart?
But now I had her in this very place,   25
Here, fast imprisoned in my glad embrace;
And while my joys beyond themselves were rapt,
I know not how, nor whither, thou'rt escaped.
Stay, and I'll follow thee!' With that he leapt
Up from the lazy couch on which he slept,   30
And, winged with passion, through his known
    purlieu
Swift as an arrow from a bow he flew,
Nor stopped until his fire had him conveyed
Where many [an] assignation he'd enjoyed,

10 *the Park*: St. James's Park.

Where finding what he sought, a mutual flame   35
That long had stayed and called before he came,
Impatient of delay, without one word,
To lose no further time, he fell aboard.
But gripped so hard he wounded what he loved,
While she in anger thus his heat reproved: 40
Cat. Forbear, foul ravisher, this rude address!
   Canst thou at once both injure and caress?
Puss. Thou hast bewitched me with thy powerful
      charms,
   And I by drawing blood would cure my harms.
Cat. He that does love would set his heart a-tilt   45
   Ere one drop of his lady's should be spilt.
Puss. Your wounds are but without, and mine within;
   You wound my heart, and I but prick your skin;
   And while your eyes pierce deeper than my claws
   You blame th'effect of which you are the cause.   50
Cat. How could my guiltless eyes your heart invade,
   Had it not first been by your own betrayed?
   Hence 'tis my greatest crime has only been
   (Not in my eyes, but yours) in being seen.
Puss. I hurt to love, but do not love to hurt.   55
Cat. That's worse than making cruelty a sport.
Puss. Pain is the foil of pleasure and delight,
   That sets it off to a more noble height.
Cat. He buys his pleasure at a rate too vain
   That takes it up beforehand of his pain.   60
Puss. Pain is more dear than pleasure, when 'tis past.
Cat. But grows intolerable if it last.
Puss. Love is too full of honour to regard
   What it enjoys, but suffers as reward.
   What knight durst ever own a lover's name   65
   That had not been half murdered by his flame?
   Or lady that had never lain at stake
   To death or force of rivals for his sake?
Cat. When love does meet with injury and pain,
   Disdain's the only medicine for disdain.   70
Puss. At once I'm happy and unhappy too
   In being pleased and in displeasing you.

43–4 See *Hudibras*, II. i. 17–18.
45 *a-tilt*: to be tilted at with lances.
60 'who borrows it against a future repayment in pain'.

Cat. Preposterous way of pleasure and of love,
 That contrary to its own end would move!
 'Tis rather hate, that covets to destroy;   75
 Love's business is to love and to enjoy.
Puss. Enjoying and destroying are all one,
 As flames destroy that which they feed upon.
Cat. He never loved at any generous rate
 That in th'enjoyment found his flame abate.   80
 As wine (the friend of love) is wont to make
 The thirst more violent it pretends to slake,
 So should fruition do the lover's fire:
 Instead of lessening, inflame desire.
Puss. What greater proof that passion does transport, 85
 When what I would die for I'm forced to hurt?
Cat. Death among lovers is a thing despised
 And far below a sullen humour prized;
 That is more scorned and railed at than the gods,
 When they are crossed in love or fall at odds.   90
 But since you understand not what you do,
 I am the judge of what I feel, not you.
Puss. Passion begins indifferent to prove,
 When love considers anything but love.
Cat. The darts of love, like lightning, wound within, 95
 And, though they pierce it, never hurt the skin;
 They leave no marks behind them where they fly,
 Though through the tenderest part of all, the eye;
 But your sharp claws have left enough to show
 How tender I have been, how cruel you.   100
Puss. Pleasure is pain; for when it is enjoyed
 All it could wish for was but to b'allayed.
Cat. Force is a rugged way of making love.
Puss. What you like best you always disapprove.
Cat. He that will wrong his love will not be nice, 105
 T'excuse the wrong he does, to wrong her twice.
Puss. Nothing is wrong but that which is ill meant.
Cat. Wounds are ill cured with a good intent.
Puss. When you mistake that for an injury
 I never meant, you do the wrong, not I.   110
Cat. You do not feel yourself the pain you give;
 But 'tis not that alone for which I grieve;

73 *preposterous*: having that last which should be first (Latin *praeposterus*, inverted).

> But 'tis your want of passion that I blame,
> That can be cruel where you own a flame.
> *Puss.* 'Tis you are guilty of that cruelty,   115
>   Which you at once outdo, and blame in me;
>   For while you stifle and inflame desire,
>   You burn and starve me in the selfsame fire.
> *Cat.* It is not I, but you, that do the hurt,
>   Who wound yourself and then accuse me for 't,   120
>   As thieves, that rob themselves 'twixt sun and sun,
>   Make others pay for what themselves have done.

121 'as thieves, who steal their own savings (by their extravagances) during the
   day . . .'.

Upon Critics who Judge of Modern Plays Precisely by the Rules of the Ancients[n]

Who ever will regard poetic fury
When it is once found idiot by a jury,[n]
And every pert and arbitrary fool
Can all poetic licence overrule,
Assume a barbarous tyranny to handle   5
The muses worse than Ostrogoth or Vandal,
Make 'em submit to verdict and report,
And stand, or fall, to th'orders of a court?
Much less be sentenced by the arbitrary
Proceedings of a witless plagiary   10
That forges old records and ordinances
Against the right and property of fancies,
More false and nice than weighing of the weather
To th'hundredth atom of the lightest feather,
Or measuring of air upon Parnassus   15
With cylinders of Torricellian glasses.[n]
   Reduce all tragedy by rules of art
Back to its antique theatre, a cart,
And make 'em henceforth keep the beaten roads
Of reverend choruses and episodes;   20
Reform and regulate a puppet-play
According to the true and ancient way
That not an actor shall presume to squeak
Unless he have a licence for 't in Greek,
Nor Whittington henceforward sell his cat in   25
Plain vulgar English without mewing Latin.[n]
No pudding shall be suffered to be witty
Unless it be in order to raise pity,[n]
Nor devil in the puppet-play b'allowed
To roar and spit fire but to fright the crowd   30
Unless some god or devil chance t'have piques
Against an ancient family of Greeks.[n]
   Others may have leave to tremble and take
     warning
How such a fatal progeny they're born in;

6 *Ostrogoth*: the east Goths conquered and ruled Italy (493–555).
27 *pudding*: jack-pudding, buffoon, clown.

For none but such for tragedy are fitted   35
That have been ruined only to be pitied,
And only those held proper to deter
Who've had th'ill luck against their wills to err;[n]
Whence only such as are of middling sizes
Between morality and venial vices   40
Are qualified to be destroyed by fate
For other mortals to take warning at;
As if the antique laws of tragedy
Did with our own municipal agree,
And served like cobwebs but t'ensnare the weak   45
And give diversion to the great to break,
To make a less delinquent to be brought
To answer for a greater person's fault
And suffer all the worst the worst approver
Can, to excuse and save himself, discover.   50
   No longer shall dramatics be confined
To draw true images of all mankind,
To punish in effigy criminals,
Reprieve the innocent and hang the false,
But a club-law [to] execute and kill   55
For nothing whomsoe'er they please at will
To terrify spectators from committing
The crimes they did, and suffered for, unwitting.
   These are the reformations of the stage,
Like other reformations of the age,   60
On purpose to destroy all wit and sense
As th'other did all law and conscience;
No better than the laws of British plays
Confirmed in th'ancient good King Howel's days,
Who made a general council regulate   65
Men's catching women by the——you know
    what,
And set down in the rubric at what time
It should be counted legal, when a crime;
Declare when 'twas and when 'twas not a sin,
And on what days it went out or came in.[n]   70
   An English poet should be tried b'his peers,
And not by pedants and philosophers,

62 i.e. the 'Thorough Reformation' of the Civil War Puritans.
67 *rubric*: heading of a statute, or direction for conduct of a religious service.
70 i.e. out of or into season.

Incompetent to judge poetic fury,
As butchers are forbid to b'of a jury;[n]
Beside the most intolerable wrong   75
To try their matter in a foreign tongue
By foreign jurymen like Sophocles,
Or *tales* falser than Euripides,
When not an English native dares appear
To be a witness for the prisoner;   80
When all the laws they use t'arraign and try
The innocent and wronged delinquent by
Were made b'a foreign lawyer and his pupils
To put an end to all poetic scruples,
And by th'advice of virtuosi-Tuscans   85
Determined all the doubts of socks and buskins,
Gave judgment on all past and future plays,
As is as apparent by Speroni's case;
Which Lope de Vega first began to steal,
And after him the French *filou* Corneille.   90
And since our English plagiaries nim
And steal their far-fet criticisms from him,[n]
And by an action falsely laid of trover
The lumber for their proper goods recover,
Enough to furnish all the lewd impeachers   95
Of witty Beaumont's poetry and Fletcher's;
Who for a few misprisions of wit
Are charged by those who ten times worse commit,
And for misjudging some unhappy scenes
Are censured for 't with more unlucky sense;   100
When all their worst miscarriages delight
And please more than the best that pedants write.

78 *tales*: bystanders empanelled to complete a jury.
83 i.e. Aristotle and his commentators.
85 *virtuosi-Tuscans*: sixteenth-century Italian commentators such as Francisco
   Robortello and Lodovico Castelvetro.
88 Sperone Speroni (1500–88) defended his tragedy *Canace* on classical principles.
89 Lope de Vega drew on Italian critics *in general* for his *Arte Nuevo de hacer
   comedias*, 1609.
90 Pierre Corneille propounded classical rules in his *discours* and *examens* (1660).
91 *nim*: steal, pilfer.
97 *misprisions*: mistakes (in law, wrong actions or omissions).

A Ballad[n]

Draw near, good people, all draw near,
  And hearken to my ditty;
    A stranger thing
    Than this I sing
  Came never to this city.   5

Had you but seen this monster,
  You would not give a farthing
    For the lions i'th' grate,
    Nor the mountain cat,
  Nor the bears in Paris Garden.   10

You would defy all pageants
  Are borne before the mayor,
    The strangest shape
    You e'er did gape
  Upon in Bartlemew Fair.   15

His face is round and decent
  As is your dish or platter,
    On which there grows
    A thing like a nose,
  But indeed it is no such matter.   20

On both sides of th'aforesaid
  Are eyes, but they're not matches,
    On which there are
    To be seen two fair
  And large well-grown moustaches.   25

---

8 *grate*: cage.
9 *mountain cat*: catamountain; leopard, panther.
10 *Paris Garden*: see *Hudibras*, I. ii. 172.
15 Bartholomew Fair at West Smithfield was held annually from 1133 to 1855.

Now this with admiration
  Does all beholders strike;
    That a beard should grow
    Upon a thing's brow,
  Did ye ever see the like?   30

He has no skull, 'tis well known
  To thousands of beholders;
    Nothing but a skin
    Does keep his brains in
  From running about his shoulders.   35

On both sides of his noddle
  Are straps o'th' very same leather;
    Ears are implied,
    But they're mere hide
  Or morsels of tripe, choose ye whether.   40

Between these two extendeth
  A slit from ear to ear,
    That every hour
    Does gape to devour
  The souse that grows so near.   45

Beneath a tuft of bristles
  As rough as a frieze-jerkin;
    If it had been a beard,
    'Twould have served a herd
  Of goats, that are of his near kin.   50

Within a set of grinders
  Most sharp and keen, corroding
    Your iron and brass
    As easy as
  They you would do a pudding.   55

But the strangest thing of all is
  Upon his rump there groweth
    A great long tail
    That useth to trail
  Upon the ground as he goeth.   60

45 *souse*: ears; literally pickled pig's ears.
52 *corroding*: eating into, gnawing away.

Part II

This monster was begotten
  Upon one of your witches
    B'an imp that came to her
    Like a man to woo her
  With black doublet and breeches.[n]   65

When he was whelped, for certain
  In divers several countries
    The hogs and swine
    Did grunt and whine,
  And the ravens croaked upon trees.   70

The winds did blow, the thunder
  And lightning loudly rumbled,
    The dogs did howl,
    Th'hollow tree in the owl——
  'Tis a good horse that ne'er stumbled.   75

As soon as he was brought forth,
  At th'midwife's throat he flew,
    And threw the pap
    Down in her lap,
  They say 'tis very true.   80

And up the walls he clambered
  With nails most sharp and keen,
    The prints whereof
    I'th' boards of the roof
  Are yet for to be seen.   85

And out at the top o'th' chimney
  He vanished, seen of none;
    For they did wink,
    Yet by the stink
  Knew which way he was gone.   90

70 See *Hudibras*, II. iii. 707–8.
73–5 See *Hudibras*, I. i. 457–8, II. i. 27–30; also p. 257 below.
88 *wink*: shut their eyes.

The country round about there
  Became like to a wildern-
    ess; for the sight
    Of him did fright
  Away men, women, and children.   95

Long did he there continue,
  And all those parts much harmed,
    Till a wise woman, which
    Some call a white witch,
  Him into a hogsty charmed.   100

There when she had him shut fast,
  With brimstone and with nitre
    She singed the claws
    Of his left paws,
  With the tip of his tail and his right ear.   105

And with her charms and ointments
  She made him tame as a spaniel;
    For she used to ride
    On his back astride,
  Nor did he do her any ill.   110

But to the admiration
  Of all, both far and near,
    He hath been shown
    In every town
  And eke in every shire.   115

And now at length he's brought
  Unto fair London city,
    Where in Fleet Street
    All those may see 't,
  That will not believe my ditty.   120

God save the King and Parliament
  And eke the Prince's Highness,
    And quickly send
    The wars an end,
  As here my song has   125

Finis.

122 Prince of Wales, later Charles II.

A Speech Made at the Rota[n]

Among the excellent orders of that glorious Senate of Rome one was that any senator, having a right to speak to every business in debate, might instead of giving his sentence to the present question (if he had no mind to declare himself) propose anything else that was in his judgment *e re publica*, of concernment to the commonwealth. This custom I humbly desire may be received into this ingenious assembly and that I may have the honour to be the first man that shall put it in practice. For I perceive we have not only heard all, and more than all, that can be said to the purpose concerning overbalance and property;[n] but like those that are out of their way, the further we go the further we are from our end, and I doubt in conclusion shall come to discover that there is no such thing at present in the English nation as either the one or the other. Besides, Sir, as all rotations and wheelings cause a kind of giddiness in the brain, so if we provide not some wholesome diversion for those that we have so often heard of, it will not be in the power of this sober and considerate coffee[n] to keep us in our wits; although if it be the black broth which the Lacedaemonians used, as some learned authors are of opinion,[n] I grant it hath a sovereign operation to strengthen politic notions—especially such as concern republics—and is the same which Lycurgus himself drank when he formed his commonwealth and, among other excellent constitutions, hit upon that excellent law that enjoins women to wear slits in their petticoats, and boys to steal bread and butter, as Plutarch writes in his life,[n] and I could wish Mr. Harrington may be desired by this assembly to introduce it into his Oceana. But this is not that which I purpose to propose at this time, but something that does more immediately concern the present government which as yet we live under, for whose service I suppose these meetings are peculiarly intended; and that is whether the late name of Rump be significant, proper, and adequate to the present Parliament. I doubt not but at first sight it will appear to most men to be nothing less; but if you please to trust me with your patience for a few minutes, I dare

Lacedaemonians: Spartans.
politic: political (but also scheming).
Lycurgus: legendary king of Sparta, to whom reforms (*c.* 600 B.C.) are ascribed.
Oceana: The Commonwealth of Oceana (1656) is Harrington's thinly disguised exposition of a model government for England.

undertake to make it appear not only out of all antiquity and the consent of all ages, but the testimony of nature herself that it is not only the most proper, apt, and significant, but the most honourable denomination that could by the wit of man be given unto it.

The learned Eben Ezra and Menasseh Ben-Israel do write that there is in the rump of man a certain bone which they call 'the bone luz'. This, they say, is of so immortal and incomprehensible a nature that at the Resurrection out of it all the rest of the bones and members shall sprout, just as a plant does out of a kernel.[n] And is there anything that can bear a nearer resemblance to this rump bone than the present Parliament, that has been so many years dead and rotten underground, to any man's thinking that the ghosts of some of the members thereof have transmigrated into other parliaments, and some into those parts from whence there is no redemption, should nevertheless at two several and respective resurrections start up, like the dragon's teeth that were sown, into living, natural, and carnal members?[n] And hence it is, I suppose, that physicians and anatomists call this bone *os sacrum* or 'the holy bone'.

The Egyptians in their hieroglyphics decyphered a prince by a bee. Now a bee, you know, does carry not only his militia or defence, but his whole politic interest in his tail; for when he has lost his sting he is presently banished that well ordered government as an unprofitable member and a drone. The Greeks call rule or empire βασιλεία, as the etymologists tell us, because it is βάσις τοῦ λαοῦ, the base or fundament of the people; for as the rump or bum in the natural body is called the fundament because it is the foundation on which all the rest of the members depend, so is the State and government in the body politic.

The philosophers say that a man is a tree inverted, and that his head is the root by which he takes in his nourishment, and his arms and legs the branches. If that be true, it must follow that his rump is the head.

It is a custom of the Eastern kings to veil their faces from public view, only to avoid prostituting the majesty of their persons to

---

those parts . . . redemption: there is no redemption from hell (proverbial); cf. Job 7:9 (Vulgate or N.E.B.).

dragon's teeth: Cadmus, in the Greek myth, sowed the teeth of the dragon he had killed. Five of the armed men who sprang up helped build the citadel, and founded the noble families, of Thebes. See Ovid, *Metamorphoses*, iii. 95–114, and *Hudibras*, I. ii. 569–72.

The Greeks . . . people: the etymology is in fact obscure; but for this conjecture see G. Curtius, *Principles of Greek Etymology*, trans. A. S. Wilkins and E. B. England, 1886, i. 439.

The philosophers . . .: Plato, *Timaeus*, 90ᵃ.

common eyes. And what is that more than the universal custom of all nations and ages hath always carefully observed to the rump? And therefore when the Philistines resolved to put the highest indignity upon David's ambassadors, they could not think of a way more ignominious than to cut their garments above their buttocks, and by that means to render those reverend parts cheap and despicable in the eyes of the rabble.

Some are of opinion that honour is seated in that part only—chiefly, at least. For it is observed that a small kick on that part does more hurt and wound honour than a cut on the head or face, or a stab or shot of a pistol on any other part of the body. And hence it is that in all combats all the rest of the members are ready to expose themselves to any danger to screen the breech, as if the whole outward man were but a life-guard to that part; and he that by turning his back exposes that to danger is ever after branded with the ignominious name of a coward.

The ancient heroes were wont to wear horse-tails in their helmets, as our young gallants do ostrich-tails in their hats; from whence we may infer that it hath been the consent of all ages that the head can receive no greater ornament than that which is conferred on it by the tail. And in all funeral pomps and public shows he that hath the longest tail to his robe is understood to be the most honourable person; and therefore when Oliver Cromwell was to be installed, his robe had a tail of six yards long, which was borne up by six young noblemen, merely in honour to that part in contemplation whereof the charge was bestowed—for all the other parts bore a nearer proportion to the body.

Is not the Chair the most honourable part of the Parliament? Then that which sits in it must of necessity be the most honourable part of the Speaker. It is an axiom in philosophy, *levia sursum, gravia deorsum*; and can anything imaginable be more grave than so venerable a senate? And hence, I suppose, the wisdom of our ancestors called it the Lower House, in relation to the place it held in the government. All birds in the air and fishes in the sea guide themselves with their tails, from the leviathan to the sprat; and the most famous of our modern philosophers hath of late made a discovery that leviathan and republic are all one.

Philistines . . . : II Samuel 10 : 4.
Some . . . body: cf. *Hudibras*, II. iii. 1065–70.
installed: i.e. as Lord Protector in 1653.
levia . . . deorsum: 'light things upwards, heavy things downwards'.
most famous . . . one: Thomas Hobbes (1588–1679), *Leviathan: Or the Matter, Form, and Power of a Commonwealth*, 1651.

The greatest honour that can be given to man is either to go before or sit above others. In sitting the whole honour is conferred on the breech; and in going before, the breech is more immediately waited upon than any other part, and therefore receives the greater respect. And from all this I doubt not but by this time it plainly appears that 'the Rump', as I said before, is not only the most honourable but most apt and proper name that can be given to those whose only business is to sit.

An Occasional Reflection on Dr. Charleton's Feeling a Dog's Pulse at Gresham College by R. B. Esq.[n]

TO LYNDAMORE

Do you observe, Lyndamore, that domestic animal, the vassal and menial servant of man, on whom he waits like a lacquey by day and watches like a constable by night, how quiet and unconcerned it stands whilst the industrious and accurate Dr. Charleton with his judicious finger examines the arterial pulsation of its left foreleg: a civil office, wherein both doctor and dog, physician and patient, with equal industry contest who shall contribute most to the experimental improvement of this learned and illustrious Society? Little doth the innocent creature know, and as little seems to care to know, whether the ingenious doctor doth it out of a sedulous regard of his patient's health or of his own proper emolument; 'tis enough to him that he does his duty; and in that may teach us to resign ourselves wholly to advance the interests and utility of this renowned and royal assembly.

Do you observe how generously he exhibits his leg? And though a dog's leg in the language of the vulgar signifies a thing worth nothing, yet even that may teach us that there's nothing so contemptible but may, if rightly applied to, contribute something to the public good of mankind and commonwealth of learning.

But if a dog be a logician, as the learned hold, and in his sagacious pursuits does use to make syllogisms,[n] we could not have made a better choice than of this animal to pursue and chase this experiment through all its operations till we have run it down to demonstration.

Nor is the diligent and solert doctor less proper for this administration as having so natural a propensity to this kind of venomous operation that it is not long since, as you well remember, when the King of Macassar's poison was sent hither, the doctor was so impatient to try the experiment solitary that, rather than attend the pleasure of the Royal Society, he adventured (though at the price of

---

sagacious: literally Latin *sagax* means 'keen-scented' (of dogs).
solert: skilful.
administration: application (of the poison) or management (of the experiment).
Macassar: a district in the Indonesian island of Celebes.
attend: await.

their displeasure) to invade it by surreption and involation, and secretly deprived the Hint-Keeper of it; for which he received I will not say whether condign punishment or severe castigation from the learned and honourable President in a grave and weighty oration pronounced by His Lordship before this celebrious and renowned assembly.[n]

Truly, Lyndamore, I am of opinion that a dog is much more proper for this experiment than that vigorous and vivid animal commonly called a cat; for a cat, you know, is said to have nine lives—that is, eight in reversion and one in possession—and it is a matter of no mean difficulty exactly to trace and observe how many of these the lethal force of this destructive medicament will reach. And therefore you may have taken notice that when we last tried this very experiment on a creature of that species, although but a weak and feeble kitten, the venomous quality proved so innocuous that the secure little beast laid itself down to sleep in the hollow concave of that emblem of our jurisdiction over the lives and limbs of dogs and cats, the mace, and in that posture, as if it had triumphed over its mortal enemy and all our hostilities, was born before the most excellent and accomplished Lord President.

You may also, Lyndamore, observe the strength of judgment and ingenuity of the acute and profound doctor in the topical application of the mortiferous unguent to that part of the dog's neck that is situate nearest to his brain and consequently to lesion, and furthest out of the reach of that natural chirurgery, as I may call it, of his tongue, that nothing may obstruct the free passage of this pernicious composition, but give it full scope to exert its efficacy in the several and respective organs of the passive animal.

You may remember, Lyndamore, what the subtle and judicious Sorbière says of a worthy member of this Society:[n] that 'tis a work of admiration to behold a person bred up in courts and camps, and at this present employed in the most weighty affairs of the State, to appear in mechanical *cuerpo* in St. James's Park and, managing the

---

invade . . . involation: seize upon the poison by stealthy removal and carrying off
   (pleonastically: to steal it by stealing and stealing).
Hint-Keeper: keeper of materials. See 'Elephant', l. 373.
President: Viscount Brouncker, President of the R. S. (1662–77) and of Gresham
   College (1664–7).
celebrious: renowned.
vivid: vigorous.
mortiferous: deadly.
chirurgery: surgery.
mechanical cuerpo: the undress (without cloak, etc.) of an artisan.

Sidrophellian tube, to muster the life-guard of Jupiter and to take an account of the spots in his belt. So we may say it is no less wonderful to behold this exquisite and solert doctor, whose province lies in the cabinet of fair ladies, and whose daily employments are to solicit the tender arteries of their ivory wrists,—that he, I say, should nevertheless condescend to animadvert the languishing diastole of an expiring mongrel.

From this, Lyndamore, we may learn that as in general nature there is neither higher nor lower, but zenith and nadir are equally on a plane as well as the poles, so we may receive matter of instruction from objects of the meanest and most contemptible quality as well as from things of higher and more sublime condition, even as the most industrious and elegant Mr. Hooke in his microscopical observations has most ingeniously and wittily made it appear that there is no difference in point of design and project between the most ambitious and aspiring politician of the world—and of our times especially—and that most importune and vexatious insect commonly called a louse.[n]

Sidrophellian tube: telescope. See *Hudibras*, II. iii. 399 ff.
life-guard of Jupiter: the four satellites then known; seen first by Galileo in 1610.
spots in his belt: Jupiter's belts are dark parallel streaks, separated by bright streaks (zones); spots at the edges of the belts may have been detected by Robert Hooke in 1664.
solicit: pay court to.
animadvert: observe.

Characters[n]

An Hypocritical Nonconformist

Is an Ambassador Extraordinary of his own making, not only from God Almighty to his Church, but from his Church to him; and, pretending to a plenipotentiary power from both, treats with himself, and makes what agreement he pleases, and gives himself such conditions as are conducible to the advantage of his own affairs. The whole design of his transaction and employment is really nothing else but to procure fresh supplies for the Good Old Cause and Covenant while they are under persecution; to raise recruits of new proselytes, and deal with all those who are, or once were, good friends to both; to unite and maintain a more close and strict intelligence among themselves against the common enemy, and preserve their general interest alive until they shall be in a condition to declare more openly for it; and not out of weakness to submit perfidiously to the laws of the land, and rebelliously endure to live in peace and quietness under the present government, in which though they are admitted to a greater share of rich and profitable employments than others, yet they will never be able to recover all their rights which they once enjoyed, and are now unjustly deprived of, but by the same expedients and courses which they then took.

The wealth of his party, of which he vapours so much to startle his governors, is no mean motive to enflame his zeal and encourage him to use the means and provoke all dangers, where such large returns may infallibly be expected. And that's the reason why he is so ready and forward to encounter all appearing terrors that may acquire the reputation of zeal and conscience: to despise the penalties of the laws, and commit himself voluntarily to prison, to draw the members of his church into a more sensible fellow-feeling of his sufferings, and a freer ministration. For so many and great have been the advantages of this thriving persecution, that the constancy and blood of the primitive martyrs did not propagate the Church more than

conducible: conducive, tending.
Good . . . Covenant: see *Hudibras*, I. i. 730 and end-note.
greater share . . .: for Butler's resentment of the Restoration settlement, see also
    p. 268.
ministration: giving of spiritual (and material) assistance.

the money and good creatures earned by these profitable sufferings
have done the discipline of the modern brethren.

He preaches the gospel in despite of itself; for though there can
be no character so true and plain of him as that which is there copied
from the scribes and Pharisees, yet he is not so weak a brother to
apply anything to himself that is not perfectly agreeable to his own
purposes, nor so mean an interpreter of Scripture that he cannot
relieve himself when he is pressed home with a text, especially where
his own conscience is judge; for what privilege have the saints more
than the wicked, if they cannot dispense with themselves in such
cases? This conscience of his (like the righteousness of the scribes
and Pharisees, from whom it is descended) is wholly taken up with
such slight and little matters that it is impossible it should ever be at
leisure to consider things of greater weight and importance. For it is
the nature of all those that use to make great matters of trifles to
make as little of things of great concernment. And therefore he
delights more to differ in things indifferent; no matter now slight and
impertinent, they are weighty enough in proportion to his judgment
to prevail with him before the peace and safety of a nation. But he has
a further artifice in it; for little petulant differences are more apt
and proper to produce and continue animosities among the rabble of
parties than things of weightier consideration (of which they are
utterly uncapable), as flies and gnats are more vexatious in hot
climates than creatures that are able to do greater mischiefs. And
they that are taught to dislike the indifferent actions of others must
of necessity abominate the greater. And as zeal is utterly lost and
has no way to show itself but in opposition, nor conscience to discover its tenderness but in seeking occasions to take offence perpetually at something (and the slighter and more trivial the better),
so that conscience that appears strict and scrupulous in small
matters will be easily supposed by the erroneous vulgar to be more
careful and severe in things of weight, though nothing has been more
false upon all experience . . . for[n] violating the laws of God as the
laws of the land, and takes more care . . . upon his conscience than
to give it any just satisfaction; for as it is apt to quarrel upon small
and trivial occasions, so it is as easily appeased with slight and trivial
pretences, and in great matters with none at all, but rather, like the
devil, tempts him to commit all manner of wickedness; for we do not
find that any possessions of the devil ever produced such horrid
actions as some men have been guilty of by being only possessed

creatures: see *Hudibras*, I. ii. 1010.
indifferent: of no consequence either way.

with their own consciences. And therefore, ever since the Act of
Oblivion reprieved him from the gallows, he endeavours to supplant
all law and government for being partial to him in his own case, as
bad men never use to forgive those whom they have injured or
received any extraordinary obligation from; for he cannot endure to
think upon repentance, as too great a disparagement for a saint to
submit to that would keep up the reputation of godliness. And because the Scripture says obedience is better than sacrifice, he believes
the less of it will serve; for he is so far from being sensible of God's
mercy and the king's for his pardon and restoration to a better condition than he was in before he rebelled, that his actions make it
plainly appear that he accounts it no better than an apostasy and
backsliding, and he expects a revolution of rebellion as obstinately
as the Turk does Mahomet's coming. For it is just with him as with
other impenitent malefactors, whom a pardon or unexpected deliver-
ance from suffering for the first crime does but render more eager to
commit the same over again; for like a losing gamester he cannot
endure to think of giving over, as long as he can by any means get
money or credit to venture again. And as the most desperate of those
people, after they have lost all, use to play away their clothes, he
offers to stake down his very skin, and not only (as some barbarous
people use) set his wife and children, but his head and four quarters
to the hangman, if he chance once more to throw out. And yet, as
stubborn and obstinate as he is to obey his lawful sovereign, of
whose grace and mercy he holds his life, he has always appeared true
and faithful to all tyrannical usurpations, without the least reluc-
tancy of conscience; for though he was fooled and cheated by them,
yet they were more agreeable to his own inclination, that does not
care to have anything founded in right, but left at large to dispensations and outgoings of Providence, as he shall find occasion to expound them to the best advantage of his own will and interest.

He cries down the Common Prayer because there is no ostentation
of gifts to be used in the reading of it, without which he esteems it no
better than mere loss of time and labour in vain, that brings him in

Act of Oblivion: the Act of Indemnity and Oblivion (1660) bestowed a general
   pardon and consigned the late hostilities to perpetual oblivion.
obedience . . . sacrifice: I Samuel 15:22.
set: wager.
head and four quarters: a traitor was liable to be hanged, drawn, beheaded, and
   quartered.
throw out: make a losing cast in the dice game of hazard (*OED*).
dispensations and outgoings: see *Hudibras*, I. ii. 1005, 1007.
Common Prayer . . .: set prayers in the Anglican liturgy precluded any display of
   personal inspiration (gifts).

no return of interest and vainglory from the rabble, who have always been observed to be satisfied with nothing but what they do not understand; and therefore the Church of Rome was fain, to comply with their natural inclinations, to enjoin them to serve God in a language of which they understand not one word; and though they abominate that, yet they endeavour to come as near it as they can, and serve God in an unknown sense, which their own godly teacher has as great a care to prepare equal and suitable to their wonderful capacities. And therefore, as the Apostles made their divine calling appear plainly to all the world by speaking languages which they never understood before, he endeavours to do the same thing most preposterously by speaking that which is no language at all, nor understood by anybody, but a collection of affected and fantastic expressions, wholly abstract from sense, as 'nothingness', 'soul-damningness and savingness', etc., in such a fustian style as the Turks and Persians use, that signify nothing but the vanity and want of judgment of the speaker, though they believe it to be the true property of the spirit and the highest perfection of all sanctity. And the better to set this off, he uses more artificial tricks to improve his spirit of utterance either into volubility or dullness, that it may seem to go of itself without his study or direction, than the old heathen orators knew, that used to liquor their throats and harangue to pipes. For he has fantastic and extravagant tones, as well as phrases, that are no less agreeable to the sense of . . . in a kind of *stilo recitativo* between singing and braying, and abhors the . . . liturgy, lest he should seem to conform to it. But as it is a piece of art to conceal art, so it is by artificial dullness to disguise that which is natural; and as his interest has always obliged him to decry human learning, reason, and sense, he and his brethren have with long and diligent practice found out an expedient to make that dullness, which would become intolerable if it did not pretend to something above nature, pass for dispensations, light, grace, and gifts. For in the beginning of the late unhappy Civil War the greatest number of those of the clergy who by the means of their parts or friends or honesty had no hopes to advance themselves to preferment in the Church took part with the Parliament against it, who were very willing to give a kind reception and encouragement to all those that offered themselves to promote the cause of reformation, which they found to be the best disguise they could possibly put upon

the Apostles . . . before: Acts 2:4–11.
stilo recitativo: recitative, rhythmical declamation in opera.
art to conceal art: proverbial (Latin, *Ars est celare artem*).
light: see *Hudibras*, ɪ. i. 476.

rebellion. And then this heavy dullness, being a public standard of
the common talents of their teachers, became, for want of a better,
a mode and afterwards a character of the power of godliness, in
opposition to the ingenuity and learning of the other clergy; and
whosoever was not naturally endued with it, or so much hypocrisy
as would serve to counterfeit it, was held unable, or suspected unfit,
to be confided in. And upon this account it has continued ever since
among the party, where it passes for a mark of distinction to discover who are gifted and who not; as among the ancient pagans,
when monsters and prodigies had gained the reputation of divine
presages, the more unnatural and deformed they appeared, they were
received with the more devout and pious regard, and had sacri-
fices accordingly appointed for their expiation. And this he finds useful to many purposes; for it does not only save him the labour of
study, which he disdains as below his gifts, but exempts him from
many other duties, and gives his idle infirmities a greater reputation
among his followers than the greatest abilities of the most industrious; while the painful heavings and straining that he uses to express himself pass for the agonies of those that deliver oracles. And
this is the reason why he is so cautious to have all his exercises seem
to be done extempore, that his spiritual talent may not be thought to
receive any assistance from natural or artificial means, but to move
freely of itself without any care or consideration of his, as if pre-
meditation and study would but render him, like other false witnesses,
the more apt to contrive and imagine how to betray and abuse the
truth. And to propagate this cheat among his hearers he omits no
little artifice that he thinks will pass unperceived: as, when he quotes
a text of Scripture, he commonly only names the chapter and about
the beginning, middle, or end of it, or about such-and-such a verse,
and then turns over the leaves of his book to find it, to show that he
had not so much preparation as to do it before, but was always surprised with his gifts and taken tardy before he was aware; and when
he happens to be out, which is not seldom, will steal a look, and
squint into his notes as cunningly as a schoolboy does into his lesson
that he is to repeat without book, that he may not be observed to
need the same means which all those that are ungifted are necessita-
ted to make use of—although his concordance supplies him with all
the gifts he has to cap texts and his adversaries' writings; with all

ingenuity: intelligence.
when monsters . . . expiation: for this Roman superstition, see also *Hudibras*,
    ii. iii. 709–14, and p. 252.
taken tardy: overtaken, caught.
to be out: to have forgotten his lines.

the doctrine and use he has, except that which is factious and seditious, which is always his own; and all that, beside nonsense, he can
justly pretend to.

The contribution which he receives from his congregation serves
him like a scale to take a just measure of the zeal and godliness of
every particular member of it, and by computing what their offerings
amount to in proportion to their abilities cast up exactly how much
grace and spiritual gifts every man is endued with. This, like auricu-
lar confession, lets him into the darkest secrets of their hearts, and
directs him how to apply his remedies according to their several
constitutions, and by finding out by observation or enquiry the
particular sins that any ... with a particular of his estate, ...
plant all his batteries against them, and deliver them over ... until
he ... ransom and be converted to an equal contribution and ...
of them all. As charity is said to cover a multitude of sins, so does
charitable contribution; and if that is wanting, it is his duty to lay
them open and impose such penances as he judges fitting, as well as
dispose of indulgences (though he does not like the word) to the
best advantage. And therefore he is an implacable enemy to all
ecclesiastical judges and officers in the Church, and would trust no
creature living with the conduct and management of men's sins but
himself and the devil, who is the only secular power that he can confide in to deliver them over to or redeem them back again at his
own rates. For he is a spiritual interloper, that steals a trade under-
hand, and by dealing in prohibited commodities can undersell and
allow better bargains of sins and absolution than those that deal
fairly and openly can afford. As for the bishops, he is rather a rival
than an enemy to them, and therefore becomes the more jealous of
them; for all the ill will he bears them is only, whatever he pretends,
for their authority and their lands, with which he is most passionately
in love, but cannot possibly get the consent of both parties to the
match, and therefore like Solomon's harlot had rather divide the
child than let the right owner have it. For his church members have
the keeping of his conscience as well as he has of theirs, and both
sealed and delivered like a pair of indentures to one another's uses;
so that he cannot, though he would, alter his judgment without
their consent—or such a valuable consideration as will secure him
against all damages that he may receive by renouncing them and his
own opinion, when he finds it most convenient to satisfy all his

charity ... sins: I Peter 4:8.
Solomon's harlot: I Kings 3:16–27.
consideration: i.e. cash payment by way of compensation.

scruples and conform. For as he parted with his benefice like a game-ster that discards and throws out a suit that is dealt him to take in a better out of the pack and mend his hand, so he can as easily by the same light and revelation be converted and change his conventicle for a better spiritual improvement when a good occasion is offered him. For how is it possible that he who cannot conform to himself should do so to anything else, or he that plants all improvements of piety in spiritual novelties be constant to anything? For he that can endure nothing that is settled, only because it is so, can never possibly settle in anything; but must, as he outgrows himself in grace, at length outgrow grace too, as the most refined of his disciples have done ordinances and government. For he differs no less from his own doctrine and discipline than from that of the Church, and is really made up of nothing but contradictions: denies free will, and yet will endure nothing but his own will in all the practice of his life; is transported with zeal for liberty of conscience, and yet is the severest imposer upon all other men's consciences in the whole world; is a professed enemy to all forms in godliness, and yet affects nothing more than a perpetual formality in all his words and actions; makes his devotions rather labours than exercises, and breaks the sabbath by taking too much pains to keep it, as he does the com-mandments of God to find out new ways for other men to keep them; calls his holding-forth 'taking of great pains', and yet pretends to do it by the spirit without any labour or study of his own. And although Christ says 'Blessed be the peacemakers', he will have none so but the peacebreakers; and because the first Christians were commanded to be obedient for conscience' sake, he commands his brother Chris-tians to be disobedient for the same reason; makes longer prayers than a Pharisee but, if the treason, sedition, nonsense, and blasphemy were left out, shorter than a publican. For he is no friend to the Lord's Prayer, for the power and full sense of it, and because it is a form and none of his own, nor of the spirit because it is learnt; and therefore prefers the Pharisaical way of tediousness and tautology. This he calls 'the gift of prayer', which he highly values himself upon, and yet delivers it in a tone that he steals from the beggars; blames the Catholics for placing devotion in the mere repetition of words, and yet makes the same the character of spiritual gifts and graces

improvement: investment, way of turning (religion) to good account .
forms: prescribed words or procedures, ceremonies.
holding-forth: preaching (Philippians 2:16).
'Blessed . . .': Matthew 5:9.
the first Christians . . . sake: Romans 13:5.
longer prayers . . . publican: Matthew 23:14 and Luke 18:13.

in himself—for he uses the old phrases of the English translation of
the Bible from the Jewish idiom as if they contained in them more
sanctity and holiness than other words that more properly signify
the same thing. He professes a mortal hatred to ceremonies, and yet
has more punctilios than a Jew; for he is of too rugged and churlish
a nature to use any respect at all to anything. And though ceremonies
are signs of submission, and very useful in the public service of God,
yet they do not turn to any considerable account, nor acquire any
opinion of gifts from the people to those that use them; and he
pretends to a nearer familiarity with his maker than to need any
ceremonies like a stranger; and indeed they are nothing agreeable to
that audacious freedom that he assumes in his applications to him.
So he condemns uniformity in the public service of God, and yet
affects nothing else in his own doctrines and uses, and cap and beard,
which are all of the same stamp. He denounces against all those that
are given over to a reprobate sense, but takes no notice of those that
are given over to a reprobate nonsense. He is an implacable enemy to
superstition and profaneness, and never gives it quarter; but is very
tender of meddling with hypocrisy—though it be far more wicked—
because the interests of it are so mixed with his own that it is very
difficult to touch the one without disordering the other. For though
hypocrisy be but a form of godliness without power, and he defies
forms above all things, yet he is content to allow of it there and disclaim it in all things else.

A Fifth Monarchy Man[n]

Is one that is not contented to be a privy counsellor of the kingdom
of heaven, but would fain be a minister of state of this world, and
translate the kingdom of heaven to the kingdom of earth. His design
is to make Christ king, as his forefathers the Jews did only to abuse
and crucify him, that he might share his lands and goods, as he did
his vicegerent's here. He dreams of a fool's paradise without a serpent in it; a golden age all of saints and no hypocrites, all holy-
court princes and no subjects but the wicked; a government of
Perkin Warbeck and Lambert Simnel saints, where every man that

the old phrases . . . thing: see *Hudibras*, I. i. 799–802.
translate: transfer.
vicegerent's: King Charles I.
Perkin Warbeck and Lambert Simnel: fraudulent pretenders to the throne of
    Henry VII (active 1491–7 and 1486–7 respectively).

had a mind to it might make himself a prince and claim a title to the crown. He fancies a Fifth Monarchy as the quintessence of all governments, abstracted from all matter and consisting wholly of revelations, visions, and mysteries. John of Leyden was the first founder of it and, though he miscarried like Romulus in a tempest, his posterity have revelations every full moon that there may be a time to set up his title again, and with better success—though his brethren that have attempted it since had no sooner quartered his coat with their own but their whole outward men were set on the gates of the City, where a head and four quarters stand as types and figures of the Fifth Monarchy.[n] They have been contriving (since experiments that cost necks are too chargeable) to try it in little, and have deposed King Oberon, to erect their monarchy in Fairyland, as being the most proper and natural region in the whole world for their government, and if it succeed there to proceed further. The devil's prospect of all the kingdoms of the earth and the glory of them has so dazzled their eyes that they would venture their necks to take him at his word and give him his price. Nothing comes so near the kingdom of darkness as the Fifth Monarchy, that is nowhere to be found but in dark prophecies, obscure mythologies, and mystical riddles, like the visions Aeneas saw in hell of the Roman Empire. Next this it most resembles Mahomet's coming to the Turks, and King Arthur's reign over the Britons in Merlin's prophecies—so near of kin are all fantastic illusions, that you may discern the same lineaments in them all. The poor wicked are like to have a very ill time under them; for they are resolved upon arbitrary government according to their ancient and fundamental revelations, and to have no subjects but slaves, who between them and the devil are like to suffer persecution enough to make them as able saints as their lords and masters. He gathers churches on the Sunday, as the Jews did sticks on their sabbath, to set the state on fire. He hums and hahs

John of Leyden: John Beuckelszoon (1509–36), a leader of the German Anabaptists at Münster. He was a fanatic, who declared himself King of Zion, and committed polygamy and murder in the name of God.

like Romulus: one explanation advanced for Romulus' disappearance was that an unnatural storm either destroyed him or concealed his murder (Plutarch, *Romulus*, xxvii. 6–8).

coat: coat of arms.

types: emblems.

The devil's . . . price: Matthew 4:8–9.

the visions . . . Empire: *Aeneid*, vi. 752–892.

Merlin's prophecies: for the prophecies of the legendary seer see Geoffrey of Monmouth, *Histories of the Kings of Britain*, vii. iii–viii. i. It was an ancient myth that King Arthur was alive in Fairyland and would return to rule Britain.

the Jews . . . sabbath: Numbers 15:32–6.

high treason, and calls upon it as gamesters do on the cast they
would throw. He groans sedition, and like the Pharisee rails when
he gives thanks. He interprets prophecies as Whittington did the
bells to speak to him,[n] and governs himself accordingly.

A Fanatic

Saint Paul was thought by Festus to be mad with too much learning;
but the fanatics of our times are mad with too little. He chooses
himself one of the elect, and packs a committee of his own party to
judge the twelve tribes of Israel. The Apostles in the Primitive Church
worked miracles to confirm and propagate their doctrine, but he
thinks to confirm his by working at his trade. He assumes a privilege
to impress what text of Scripture he pleases for his own use, and
leaves those that make against him for the use of the wicked. His
religion, that tends only to faction and sedition, is neither fit for
peace nor war, but times of a condition between both—like the sails of
a ship, that will not endure a storm and are of no use at all in a
calm. He believes it has enough of the Primitive Christian if it be
but persecuted as that was—no matter for the piety or doctrine of
it—as if there were nothing required to prove the truth of a religion
but the punishment of the professors of it, like the old mathematicians, that were never believed to be profoundly knowing in
their profession until they had run through all punishments and just
escaped the fork. He is all for suffering for religion, but nothing for
acting; for he accounts good works no better than encroachments
upon the merits of free believing, and a good life the most troublesome and unthrifty way to heaven. He canonizes himself a saint in
his own lifetime, as the more sure and certain way, and less troublesome to others. He outgrows ordinances as a prentice that has served
out his time does indentures and, being a freeman, supposes himself
at liberty to set up what religion he pleases. He calls his own supposed abilities 'gifts', and disposes of himself like a foundation
designed to pious uses, although like others of the same kind they
are always diverted to other purposes. He owes all his gifts to his

the Pharisee: Luke 18:11.
Saint . . . learning: Acts 26:24.
committee: see end-note to *Hudibras*, I. i. 76.
His religion: cf. *Hudibras*, I. i. 187–204.
mathematicians . . . fork: astrologers . . . gallows; see Juvenal, *Satires*, vi. 560–4.
'gifts': cf. *Hudibras*, I. i. 476.

ignorance, as beggars do the alms they receive to their poverty. They are such as the fairies are said to drop in men's shoes and, when they are discovered, to give them over and confer no more; for when his gifts are discovered they vanish and come to nothing. He is but a puppet saint, that moves he knows not how, and his ignorance is the dull leaden weight that puts all his parts in motion. His outward man is a saint, and his inward man a reprobate; for he carries his vices in his heart, and his religion in his face.

A Ranter

Is a fanatic hector that has found out by a very strange way of new light how to transform all the devils into angels of light; for he believes all religion consists in looseness, and that sin and vice is the whole duty of man. He puts off the old man, but puts it on again upon the new one, and makes his pagan vices serve to preserve his Christian virtues from wearing out; for if he should use his piety and devotion always, it would hold out but a little while. He is loth that iniquity and vice should be thrown away, as long as there may be good use of it; for if that which is wickedly gotten may be disposed to pious uses, why should not wickedness itself as well? He believes himself shot-free against all the attempts of the devil, the world, and the flesh, and therefore is not afraid to attack them in their own quarters and encounter them at their own weapons. For as strong bodies may freely venture to do and suffer that, without any hurt to themselves, which would destroy those that are feeble, so a saint that is strong in grace may boldly engage himself in those great sins and iniquities that would easily damn a weak brother, and yet come off never the worse. He believes deeds of darkness to be only those sins that are committed in private, not those that are acted openly and owned. He is but an hypocrite turned the wrong side outward; for as the one wears his vices within and the other without, so when they are counterchanged the ranter becomes an

A RANTER: the Ranters were a wild antinomian sect, which maintained that the moral law was not binding upon true Christians. Ralpho uses antinomian arguments in *Hudibras* II. ii. 233–50.

the whole duty of man: title of an enormously popular devotional work, pub. 1658.

He puts . . . new one: Ephesians 4:22–4.

shot-free: bullet-proof.

hypocrite, and the hypocrite an able ranter. His church is the devil's chapel; for it agrees exactly both in doctrine and discipline with the best-reformed bawdy-houses. He is a monster produced by the madness of this latter age; but if it had been his fate to have been whelped in old Rome, he had passed for a prodigy and been received among raining of stones and the speaking of bulls, and would have put a stop to all public affairs until he had been expiated. Nero clothed the Christians in the skins of wild beasts; but he wraps wild beasts in the skins of Christians.

A Sceptic

Is a critic that deals in wholesale. He never censures but in gross, as being the most thriving and easy trade of wit; for the discovery of particular errors in knowledge requires deeper insight, has more of difficult subtlety, and less of glory; as it is easier by much to cry down a science than to understand it, and more brave to appear above it than skilful in it. He has a natural inclination and ambition to knowledge; but, being unfortunate in a temper of wit not capable of it, derives his glory from the remedy of his defects (as men do their bravery from their nakedness) and, undervaluing that which he cannot attain to, would make his necessity appear a virtue, and his ignorance the choice of his judgment. Much of this proceeds from his envy, which is so impatient of seeing any man exceed him in that which he would gladly pretend to that, with Caesar, he had rather destroy the commonwealth of letters than endure another to be greater than himself in it. If it be his misfortune to be engaged in an argument, his constant method is catechism; for he will be sure to ask questions only, and put others to answer—a game at which the dullest idiot may play with the wisest in the world, and be too hard for him. And when with his pedigree of questions that beget one another he has driven you as far as the wit of man can reach, because you can go no further he will conclude you have not moved at all—as, if you should tell him of the siege of Troy, and do not begin (as Horace's poetaster did) with the hatching of Castor and Pollux,[n] he will not believe you can say anything of Hector and

---

His . . . chapel: alluding to the proverb, 'Where God has his church the devil has his chapel.'

Nero . . . beasts: see *Hudibras*, I. i. 789–92 and note p. 292

Caesar . . . it: Caligula (emperor A.D. 37–41) contemplated the destruction of works by Homer, Virgil, and Livy (Suetonius, *Caligula*, xxxiv. 2).

Ajax. He is a worse tyrant than Caligula wished himself; for in denying reason, sense, and demonstration he cuts off all the best heads of mankind at a blow.

An Astrologer

Is one that expounds upon the planets, and teaches to construe the accidents by the due joining of stars in construction. He talks with them by dumb signs, and can tell what they mean by their twinkling and squinting upon one another as well as they themselves. He is a spy upon the stars, and can tell what they are doing by the company they keep and the houses they frequent; they have no power to do anything alone, until so many meet as will make a quorum. He is clerk of the committee to them, and draws up all their orders that concern either public or private affairs. He keeps all their accounts for them, and sums them up, not by debtor, but creditor alone—a more compendious way. They do ill to make them have so much authority over the earth, which perhaps has as much as any one of them but the sun, and as much right to sit and vote in their councils as any other; but because there are but seven electors of the German Empire, they will allow of no more to dispose of all other, and most foolishly and unnaturally depose their own parent of its inheritance rather than acknowledge a defect in their own rules. These rules are all they have to show for their title, and yet not one of them can tell whether those they had them from came honestly by them. Virgil's description of Fame, that reaches from earth to the stars, *tam ficti pravique tenax*, to carry lies and knavery, will serve astrologers without any sensible variation. He is a fortune-seller, a retailer of destiny, and petty chapman to the planets. He casts nativities as gamesters do false dice, and by slurring and palming sextile, quartile,

Caligula wished himself: 'If only the Roman people had but one neck!' (Suetonius, *Caligula*, xxx. 2).

construe ... construction: 'interpret casual occurrences by combining the stars in a scheme the same way as a grammarian construes words by establishing syntactical connections' (with a possible pun on 'accidence').

squinting: suggesting their oblique angles one to another.

debtor ... creditor: what they owe to the world ... what the world owes to them.

compendious: expeditious.

they will allow ...: astrologers will allow only the seven Ptolemaic planets (as the earth would make eight) ...

tam ... t enax: 'so tenacious of false and wicked news'—as much as of truth (*Aeneid*, iv. 188).

slurring: sliding the dice from the box so that they do not turn.

sextile ... trine: aspects of heavenly bodies 60, 90, and 120° apart.

and trine like size, quater, trois, can throw what chance he pleases.
He sets a figure as cheats do a main at hazard, and gulls throw away
their money at it. He fetches the grounds of his art so far off, as well
from reason as the stars, that like a traveller he is allowed to lie by
authority. And as beggars, that have no money themselves, believe
all others have, and beg of those that have as little as themselves,
so the ignorant rabble believe in him, though he has no more reason
for what he professes than they.

A Small Poet

Is one that would fain make himself that which nature never meant
him, like a fanatic that inspires himself with his own whimsies. He
sets up haberdasher of small poetry with a very small stock and no
credit. He believes it is invention enough to find out other men's wit,
and whatsoever he lights upon, either in books or company, he
makes bold with as his own. This he puts together so untowardly
that you may perceive his own wit has the rickets by the swelling
disproportion of the joints. Imitation is the whole sum of him, and
his vein is but an itch or clap that he has catched of others, and his
flame like that of charcoals that were burnt before. But as he wants
judgement to understand what is best, he naturally takes the worst,
as being most agreeable to his own talent. You may know his wit
not to be natural, 'tis so unquiet and troublesome in him; for as
those that have money but seldom are always shaking their pockets
when they have it, so does he when he thinks he has got something
that will make him appear. He is a perpetual talker, and you may
know by the freedom of his discourse that he came lightly by it, as
thieves spend freely what they get. He measures other men's wits
by their modesty, and his own by his confidence. He makes nothing
of writing plays, because he has not wit enough to understand the
difficulty. This makes him venture to talk and scribble as chouses do
to play with cunning gamesters until they are cheated and laughed at.
He is always talking of wit, as those that have bad voices are always
singing out of tune, and those that cannot play delight to fumble on
instruments. He grows the unwiser by other men's harms; for the
worse others write, he finds the more encouragement to do so too.

size . . . trois: six, four, and three on the dice.
main: in hazard the number called by the 'setter', which must then be cast for.
fetches: derives
chouses: dupes.

His greediness of praise is so eager that he swallows anything that comes in the likeness of it, how notorious and palpable soever, and is as shot-free against anything that may lessen his good opinion of himself—this renders him incurable, like diseases that grow insensible.

If you dislike him, it is at your own peril. He is sure to put in a caveat beforehand against your understanding and, like a malefactor in wit, is always furnished with exceptions against his judges. This puts him upon perpetual apologies, excuses, and defences, but still by way of defiance in a kind of whiffling strain, without regard of any man that stands in the way of his pageant. Where he thinks he may do it safely, he will confidently own other men's writings, and where he fears the truth may be discovered, he will by feeble denials and feigned insinuations give men occasion to suppose so.

If he understands Latin or Greek, he ranks himself among the learned, despises the ignorant, talks criticisms out of Scaliger, and repeats Martial's bawdy epigrams, and sets up his rest wholly upon pedantry. But if he be not so well qualified, he cries down all learning as pedantic, disclaims study, and professes to write with as great facility as if his muse was sliding down Parnassus. Whatsoever he hears well said he seizes upon by poetical licence, and one way makes it his own—that is by ill repeating of it. This he believes to be no more theft than it is to take that which others throw away. By this means his writings are like a tailor's cushion of mosaic work, made up of several scraps sewed together. He calls a slovenly, nasty description 'great nature', and dull flatness 'strange easiness'. He writes down all that comes in his head, and makes no choice, because he has nothing to do it with—that is, judgement. He is always repealing the old laws of comedy and, like the Long Parliament, making ordinances in their stead, although they are perpetually thrown out of coffee-houses and come to nothing. He is like an Italian thief, that never robs but he murders to prevent discovery, so sure is he to cry down the man from whom he purloins that his

---

insensible: incapable of feeling or sensation, unresponsive.

exceptions against: objections to.

whiffling: shifting, evasive; also clearing the way for a procession.

Scaliger: J. C. Scaliger, author of *Poetics*, 1561.

Martial's bawdy epigrams: obscenity apart, Martial's *Epigrams* (pub. A.D. 86–102) would not demand sustained concentration (just as Scaliger would be easier reading than Aristotle).

the Long Parliament . . .: the Acts of the Long Parliament after 1641, which did not receive royal assent, were initially called Ordinances.

petty larceny of wit may pass unsuspected. He is but a copier at best, and will never arrive to practise by the life; for bar him the imitation of something he has read, and he has no image in his thoughts. Observation and fancy, the matter and form of just wit, are above his philosophy.

He appears so over-concerned in all men's wits as if they were but disparagements of his own, and cries down all they do as if they were encroachments upon him. He takes jests from the owners, and breaks them as justices do false weights and pots that want measure; when he meets with anything that is very good, he changes it into small money, like three groats for a shilling, to serve several occasions. He disclaims study, pretends to take things in motion, and to shoot flying, which appears to be very true by his often missing of his mark. His wit is much troubled with obstructions, and he has fits as painful as those of the spleen. He fancies himself a dainty, spruce shepherd, with a flock and a fine silken shepherdess that follows his pipe as rats did the conjurers in Germany.

As for epithets, he always avoids those that are near akin to the sense; such matches are unlawful, and not fit to be made by a Christian poet. And therefore all his care is to choose out such as will serve, like a wooden leg, to piece out a maimed verse that wants a foot or two; and if they will but rhyme now and then into the bargain, or run upon a letter, it is a work of supererogation.

As for similitudes, he likes the hardest and most obscure best; for as ladies wear black patches to make their complexions seem fairer than they are, so when an illustration is more obscure than the sense that went before it, it must of necessity make it appear clearer than it did; for contraries are best set off with contraries.

He has found out a way to save the expense of much wit and sense; for he will make less than some have prodigally laid out upon five or six words serve forty or fifty lines. This is a thrifty invention and very easy, and (if it were commonly known) would much increase the trade of wit and maintain a multitude of small poets in constant employment. He has found out a new sort of poetical georgics, a trick of sowing wit like clover-grass on barren subjects which would yield nothing before. This is very useful for the times wherein, some men say, there is no room left for new invention. He will take three

---

just wit: see p . 272–3 below.
shoot flying: shoot (birds) on the wing.
obstructions: constipation.
rats . . . Germany: as in the Pied Piper of Hamelin legend.
run upon a letter: alliterate.

grains of wit like the elixir, and, projecting it upon the iron age, turn it immediately into gold: all the business of mankind has presently vanished, the whole world has kept holiday; there has been no men but heroes and poets, no women but nymphs and shepherdesses; trees have borne fritters, and rivers flowed plum-porridge.

We read that Virgil used to make fifty or sixty verses in a morning, and afterwards reduce them to ten. This was an unthrifty vanity, and argues him as well ignorant in the husbandry of his own poetry as Seneca says he was in that of a farm; for, in plain English, it was no better than bringing a noble to ninepence. And as such courses brought the Prodigal Son to eat with hogs, so they did him to feed with horses, which were not much better company, and may teach us to avoid doing the like. For certainly it is more noble to take four or five grains of sense and, like a gold-beater, hammer them into so many leaves as will fill a whole book than to write nothing but epitomes, which many wise men believe will be the bane and calamity of learning.

When he writes, he commonly steers the sense of his lines by the rhyme that is at the end of them, as butchers do calves by the tail. For when he has made one line, which is easy enough, and has found out some sturdy hard word that will but rhyme, he will hammer the sense upon it, like a piece of hot iron upon an anvil, into what form he pleases.

There is no art in the world so rich in terms as poetry; a whole dictionary is scarce able to contain them. For there is hardly a pond, a sheep-walk, or a gravel-pit in all Greece but the ancient name of it is become a term of art in poetry. By this means small poets have such a stock of able hard words lying by them, as *dryades, hamadry-ades, Aonides, fauni, nymphae, sylvani*, etc., that signify nothing at all, and such a world of pedantic terms of the same kind as may serve to

projecting: the alchemical term for throwing the powder of the philosopher's stone (the elixir) upon metal in fusion, so as to transmute it.

We . . . ten: see *Vergilii Vita Donatiana*, rec. J. Brummer (app. to Donatus, *Interpretationes Vergilianae*, ed. H. Georgii, 1969), p. 6.

Seneca . . . farm: Seneca corrects Virgil on points of husbandry and doubts that the *Georgics* were intended to teach farmers (*Epistles*, lxxxvi. 15–16).

bringing . . . ninepence: a proverbial description of prodigality. A noble was worth about 6*s*.

the Prodigal Son: Luke 15:11 ff.

so . . . horses: alluding to the young Virgil's curing Augustus' horses (*Vergilii Vita Donatiana*, ed. cit., p. 21).

many wise men: see Bacon, *Works*, 1857–74, iii. 483–4.

Aonides: the Muses (maidens from Aonia).

sylvani: the gods of woods and fields.

furnish all the new inventions and thorough reformations that can happen between this and Plato's Great Year.

When he writes, he never proposes any scope of purpose to himself, but gives his genius all freedom; for as he that rides abroad for his pleasure can hardly be out of his way, so he that writes for his pleasure can seldom be beside his subject. It is an ungrateful thing to a noble wit to be confined to anything; to what purpose did the ancients feign Pegasus to have wings, if he must be confined to the road and stages like a pack-horse, or be forced to be obedient to hedges and ditches? Therefore he has no respect to decorum and propriety of circumstance—for the regard of persons, times, and places is a restraint too servile to be imposed upon poetical licence—like him that made Plato confess Juvenal to be a philosopher, or Persius, that calls the Athenians *quirites*.

For metaphors he uses to choose the hardest and most far-fet that he can light upon; these are the jewels of eloquence, and therefore the harder they are the more precious they must be.

He'll take a scant piece of coarse sense, and stretch it on the tenterhooks of half a score rhymes until it crack that you may see through it, and it rattle like a drumhead. When you see his verses hanged up in tobacco shops, you may say, in defiance of the proverb, that the weakest does not always go to the wall; for 'tis well known the lines are strong enough, and in that sense may justly take the wall of any that have been written in our language. He seldom makes a conscience of his rhymes, but will often take the liberty to make 'preach' rhyme with 'cheat', 'vote' with 'rogue', and 'committee-man' with 'hang'.

He'll make one word of as many joints as the tin pudding that a juggler pulls out of his throat and chops in again; what think you of *glad-fum-flam-hasta-minantes*? Some of the old Latin poets bragged

---

Plato's Great Year: a Great Year would be completed when all the heavenly bodies in their orbits returned to the same relative positions (*Timaeus*, 39^d).

scope of purpose: calculated end in view.

him . . . philosopher: unidentified.

Persius . . . quirites: Satires, iv. 8. *Quirites* means Romans (in their civilian, as opposed to political and military, capacity).

far-fet: far-fetched.

strong: 'strong lines' referred to the concentration and difficulty in earlier writers such as Donne.

tin pudding: imitation string of sausages, made of tin.

chops: thrusts.

glad-fum-flam-hasta-minantes: elided pronunciation of *gladius-fumus-flamma* . . .: 'sword-smoke-flame-spear-threatening'.

Some . . . brass: Horace refers to his verse as 'a monument more lasting than bronze' (*Odes*, III. xxx. 1).

that their verses were tougher than brass and harder than marble; what would they have done if they had seen these? Verily, they would have had more reason to wish themselves an hundred throats than they then had—to pronounce them.

There are some that drive a trade in writing in praise of other writers (like rooks that bet on gamesters' hands), not at all to celebrate the learned author's merits, as they would show, but their own wits, of which he is but the subject. The lechery of this vanity has spawned more writers than the civil law; for those whose modesty must not endure to hear their own praises spoken may yet publish of themselves the most notorious vapours imaginable. For if the privilege of love be allowed—*Dicere quae puduit, scribere iussit amor*—why should it not be so in self-love too? For if it be wisdom to conceal our imperfections, what is it to discover our virtues? It is not like that nature gave men great parts upon such terms as the fairies use to give money: to pinch and leave them if they speak of it. They say praise is but the shadow of virtue; and sure that virtue is very foolish that is afraid of its own shadow.

When he writes anagrams, he uses to lay the outsiders of his verses even, like a bricklayer, by a line of rhyme and acrostic, and fill the middle with rubbish. In this he imitates Ben Jonson, but in nothing else.

There was one that lined a hat-case with a paper of Benlowes's poetry.[n] Prynne bought it by chance, and put a new demi-castor into it. The first time he wore it he felt only a singing in his head, which within two days turned to a vertigo. He was let blood in the ear by one of the state physicians, and recovered; but before he went abroad he writ a poem of rocks and seas in a style so proper and natural that it was hard to determine which was ruggeder.

There is no feat of activity, nor gambol of wit, that ever was performed by man, from him that vaults on Pegasus to him that tumbles through the hoop of an anagram, but Benlowes has got the

---

wish . . . throats: Virgil declares that a hundred mouths could not describe hell (*Aeneid*, vi. 625–7. Cf. *Georgics*, ii. 42–4).

rooks . . . hands: sharpers not handling cards themselves, but betting on the fortunes of gamblers who are playing.

Dicere . . . amor: 'Love orders me to write what I was ashamed to say' (Ovid *Heroides*, iv. 10).

Ben Jonson: Jonson was for a time a bricklayer.

Prynne: see *Hudibras*, I. i. 640 and note p. 291.

demi-castor: a hat made from a mixture of beaver's and other fur.

let blood . . .: see *Hudibras*, I. iii. 153–4 and note p. 296.

mastery in it, whether it be high-rope wit or low-rope wit.[n] He has all sorts of echoes, rebuses, chronograms, etc., besides carwitchets, clenches, and quibbles. As for altars and pyramids in poetry, he has outdone all men that way; for he has made a gridiron and a frying-pan in verse that, beside the likeness in shape, the very tone and sound of the words did perfectly represent the noise that is made by those utensils, such as the old poet called *sartago loquendi*. When he was a captain, he made all the furniture of his horse, from the bit to the crupper, in beaten poetry, every verse being fitted to the proportion of the thing, with a moral allusion of the sense to the thing (as 'the bridle of moderation', 'the saddle of content', and 'the crupper of constancy'); so that the same thing was both epigram and emblem, even as a mule is both horse and ass.

Some critics are of opinion that poets ought to apply themselves to the imitation of nature, and make a conscience of digressing from her; but he is none of these. The ancient magicians could charm down the moon, and force rivers back to their springs, by the power of poetry only; and the moderns will undertake to turn the inside of the earth outward (like a juggler's pocket) and shake the chaos out of it, make nature show tricks like an ape, and the stars run on errands; but still it is by dint of poetry. And if poets can do such noble feats, they were unwise to descend to mean and vulgar; for where the rarest and most common things are of a price, as they are all one to poets, it argues disease in judgment not to choose the most curious. Hence some infer that the account they give of things deserves no regard, because they never receive anything as they find it into their compositions, unless it agree both with the measure of their own fancies and the measure of their lines, which can very seldom happen; and therefore when they give a character of any thing or person, it does commonly bear no more proportion to the subject than the fishes and ships in a map do to the scale. But let such know that poets as well as kings ought rather to consider what is fit for them to give than others to receive; that they are fain to have regard to the exchange of language, and write high or low according as that runs; for in this age, when the smallest poet seldom

---

carwitchets, clenches, and quibbles: all mean plays upon words.
sartago loquendi: 'hotchpotch of language' (Persius, *Satires*, i. 80); *sartago* is, literally, a frying-pan.
captain: Benlowes was a captain of horse in 1648.
The ancient . . . only: cf. *Hudibras*, ii. iii. 599–601.
of a price: equally priced.
curious: exquisite, noteworthy.

goes below more the most, it were a shame for a greater and more noble poet not to out-throw that cut a bar.[n]

There was a tobacco-man that wrapped Spanish tobacco in a paper of verses which Benlowes had written against the Pope, which by a natural antipathy that his wit has to anything that's Catholic spoiled the tobacco; for it presently turned mundungus. This author will take an English word and, like the Frenchman that swallowed water and spit it out wine, with a little heaving and straining would turn it immediately into Latin—as *plunderat ille domos, mille hocopokiana,* and a thousand such.

There was a young practitioner in poetry that found there was no good to be done without a mistress; for he that writes of love before he hath tried it doth but travel by the map, and he that makes love without a dame does like a gamester that plays for nothing. He thought it convenient, therefore, first to furnish himself with a name for his mistress beforehand that he might not be to seek when his merit or good fortune should bestow her upon him; for every poet is his mistress's godfather, and gives her a new name like a nun that takes orders. He was very curious to fit himself with a handsome word of a tunable sound, but could light upon none that some poet or other had not made use of before. He was therefore forced to fall to coining, and was several months before he could light on one that pleased him perfectly. But, after he had overcome that difficulty, he found a greater remaining: to get a lady to own him. He accosted some of all sorts, and gave them to understand, both in prose and verse, how incomparably happy it was in his power to make his mistress; but could never convert any of them. At length he was fain to make his laundress supply that place as a proxy until his good fortune or somebody of better quality would be more kind to him, which after a while he neither hoped nor cared for; for how mean soever her condition was before, when he had once pretended to her, she was sure to be a nymph and a goddess. For what greater honour can a woman be capable of than to be translated into precious stones and stars? No herald in the world can go higher. Besides he found no man can use that freedom of hyperbole in the character of a person commonly known, as great ladies are, which he[n] can in describing one so obscure and unknown that nobody can disprove him. For he that writes but one sonnet upon any of the public persons shall be sure to have his reader at every third word cry out:

a paper . . . Pope: *Papa Perstrictus* (1645).
mundungus: a slang expression, used to describe ill-smelling tobacco.
plunderat . . .: 'he plunders the houses'; 'a thousand hocus-pocuses'.

'What an ass is this to call Spanish paper and ceruse "lilies and roses"!
—Or claps "influences"!—To say "the Graces are her waiting-
women" when they are known to be no better than her bawds!—
That "day breaks from her eyes" when she looks asquint!—Or
that "her breath perfumes the Arabian winds" when she puffs
tobacco!'

It is no mean art to improve a language and find out words that
are not only removed from common use, but rich in consonants,
the nerves and sinews of speech, to raise a soft and feeble language
like ours to the pitch of High Dutch, as he did that writ

> Art's rattling foreskins shrilling bagpipes quell.

This is not only the most elegant, but most poetic way of writing
that a poet can use; for I know no defence like it to preserve a poem
from the torture of those that lisp and stammer. He that wants teeth
may as well venture upon a piece of tough, horny brawn as such
a line; for he will look like an ass eating thistles.

He never begins a work without an invocation of his muse; for it
is not fit that she should appear in pubic to show her skill before she
is entreated, as gentlewomen do not use to sing until they are applied
to and often desired.

I shall not need to say anything of the excellence of poetry, since it
has been already performed by many excellent persons, among whom
some have lately undertaken to prove that the civil government
cannot possibly subsist without it—which, for my part, I believe to
be true in a poetical sense, and more probable to be received of it
than those strange feats of building walls and making trees dance
which antiquity ascribes to verse. And though philosophers are of a
contrary opinion, and will not allow poets fit to live in a commonwealth, their partiality is plainer than their reasons; for they have no
other way to pretend to this prerogative themselves, as they do, but
by removing poets, whom they know to have a fairer title; and this
they do so unjustly that Plato, who first banished poets his republic,
forgot that that very commonwealth was poetical. I shall say nothing
to them, but only desire the world to consider how happily it is like
to be governed by those that are at so perpetual a civil war among
themselves that, if we should submit ourselves to their own resolution

---

Spanish paper and ceruse: cosmetics; rouge and white (lead) respectively.
Art's . . . quell: author unidentified; perhaps imaginary.
some . . . without it: see *Hudibras*, I. ii. 399–400 and note p. 294.
poetical: fabulous, fictional.
strange feats . . .: see Ovid, *Metamorphoses*, xi. 1–2.
Plato . . . republic: *Republic*, 398^d, 608^a.

of this question, and be content to allow them only fit to rule if they could but conclude it so themselves, they would never agree upon it. Meanwhile there is no less certainty and agreement in poetry than the mathematics; for they all submit to the same rules without dispute or controversy. But whosoever shall please to look into the records of antiquity shall find their title so unquestioned that the greatest princes in the whole world have been glad to derive their pedigrees, and their power too, from poets. Alexander the Great had no wiser a way to secure that empire to himself by right which he had gotten by force than by declaring himself the son of Jupiter; and who was Jupiter but the son of a poet? So Caesar and all Rome was transported with joy when a poet made Jupiter his colleague in the Empire; and when Jupiter governed, what did the poets that governed Jupiter?

A Play-Writer

Of our times is like a fanatic, that has no wit in ordinary easy things, and yet attempts the hardest task of brains in the whole world, only because, whether his play or work please or displease, he is certain to come off better than he deserves and find some of his own latitude to applaud him, which he could never expect any other way, and is as sure to lose no reputation, because he has none to venture—

> Like gaming rooks, that never stick
> To play for hundreds upon tick,
> 'Cause, if they chance to lose at play,
> They've not one halfpenny to pay,
> And, if they win a hundred pound,
> Gain if for sixpence they compound.

Nothing encourages him more in his undertaking than his ignorance; for he has not wit enough to understand so much as the difficulty of what he attempts; therefore he runs on boldly like a foolhardy wit, and fortune, that favours fools and the bold, sometimes takes

Alexander . . . of Jupiter: Alexander visited the temple of Ammon in Egypt, where he was recognized by the oracle as Ammon's son. Ammon was identified with Jupiter by the Romans.
son of a poet: i.e. invention of.
Caesar . . . Empire: probably Caligula, himself the 'poet', proclaiming his intimacy with Jupiter (Suetonius, *Caligula*, xxii. 4).
latitude: (mental) capacity; also laxity.
stick: scruple, hesitate.

notice of him for his double capacity, and receives him into her good graces. He has one motive more, and that is the concurrent ignorant judgment of the present age, in which his sottish fopperies pass with applause, like Oliver Cromwell's oratory among fanatics of his own canting inclination.

He finds it easier to write in rhyme than prose; for the world being overcharged with romances, he finds his plots, passions, and re-partees ready made to his hand, and if he can but turn them into rhyme the thievery is disguised, and they pass for his own wit and invention without question, like a stolen cloak made into a coat or dyed into another colour. Besides this he makes no conscience of stealing anything that lights in his way, and borrows the advice of so many to correct, enlarge, and amend what he has ill-favouredly patched together that it becomes like a thing drawn by council and none of his own performance, or the son of a whore, that has no one certain father. He has very great reason to prefer verse before prose in his compositions; for rhyme is like lace, that serves excellently well to hide the piecing and coarseness of a bad stuff, contributes mightily to the bulk, and makes the less serve by the many imper-tinencies it commonly requires to make way for it; for very few are endowed with abilities to bring it in on its own account. This he finds to be good husbandry and a kind of necessary thrift; for they that have but a little ought to make as much of it as they can. His prologue, which is commonly none of his own, is always better than his play (like a piece of cloth that's fine in the beginning and coarse afterwards), though it has but one topic, and that's the same that is used by malefactors when they are tried: to except against as many of the jury as they can.

A Romance Writer

Pulls down old histories to build them up finer again after a new model of his own designing. He takes away all the lights of truth in history to make it the fitter tutoress of life; for truth herself has little or nothing to do in the affairs of the world although all matters of the greatest weight and moment are pretended and done in her name, like a weak princess that has only the title, and falsehood all the power. He observes one very fit decorum in dating his histories in the days of old, and putting all his own inventions upon ancient times; for when the world was younger it might perhaps love and fight and do generous things at the rate he describes them; but since it is grown old all these heroic feats are laid by and utterly given over, nor ever like to come in fashion again; and therefore all his images of those virtues signify no more than the statues upon dead men's tombs, that will never make them live again. He is like one of Homer's gods, that sets men together by the ears and fetches them off again how he pleases; brings armies into the field like Janello's leaden soldiers,[n] leads up both sides himself, and gives the victory to which he pleases, according as he finds it fit the design of his story; makes love and lovers too, brings them acquainted and appoints meetings when and where he pleases, and at the same time betrays them in the height of all their felicity to miserable captivity or some other horrid calamity, for which he makes them rail at the gods and curse their own innocent stars, when he only has done them all the injury; makes men villains, compels them to act all barbarous inhumanities by his own directions, and after inflicts the cruellest punishments upon them for it. He makes all his knights fight in fortifications and storm one another's armour before they can come to encounter body for body, and always matches them so equally one with another that it is a whole page before they can guess which is likely to have the better; and he that has it is so mangled that it had been better for them both to have parted fair at first. But when they encounter with those that are no knights, though ever so well armed and mounted, ten to one goes for nothing. As for the ladies, they are every one the most beautiful in the whole world, and that's the reason why no one of them, nor all together with all their charms, have power to tempt away any knight from another. He differs from a just historian as a joiner does from a carpenter: the one does things plainly and substantially for use, and the other carves and polishes merely for show and ornament.

A Modern Critic

Is a corrector of the press gratis, and as he does it for nothing so it is to no purpose. He fancies himself Clerk of Stationers' Hall, and nothing must pass current that is not entered by him. He is very severe in his supposed office, and cries 'Woe to ye scribes' right or wrong. He supposes all writers to be malefactors without clergy

fair: peaceably.
Woe to ye scribes: Matthew 23:13.

that claim the privilege of their books, and will not allow it where the law of the land, and common justice, does.[n] He censures in gross, and condemns all without examining particulars; if they will not confess and accuse themselves, he will rack them until they do. He is a committee-man in the commonwealth of letters, and as great a tyrant; so is not bound to proceed but by his own rules, which he will not endure to be disputed. He has been an apocryphal scribbler himself; but his writings wanting authority, he grew discontent and turned apostate, and thence becomes so severe to those of his own profession. He never commends anything but in opposition to something else, that he would undervalue, and commonly sides with the weakest, which is generous anywhere but in judging. He is worse than an *index expurgatorius*; for he blots out all, and when he cannot find a fault makes one. He demurs to all writers, and when he is overruled will run into contempt. He is always bringing writs of error like a pettifogger, and reversing of judgments, though the case be never so plain. He is a mountebank that is always quacking of the infirm and diseased parts of books to show his skill, but has nothing at all to do with the sound. He is a very ungentle reader; for he reads sentence on all authors that have the unhappiness to come before him; and therefore pedants that stand in fear of him always appeal from him beforehand by the name of Momus and Zoilus, complain sorely of his extrajudicial proceedings, and protest against him as corrupt and his judgment void and of none effect, and put themselves into the protection of some powerful patron, who like a knight errant is to encounter with the magician and free them from his enchantments.

A Duke of Bucks[n]

Is one that has studied the whole body of vice. His parts are disproportionate to the whole, and like a monster he has more of some and less of others than he should have. He has pulled down all that fabric that nature raised in him, and built himself up again after a model of his own. He has dammed up all those lights that nature made into the noblest prospects of the world, and opened other little

committee-man: see *Hudibras*, I. i. 76 and note p. 289.
writs of error: see *Hudibras*, I. ii. 163 and note p. 293.
Momus: Greek god of ridicule; hence a fault-finder.
Zoilus: early critic of Homer; hence a carping critic.

blind loop-holes backward, by turning day into night and night into day. His appetite to his pleasures is diseased and crazy like the pica in a woman that longs to eat that which was never made for food, or a girl in the greensickness that eats chalk and mortar. Perpetual surfeits of pleasure have filled his mind with bad and vicious humours (as well as his body with a nursery of diseases), which makes him affect new and extravagant ways, as being sick and tired with the old. Continual wine, women, and music put false values upon things, which by custom become habitual and debauch his understanding so, that he retains no right notion nor sense of things; and as the same dose of the same physic has no operation on those that are much used to it, so his pleasures require a larger proportion of excess and variety to render him sensible of them. He rises, eats, and goes to bed by the Julian account—long after all others, that go by the new style—and keeps the same hours with owls and the antipodes. He is a great observer of the Tartar's customs, and never eats till the Great Cham, having dined, makes proclamation that all the world may go to dinner. He does not dwell in his house but haunt it, like an evil spirit that walks all night to disturb the family and never appears by day. He lives perpetually benighted, runs out of his life, and loses his time as men do their ways in the dark; and as blind men are led by their dogs, so is he governed by some mean servant or other that relates to his pleasures. He is as inconstant as the moon which he lives under, and although he does nothing but advise with his pillow all day, he is as great a stranger to himself as he is to the rest of the world. His mind entertains all things very freely that come and go; but like guests and strangers they are not welcome if they stay long. This lays him open to all cheats, quacks, and impostors, who apply to every particular humour while it lasts, and afterwards vanish. Thus with St. Paul, though in a different sense, he 'dies daily', and only lives in the night. He deforms nature while he intends to adorn her, like Indians that hang jewels in their lips and noses. His ears are perpetually drilled with a fiddlestick. He endures pleasures with less patience than other men do their pains.

blind: from which the light or view is cut off.
pica: perverted appetite.
nursery: collection (as of plants in a nursery-garden).
Julian ... new style: the Julian Calendar was running ten days behind the Gregorian, or New Style.
Great Cham ... : See Sir Thomas Herbert, *A Relation of Some Years Travel*, 1634 (fac. 1971), p. 130.
dies daily: 1 Corinthians 15:31.

Miscellaneous Observations[n]

All beauty and the ornaments of it are naturally designed for the outsides of things and not their inward parts; for if the inside of the beautifullest creature in the world were turned outward nothing could appear more ghastly and horrible. And so it is in all the affairs of the world, by which nature seems to provide for the decency and comeliness (at least) of the world, but leaves it to itself in all other matters.

All innovations in Church and State are like new-built houses: unwholesome to live in until they are made healthful and agreeable by time.

The Hobbists will undertake to prevent civil wars by proving that mankind was born to nothing else; to reduce men to subjection and obedience by maintaining that nature made them all equal; secure the rights of princes by asserting that whosoever can get their power from them has right enough to it; and persuade them and their subjects to observe imaginary contracts by affirming that they are invalid as soon as made.[n]

That justice that is said to establish the throne of a prince consists no less in the justness of his title than the just administration of his government; for an unjust title cannot be supported but by unjust means; and for want of this all our late usurpations miscarried.

Rebels have been used in this kingdom like sinners in the kingdom of heaven, where there is more rejoicing over one sinner than forty just men that need no repentance.

As soon as a man has taken an oath against his conscience and done his endeavour to damn himself he is capable of any trust or employment in the government, so excellent a quality is perjury to render the most perfidious of men most fit and proper for public charges of the greatest consequence; and such as have ever so little restraint laid upon them by conscience or religion or natural integrity are declared insufficient and unable to hold any office or public trust in the nation. And this is the modern way of test, as they call it,[n]—to take measure of men's abilities and faith by their alacrity in swearing—and is indeed the most compendious way to exclude all those that have any conscience and to take in such as have none at all.

sinners . . . repentance: see Luke 15:7.

All the designs and practices of Popish priests upon the Protestant religion are never in probability so like to reduce the Church of England to lick up its old vomit as those of our own dignitaries at home. For ever since the Church lands were sold in the Presbyterian times they have so terrible an apprehension that the same thing may be done again some time or other—especially where there is so late a precedent for it—that there is nothing they would not submit to, and believe, to insure their spiritual dignities. And as nothing can perform that so certainly as the introduction of the Romish religion, that has so great a power over all governments where it is received, so there is no course nor means which they would not willingly use, and contribute anything (but money), to re-establish it here again. And hence it is that in the late contest between the King and Parliament about indulgence to be granted to the Catholics for the free exercise of their religion as well as the Fanatics (who were only brought in as stales) some of the prelates appeared openly for them in the House of Lords.[n] And this, being their certain interest, they will never forget, nor omit to promote, especially when it is like to bring with it so great an additional increase of power and revenue. And this they have a further reason to advance, considering the general ill will and hatred they have contracted from the people of all sorts by their imprudent demeanour and the unjust dealing they have used since their restoration, beside the envy they have drawn upon themselves by the vast sums of money they have gained and the few charitable works they have done with it. For these officers and commanders of the Church militant are like soldiers of fortune that are free to serve on any side that gives the best pay.

The inhabitants of the city of London, who generally had run away from the Plague and deserted their houses more than those of the suburbs, were the next year burnt down by the Fire, and those who had suffered before under the one judgment were spared by the other.[n]

The world is more beholden to fools than wise men; for they maintain the greatest part of it, that would be in a very sad condition but for the encouragement it perpetually receives from them. All the great and honourable professions, and most of the richest and right worshipful mysteries, would have very little to do without their custom and the constant employment which they never fail to receive from them. For prodigality and luxury and vanity are great consumers, not only of themselves, but of all commodities of the growth of any nation, which (as men of politics affirm) is the only way to distribute and propagate trade among all people.[n] And although those extravagant follies are destructive always to those that use them (and to those only), yet they are very beneficial to all others that have to do with them; and when their disorders produce diseases and infirmities in their bodies or estates, employ two professions to manage and govern them to their own best advantages. And as for those fools whose natural weakness and want of reason renders them credulous and apt to devour anything that is imposed upon them by those that have ever so little more wit, or rather craft, than themselves: there are innumerable impostors that live upon them, as the varieties of folly and ignorance are infinite. And although those two different sorts of follies disdain one another's extravagancies in their several ways, yet both tend to the same end and purpose, which is nothing but what philosophers affirmed so long since: that all men are born to live and die for the service of their native countries.

The tradition that the earth will in the end be destroyed by fire is not improbable in nature. For as the sea has visibly and apparently in few years decayed, and left many havens some miles from the shore in almost all countries that border upon it, it follows that in length of time (supposing the same order of nature still continuing) it must of necessity be utterly exhausted. And then, there being no moisture left to produce and preserve plants, all vegetables will be naturally dried, and rendered combustible, and inevitably set on fire by the beams of the sun. And as at the Flood, when the sea had all those vast quantities of water which are since spent, the earth was perhaps naturally drowned, so when it has too little it will probably be as naturally burnt. Nor is it improbable that what the sea loses the earth gains, and therefore daily grows bigger; for as the greatest part, if not all, the supply of matter in all natural productions comes from the sun and the sea, the fountains of all heat and moisture (for all places that lie too remote from the sea to receive a constant share of rain become deserts and produce nothing), so little or nothing of that moisture is ever returned back again from whence it came, but resolved into earth, as all natural bodies by corruption are, and so must of necessity add perpetually to the bulk of the earth; as we see about all great and ancient cities the earth increased some yards in depth (notwithstanding the vast quantities

The tradition . . . fire: 2 Peter 3:10.
For as the sea . . .: see 'Upon the Royal Society', ll. 81–2.
resolved into earth: the element water *becomes* the element earth in accordance with Aristotelian theory.

of materials that are taken out of it for the uses of building), and in all fens and marshes and woodlands uninhabited a great deal more. Besides the rains carry a great deal of earth from the tops of mountains down into valleys, which may be one reason why the Adriatic Sea has lost so much of its ancient shore, lying in the midst of so many mountains.

The tides of the sea may seem to be caused by the motion of the earth; for if it always moves eastward, as some believe, it causes the great ocean to move westward until it meets with the opposite motion (for all the opposite parts of a wheel in motion move contrary to one another), and then the great bulk of the sea turns back again. What operation the moon has upon the sea may in probability be collected from the course she keeps with the sun. Nor is there any way so likely to conceive how the sea should have such variety of currents but as this great motion meets with variety of diversions, as we see the wind does among mountains. All the motions that we can observe great bodies of water naturally to have proceed either from the declivity of the earth or the impulse of violent winds, but the tides are far from having any of those causes; for they move equally backwards and forwards almost as equally with or against both.

Whatsoever it is, it must be something of prodigious force that can move so great a weight as that of the sea; and if the influence of the moon can do it, as some believe, it is probable that the influence of the sun, being so many times more powerful, may have the same operation upon the earth. As for the reasons some give for the rapid motion of the sun from the quick motion of light, that appears at any distance [at] which it may be seen the very instant it is lighted, that does not at all concern the diurnal motion of the body of the sun; for a torch that appears at a great distance the same moment it is held up, yet if it be carried from one place to another, does not appear to move faster, but rather slower (by reason of the distance), than the person that bears it. And if the body of the sun did move with that velocity as it must of necessity to pass so vast a space, it must by the same necessity draw a tail after it like a comet, which it does not, and therefore in probability stands still. And if the rest of the planets do not do so, it is because they are only illuminated by the sun, and therefore not subject to any such impression by their quick motions through the ether more than the most violent winds are able to move the sunbeams when it shines upon the earth. And

The tides . . . : see 'Upon the Royal Society', ll. 37–40 and note p. 305, and cf. ll. 73–6.
the quick . . . lighted: see Lucretius, *De Rerum Natura*, iv. 198–215.
And if the body . . . : see 'Upon the Royal Society', ll. 63–8.

therefore they who affirm the sun to be the same with our artificial fire are mistaken; for then the sunbeams would be as liable to be moved by the air as our fire is.

The truth is, though our fire be made of the beams of the sun, yet it is mixed with grosser matter, which renders it not so fine and pure as those rays are naturally of themselves, and consequently subject to the impulse of grosser bodies. But if any man shall suppose from hence that the sun, being of so pure a substance and passing how rapid soever through the pure ether, is not capable of meeting with that opposition that can cause him to change his figure, yet we see that comets, which pass through as pure and subtle an air, do nevertheless draw tails after them of many thousand miles in length. And if the sun can draw out of the sea that vast quantity of water that is contained in the clouds and out of the earth all plants and trees of the largest size, all tending towards itself, it is not improbable but it may with less difficulty cause the earth to turn round towards itself, being equally poised in the air, and no impediment that we know of to stop its circulation.

The beams of the sun move downwards towards the earth empty and upwards when they are laden with exhalations, as water in the inside of the earth moves upwards towards the tops of mountains, where the heads of great rivers are usually found, and downwards on the outside.

All the stars that twinkle seem to be flames and consequently suns, and those that do not other worlds like the moon, who when shining ever so bright is never seen to twink as the sun does.

The end of all knowledge is to understand what is fit to be done; for to know what has been, and what is, and what may be, does but tend to that.

Reason is a faculty of the mind, whereby she puts the notions and images of things (with their operations, effects and circumstances) that are confused in the understanding, into the same order and condition in which they are really disposed by nature or event. The right performance of this is called truth, to which reason naturally tends in a direct line, although she sometime miscarry and fail by the subtlety of the object or her own imperfection, and that we call error or falsehood. Between this and truth lies the proper sphere of wit, which, though it seem to incline to falsehood, does it only to

water . . . outside: see 'Upon the Royal Society', ll. 49–52 and note p. 305.
All the stars . . .: see 'Elephant', ll. 189–94 and note p. 304.

give intelligence to truth. For as there is a trick in arithmetic by giving a false number to find out a true one, so wit by a certain sleight of the mind delivers things otherwise than they are in nature by rendering them greater or less than they really are (which is called hyperbole) or by putting them into some other condition than nature ever did (as when the performances of sensible and rational beings are applied to senseless and inanimate things, with which the writings of poets abound). But when it employs those things which it borrows of falsehood to the benefit and advantage of truth—as in allegories, fables and apologues—it is of excellent use, as making a deeper impression into the minds of men than if the same truths were plainly delivered. So likewise it becomes as pernicious when it takes that from truth which it uses in the service of error and falsehood, as when it wrests things from their right meaning to a sense that was never intended.

The original of reason proceeds from the divine wisdom, by which the order and disposition of the universe was immediately contrived, every part of which has so rational a relation to every other in particular and the whole in general that, though it consist of innumerable pieces and joints, there is not the least flaw imaginable in the whole. Hence it follows that the order of nature is but a copy which the divine wisdom has drawn of itself and committed to the custody of nature, of which she is so constant and faithful an observer that her very deviations and miscarriages are arguments of her loyalty to it. For in those she is as rationally obedient to her instructions as in her regular operations, and by preserving the religion of causes (wheresoever they meet) inviolate, though with the miscarriage of the intended effect (as if she killed the child to save the mother), does but tell us that she had rather fail of her own purposes and make monsters or destroy mankind than digress the least minute from those rules which the divine pleasure has prescribed her. This book of nature man only of all mortal creatures has the honour and privilege to read, which leads him immediately to God and is the greatest demonstration he hath given of himself to nature and the nearest visible access to his divine presence humanity is capable of. For in the first characters and single elements of the creation we cannot so perfectly read God as we can where those letters are joined together and become words and sense, as they do in the

religion: devotion to some principle (in this case the laws governing the several causes independently).
causes: Butler thinks in terms of the four Aristotelian causes—efficient, material, formal, and final.

rational distribution of all the parts of nature. This order is the universal apostle of the whole world, that perpetually preaches God to mankind (and to mankind only) everywhere and has hardly found any nation so barbarous where some have not become proselytes— and for others, nothing but this can encounter with them upon their own grounds. This is the foundation of all religion; for no man that is not certain there is a God can possibly believe or put his trust in him.

All the works of nature are miracles, and nothing makes them appear otherwise but our familiarity with them; for there is nothing in nature but, being rightly considered, would carry us beyond admiration to amazement. But these wonders are methodical and confined to order, to which they are so constant and certain that the ignorance of mankind accounts nothing miraculous but the deviations or diversions of them.

They who suppose the world was made by chance, as Epicurus etc. did, do but acknowledge that the foundation of that opinion must be so too. For if it be possible for all things to fall into so excellent an order by trying infinite experiments *in vacuo* from all eternity, it follows that that opinion can proceed from nothing but mere chance, and therefore can have no reason to depend upon; and consequently all that we find by experiment to be constantly true and certain does but fall out to be so by chance. For the opinions and judgments of men can have no better nor other foundation than that of nature, from whence they are, or should be, derived if they are true; but if false from error and mistake, the common productions of chance and accident. For the mind and understanding of man is but a mirror that receives and represents the images of those objects that nature sets before it at a just distance, as far as it is able to receive them. And therefore the more remote things are, the more uncapable it is to entertain them; and if it ever hap to be in the right, it is like a lucky cast at dice, but by mere chance and haphazard.

The way of attaining mystical knowledges is equally extravagant with that sottish story of Democritus, who is said to have put out his own eyes that he might contemplate the better; an excellent

---

Epicurus: Greek philosopher (341–270 B.C.) who accepted the theory of atomism and whose doctrines were later expounded by Lucretius (*c.* 99–*c.* 55 B.C.) in his poem *De Rerum Natura*.

Democritus: Greek philosopher (b. *c.* 460 B.C.) who worked out the theory of atomism invented by Leucippus and later taken over by Epicurus. The source of this story is Aulus Gellius, *Noctes Atticae*, x. 17.

preparative to his discovery of the world's being made by the accidental rencounter of atoms *in vacuo*, which no man could ever have hit upon that had not been mad enough to put out his own eyes upon any account whatsoever. Nevertheless this freak of the philosopher [was received] with great reverence and admiration by the learned, as many others of the same kind are, and no less celebrated than Socrates his dying for his religion or enduring to be beaten by his wife, in which he was but a confessor of virtue, but in the other a pagan schismatic and martyr to his own opinion.

Logicians cannot teach men solid and substantial reason, but only little tricks and evasions that are worse than nothing, like stamping on the floor of a fencing school, that goes for nothing upon the grass.

There is nothing more necessary and useful to reason than distinguishing, and therefore the word 'discretion' signifies nothing else. And yet there is nothing that is rendered so much the cause of ignorance, error, and nonsense as School distinctions; for no distinctions can be good but those that are so plain that they make themselves. For the best things when they are abused become the worst.

The bigger the volumes of conciliators are, the less credit they deserve; for the difference must of necessity be very great where there is so much difficulty to compound it. Things that have any natural relation are easily made to agree.

Notions are but pictures of things in the imagination of man, and if they agree with their originals in nature they are true, and if not, false. And yet some men are so unwary in their thoughts as to confound them, and mistake the one for the other, as if the picture of a man were really the person for whom it was drawn.

Aristotle thought to reduce nature to his own notions rather than to suit them agreeable to her, and studied her more in the metaphysics of his own brain than her own certain operations, as if his

Socrates . . . wife: the philosopher was sentenced to death in 399 B.C. He had been accused of refusing to recognize the state gods and of introducing other new deities; also of corrupting youth. His wife Xanthippe was a notorious scold. (Diogenes Laertius, ii. 40 and ii. 36–7.)

Logicians . . .: see *Hudibras*, I. i. 65–80.

'discretion': separation or distinction (from the original Latin meaning of *discretio*), as well as discernment (a late Latin sense).

School distinctions: those made in the formal logic of medieval schoolmen, and attempted by Hudibras in the synods-bears debate.

Notions . . .: see *Hudibras*, I. i. 139–42.

chiefest care had been to make his systems of her rather artificial than true, and to agree among themselves very prettily, but perhaps without any great regard to truth or nature. This made him so overartificial that some have believed the use and profit men receive from his writings will not bear the charges of the pains and study that must be bestowed upon them.

There is a great deal of difference between those actions that reason performs freely and of her own accord and those wherein she is prescribed to and forced, the former being commonly clear and open and the other obscure and intricate, as the stream of a river differs from the pipes of an aqueduct. For when opinion, that should wait upon reason, does govern and dictate to it, the disorder is so preposterous, and the restraint so ungrateful to reason (that like a conjurer must not stir out of a circle), that commonly her best performances are but canting and imposture. When the imagination is broken loose from the obedience of reason, it becomes the most disordered and ungoverned thing in the world; it cheats the senses, and raises the passions to that prodigious height that the strength of the body—as if it gained what the mind loses—becomes more than treble to what it was before. It transports a man beyond himself, and does things so far beside the ordinary course of nature and the understanding of the wisest that—as if they had lost their wits too by contagion—it often passes for possessions of the devil.

Reason is the only helm of the understanding; the imagination is but the sail, apt to receive and be carried away with every wind of vanity, unless it be steered by the former. And although like the loadstone it have some variations, it is the only compass man has to sail by. Nor is it to be contemned because it sometimes leads him upon a rock; that is but accidental, and he is more apt to hit upon those without it. For all the variations of reason that do not proceed from the disproportion of men's wits, which can never be reduced to a standard, are rather imposed by passion, concernment, melancholy, custom, and education (which very few can ever redeem themselves from) than intended by nature. And for the cheats and impostures that are wrought by it, they are no other than the greatest blessings which God and nature have bestowed upon mankind are

artificial: according to rules of art.
some have believed . . .: a deliberate understatement, the criticism of Aristotle's 'artificiality' being a common seventeenth-century theme.
ungrateful: distasteful.
variations: deviations from the true north–south line.
concernment: interest.

usually made serviceable to; and if we will disclaim reason for being no better dealt with, I do not know how we can excuse the Gospel, physic, wealth, liberty, wine, and love, which were destined to the happiness and well-being of man, but most commonly become the fatal causes of his ruin and destruction.

Though probability, like one that squints, look several ways at once, it is much better than blind fancy or credulity; for he that puts out his eyes because he cannot [see] so well as he would inflicts a just punishment upon his own folly. Nonsense is as well proof against contradiction as demonstration is; for no man can say more against that which he does not understand than against that which is manifest. There is a great deal of difference between that which may be proved and that which cannot be disproved; for though doubt always attends probability, yet in knowing persons, being the effect of reason and discourse, it is of a nobler nature than mere opinion, or implicit credulity, which is but the apostasy of doubt. Credulity and demonstration are different ends of doubt, as death and health[n] are of pain; but he that thinks to cure himself of that malady by the former deserves it.

Demonstration is the proper business of knowledge, and probability of belief; and as there is no certain knowledge without demonstration, so there is no safe belief without probability.

Faith can determine nothing of reason, but reason can of faith. And therefore if faith be above reason (as some will have it), it must be reason only that can make it appear to be so; for faith can never do it. So that faith is beholden to reason for this prerogative, and sure it cannot be much above that from which it receives its credit. Faith cannot define reason, but reason can faith, and therefore it should seem to be the larger, as the comprehending must be greater than that it comprehends. But howsoever we should grant it to be above reason, certainly the less it is above it, it is justly esteemed the better; else divines and schoolmen of all ages would never have taken so much pains as they have to bring it as near to reason as they can, if it had been better at a distance. The very being of faith depends upon reason, for no irrational creature is capable of it; and if we will not allow this, we must of necessity acknowledge that it depends upon ignorance—which is worse—for no man can believe anything but because he does not know it.[n] But faith always differs

discourse: 'the act of understanding, by which it passes from premises to consequences' (Johnson, *Dictionary*).
the comprehending: that which includes or contains something else.

from itself according as it falls upon persons; for that which is one man's faith may be another man's knowledge; so that the less any man knows, the more he hath to believe.

Faith is so far from being above reason and knowledge that it is below ignorance, which it depends upon; for no man can believe and not be ignorant, but he may be ignorant and not believe. Whensoever reason and demonstration appears, faith and ignorance vanish together.[n]

They that dispute matters of faith into nice particulars and curious circumstances do as unwisely as a geographer that would undertake to draw a true map of *terra incognita* by mere imagination; for though there is such a part of the earth, and that not without mountains and vallies and plains and rivers, yet to attempt the description of these and assign their situations and tracts without a view of the place is more than ridiculous.

He that believes in the Scriptures is mistaken if he therefore thinks he believes in God; for the Scriptures are not the immediate word of God. For they were written by men, though dictated by divine revelation; of which since we have no testimony but their own, nor any other assurance, we do not believe them because they are the word of God; for we must believe them before we believe that which we receive only from them. And if we believe God because we believe them, we believe in him but at the second hand, and build the foundation of our faith in God upon our faith in men. So if we imagine we believe in God because we believe in the Scriptures, we deceive ourselves; for if I tell a man something of a third person, which he believes, he does not believe that third person, but me that tell it him.

The Papists say they believe as the Church believes, and the Protestants laugh at them for it, but do the very same thing themselves; all the difference is the first believe by wholesale and the last by retail. The Papists believe something, but they know not what; the Protestant believes this or that, but he knows not what it is. The Papist believes what he cannot understand, without examination; the Protestant will examine (though he cannot understand) before he will believe; so that, though they differ in words, they agree in the same thing. The Protestant will not allow the Scripture to be read in an unknown tongue, but is content to have it read in an unknown sense, which is all one. They will not have God described to the eye in any corporeal shape, but are willing he should be expressed to the ear by several parts of man's body, as it is frequently found in the Scripture.

There is a trick in arithmetic by giving a false number to find out a true one; so there is no way to come nearer to truth than by fable, allegories and apologues that have no truth at all in them.

Allegories are only useful when they serve as instances to illustrate some obscure truth. But when a truth, plain enough, is forced to serve an allegory, it is a preposterous mistake of the end of it— which is to make obscure things plain, not plain things obscure— and is no less foolish than if we should look upon things that lie before us with a perspective, which is so far from assisting the sight that it utterly obstructs it; beside the preposterous difficulty of forcing things against their natural inclinations, which at the best does but discover how much wit a man may have to no purpose, there being no such argument of a slight mind as an elaborate trifle.

There is scarce any one thing in which men are generally more apt to mistake than in their censure of styles. For as style is nothing (as it is taken) but a proper, natural, and significant way of expressing our conceptions in words, and as it agrees or disagrees with those is either good or bad, so he that takes it for good or bad of itself is very much mistaken, and erroneously takes the music for the instrument it is played upon, and according as that is in or out of tune commends or cries down the composition. For though good things may be blemished by being ill delivered, yet that which is bad of itself can never be rendered good by any language of itself. And although the plainest and most significant style be undoubtedly the best, yet it is only so where the excellency of the sense will bear it, as it is a superfluous thing to lace or embroider that which is richer without it. But where the sense is vulgar and common it does require something extraordinary in the expression to set if off with a greater grace, and disguise the natural homeliness of the thing, and (if it be possible) to render it as becoming as if it were naturally so of itself. For that which is old and worn-out may be made new by a new way of expression or application, and no less witty than if it were fresh and never heard of before. But this is impossible to be done in some arguments, and no way but in one fashion of writing.

preposterous: having last that which should be first (Latin *praeposterus*, inverted).
perspective: an optical instrument.

My writings are not set off with the ostentation of prologue, epilogue, nor preface; nor sophisticated with songs and dances, nor music nor fine women between the cantos; nor have anything to commend them but the plain downrightness of the sense.

A satire is a kind of knight-errant, that goes upon adventures to relieve the distressed damsel Virtue, and redeem Honour out of enchanted castles, and oppressed Truth and Reason out of the captivity of giants and magicians; and though his meaning be very honest, yet some believe he is no wiser than those wandering heroes used to be, though his performances and achievements be ever so renowned and heroical. And as those worthies, if they lived in our days, would hardly be able to defend themselves against the laws against vagabonds, so our modern satire has enough to do to secure himself against the penalties of *scandalum magnatum* and libels.

There is nothing that provokes and sharpens wit like malice and anger—*Si natura negat, facit indignatio,* etc. And hence perhaps came the first occasion of calling those raptures 'poetical fury'. For malice is a kind of madness (for if men run mad for love, why should they not as well do so for hate?), and as madmen are said to have in their fits double the strength they had before, so have malicious men the wit. He who first found out iambics, and before with all his wit and fancy could not prevail with the father of his mistress to keep but his promise with him, had no sooner turned his love into hate but he forced him with the bitterness of his new rhymes to hang himself—so much power has malice above all other passions to heighten wit and fancy; for malice is restless and never finds ease until it has vented itself. And therefore satires, that are only provoked with the madness and folly of the world, are found to contain more wit and ingenuity than all other writings whatsoever, and meet with a better reception from the world—that is always more delighted to hear the faults and vices, though of itself, well described—than all

sophisticated: adulterated, deprived of natural simplicity. Butler is thinking here of Restoration stage practice.

scandalum magnatum: 'the publication of a malicious report against any person holding a position of dignity' (*OED*).

Si natura . . .: Juvenal, *Satires*, i. 79 ('. . . indignatio versum': 'if nature refuses, indignation makes the verse').

'*poetical fury*': inspired frenzy of the poet.

He . . . iambics: Archilochus, Greek poet (probably eighth century B.C.), who developed in its early form the iambic metre, especially suited to satire.

hang himself: tradition has it that both the father Lycambes and the daughter Neobule hanged themselves as a consequence of Archilochus' satires.

the panegyrics that ever were, which are commonly as dull as they are false, and no man is delighted with the flattery of another.

Among all sports and shows that are used none are so delightful as the military, that do but imitate and counterfeit fights; and in heroical poetry, that has nothing to do with satire, what is there that does so much captivate the reader as the prodigious feats of arms of the heroes and the horrid destruction they make of their enemies? There is no sort of cunning in the world so subtle and curious as that which is used in doing of mischief, nor any true wisdom and polity so ingenious as the artifices of cheats and impostors, against which all the wisdom of laws is so unable to prevail that they will turn all their best and surest guards upon themselves, in spite of all the caution and care which the wisest governments can possibly contrive. How far more cunning and crafty have the wits of men been in finding out that prodigious variety of offensive weapons, in comparison of those few that have [been] invented only for defence, though their own preservation ought in reason to be more considerable to them than the destruction of others. What made the serpent so subtle as to outwit Adam in Paradise, though a copy drawn from the original of wisdom itself, but only the malice of his design, so active and industrious is the Devil to do mischief? For malice is the reason of state of hell, as charity is of heaven, and therefore the proceedings of both are directly contrary. For God, who made the world and all that is in it in six days, was forty days and nights too in drowning of it, beside so many years in executing what he had resolved—whose punishments extend but to the third or fourth generation, but his mercy unto thousands. Malice is so great an odds in any contest between man and man that the law does not condemn one man for killing another for any reason so much as for having malice prepensed on his side, as if it were one of those illegal weapons which the statute of stabbing provides against. What a stupendous operation has the malice of witches (for nothing else qualifies them to be such), who, if the laws of the land are but true and just, are able to do feats which the wisest men in the world are not able to understand. And hence it is that envy and emulation,

a copy . . . itself: Genesis 1:26–7.
forty days and nights: Genesis 7:12.
whose punishments . . . thousands: Exodus 20:5–6.
prepensed: the earlier form of the modern 'prepense' (planned beforehand).
statute of stabbing: this enacted (1604) that if a man stab another (who has no weapon drawn or has not struck first) who dies within six months, the stabber is guilty of wilful murder. Hence stabbing weapons were in effect more 'illegal' than shooting or cudgelling weapons.

which is but a kind of malice, has power to enable some men to do things which had otherwise been far above their natural abilities.

It is not only a wicked vice, but its own punishment also; for it always afflicts those more that bear it than those for whose sakes they endure the slavery to maintain it. He who in a rage threw his pencil at his picture, because he could not please himself in drawing the foam of a mad dog, came nearer to nature both in his performance and the way of doing it than all his sober study and care could ever have brought him. For all the best productions of most judicious men's studies proceed from nothing more than their restless vexation of thought, which all passions naturally produce in the mind, and put the spirits into a quicker motion than they are capable of in a quiet temper. But, notwithstanding the many advantages that wit receives from passion, there is nothing in nature so pernicious and destructive to all manner of judgement; for all passion is so partial and prepossessed that it is not capable of making a true judgement of anything, though ever so plain and easy. And although there are but few passions the natural temper of judgement, as fear, sorrow, shame, etc., yet where they prevail they are as averse to it, and sometime more, than those of a direct contrary nature. For judgement is like a balance that measures all things by weight, and therefore the more light and less solid anything is, the less apt it is to be examined that way.

Men of the quickest apprehensions and aptest geniuses to anything they undertake do not always prove the greatest masters in it. For there is more patience and phlegm required in those that attain to any degree of perfection than is commonly found in the temper of active and ready wits, that soon tire and will not hold out, as the swiftest race-horse will not perform a long journey so well as a sturdy, dull jade. Hence it is that Virgil, who wanted much of that natural easiness of wit that Ovid had, did nevertheless with hard labour and long study in the end arrive at a higher perfection than the other, with all his dexterity of wit but less industry, could attain to. The same we may observe of Jonson and Shakespeare.[n] For he that is able to think long and judge well will be sure to find out better things than another man can hit upon suddenly, though of more quick and ready parts, which is commonly but chance, and the other art and judgement.

He who in a rage threw . . .: Protogenes. Pliny reports his throwing a paint-sodden sponge (*Natural History*, xxxv. xvi).

Few men's wits and judgements, how excellent soever in their kinds, will ever be brought to stand in tune together; for good wits do not always jump. There is no theft so easy as that of wit, that is so cheap it will not bear the charges of being locked up or looked after. But though it be less difficult than to rob an orchard that is unfenced, yet he who thinks he can steal judgement is as ridiculous as he that believes he can run away with the trees, or because he can steal the ore supposes he can convey away the mine. For there is no true wit that is not produced by a great deal of judgement. For wit and fancy are but the clothes and ornaments of judgement, and when they are stolen by those whom they will not fit they serve them to no purpose, or that which is worse than none, to make them ridiculous. For almost all plants, and animals too, degenerate where they are not naturally produced, and he that believes otherwise of wit is as ignorant as those silly Indians that buy gunpowder of our merchants and sow it in the earth, believing it will grow there.

Wit is very chargeable and not to be maintained in its necessary leisure and expenses at an ordinary rate. It is the worst trade in the world to live upon and a commodity that no man thinks he has need of. For those who have the least believe they have as much as the best, and enjoy greater privileges; for as they are their own judges they are subject to no censures which they cannot easily reverse, and it is incredible how much upon that account they will despise all the world; which those who have more wit dare not do, and the more wit they have, are but the more severe to themselves and their own performances, and have just confidence enough to keep them from utterly renouncing of it, which they are apt to do upon the smallest check if something else than their own inclinations did not oppose them in it.

Wit is, like science, not of particulars but universals; for as arguments drawn from particulars signify little to universal nature, which is the proper object of science, so wit that is raised upon any one particular person goes no further unless it be from thence extended to all human nature.

Dr. Donne's writings are like voluntary or prelude, in which a man is not tied to any particular design of air, but may choose his key or mood at pleasure; so his compositions seem to have been written without any particular scope.

those silly Indians . . . : in Virginia (Purchas, *Pilgrimes,* IV. ix. iv. ii. 1709).
scope: end in view.

There are two ways of quibbling: the one with words and the other with sense, like the *figurae dictionis et figurae sententiae* in rhetoric. The first is done by showing tricks with words of the same sound but different senses; and the other by expressing of sense by contradiction and riddle. Of this Mr. Waller[n] was the first, most copious author, and has so infected our modern writers of heroics with it that they can hardly write any other way, and if at any time they endeavour to do it, like horses that are put out of their pace they presently fall naturally into it again. *Trotto d'asino dura poco.*

They that write plays in rhyme tell us that the language of comedy ought to be common discourse such as men speak in familiar conversation—as if verse were so.[n]

It is much easier to write plays in verse than prose, as it is harder to imitate nature than any deviation from her, and prose requires a more proper and natural sense and expression than verse, that has something in the stamp and coin to answer for the alloy and want of intrinsic value.

They are very weak critics who suppose a poet that writes a play ought, like one that rides post with a halter about his neck, to bring all his design and contrivance within so many hours, or else be hanged for it—as if things of greater importance, and much more to the purpose, were to be omitted for a mere curiosity which few or none but the capricious take notice of.

Our modern authors write plays as they feed hogs in Westphalia, where but one eats pease or acorns, and all the rest feed upon his and one another's excrement. So the Spaniard first invents and designs plays; the French borrow it from them; and the English from the French.

Dryden weighs poets in the virtuoso's scales that will turn with the hundredth part of a grain,[n] as curiously as Juvenal's lady-pedantess

---

figurae dictionis et figurae sententiae: figures of speech and figures of thought.
words of the same sound: the punning which Restoration readers found offensive in Jacobean drama and metaphysical poetry.
heroics: heroic couplets, rhymed iambic pentameters.
Trotto . . .: 'An ass's trot doesn't last long' (Italian proverb, of good intentions not maintained).
coin: the device stamped upon money.
virtuoso's scales: the Royal Society 'virtuosi' had invented 'a very exact pair of scales, for trying a great number of magnetical experiments' (Thomas Sprat, *History of the Royal Society*, 1667 (fac. 1958), p. 247).

> Committit vates et comparat, inde Maronem,
> Atque alia parte in trutina suspendit Homerum.

He complained of B. Jonson for stealing forty scenes out of Plautus.
Set a thief to find out a thief.[n]

Monsieur Montaigne, the essayist, seems when he wrote to have
been either a little warmed with wine or naturally hot-headed.

The historian of Gresham College endeavours to cry down oratory
and declamation while he uses nothing else.

The Greek tongue is of little use in our times, unless to serve
pedants and mountebanks to smatter withal; to coin foolish titles
for medicines, and books of all languages; and furnish preachers
with sentences to astonish the ignorant, and lose time withal in
translating it over again into the vulgar and nonsense. It is in itself
a very untoward language that abounds in a multitude of impertinent
declinations, conjugations, numbers, times, anomalies, and form-
ings of verbs, but has little or no construction. And though no language is so curious in the contrivance of long and short vowels, yet
they are so confounded by the accent that they are rendered of no
use at all; and in verse the accent is again so confounded by the
quantity of the syllable that the language becomes another thing.

Bodin admires Guicciardine for the best of historians, and calls
him *parens historiae*; but in the end of his encomion discovers the
true reason of it, when, commending his ingenuity and candour, he
says he was so just to truth that, speaking of the original of the
French pox, he takes the scandal off that nation and very impartially
lays it upon the Neapolitans.

Printers find by experience that one murder is worth two monsters,
and at least three walking spirits. For the consequence of murder is
hanging, with which the rabble is wonderfully delighted. But where

Committit . . .: *Satires*, vi. 436–7 ('brings together and compares the poets,
   suspends Virgil in one scale and Homer in the other').
The historian . . .: Thomas Sprat, *History*, esp. pp. 111–13. The Society, which
   held meetings at Gresham College, aimed at 'mathematical plainness' in
   language.
the vulgar: the vulgar tongue, English.
declinations: declensions.
anomalies: deviations from its grammatical rules. Butler's spelling is 'anomulas'.
Bodin . . . Guicciardine: Jean Bodin, *Method for the Easy Comprehension of History* (1566), trans. B. Reynolds, 1945, pp. 61, 74; commenting on Francesco
   Guicciardini, *History of the Wars of Italy*, trans. G. Fenton, 1579, p. 128.
encomion: encomium.

murders and walking spirits meet, there is no other narrative can come near it.

Men that are mad upon many things are never so extravagant as those who are possessed with but one; for one humour diverts another and never suffers the caprice to fix. And as those who apply themselves to many studies never become excellent in any one, so those that are distracted with several sorts of freaks are never so solidly and profoundly mad as those that are wholly taken up with some one extravagance. For sottishness and folly, which is nothing else but natural madness, is neither so ridiculous nor serious in its way as that which men fall into by accident or their own ungoverned passions. And although a madman in his intervals is much wiser than a natural fool, yet a fool (if he be not very stupid) has, all things considered, much the advantage of him. For nature never made anything so bad as the deviations from her have rendered it; nor is she more improved by art and ingenuity than impaired by artificial folly and industrious ignorance. And therefore the author of *Don Quixote* makes Sancho, though a natural fool, much more wise and politic than his master with all his studied and acquired abilities.

There is no better argument to prove that the Scriptures were written by divine inspiration than that excellent saying of Our Saviour: 'If any man will go to law with thee for thy cloak, give him thy coat also.'

Christ told the woman whom he cured that her faith had made her well; but the faith of patients in the doctors and empirics of our times is often found to be the cause of their destruction.

Among all diseases incident to mankind three parts of four are so naturally curable (except in epidemical maladies) that they recover of themselves, especially in places where there are few physicians; and of that fourth, one half at least miscarry either by disorder, or want of necessary help and care or too much; so that there is but one eighth that is naturally mortal. As for the rest, whatsoever course is used, either by application of medicines that do no hurt or charms that do as little good, the cure never fails to be imputed (though done by nature) to that which was last used. And that is one reason why there are so great varieties of medicines (especially among empirics and old women) for one and the same disease, of all

---

in his intervals: between his fits.
'*If any man . . .*': Matthew 5:40.
Christ told the woman: Mark 5:34.

which not one perhaps ever wrought the effect, but only happened to be applied at that time when nature was doing her own work, and so carried the credit of the cure from her; while the best and most proper medicines in nature, being applied to incurable diseases, are as falsely supposed to kill and as idly laid by as the other are received.

Monasteries are but a kind of civil bedlams, where those that would be otherwise troublesome to the world are persuaded to shut up themselves.

They that profess religion and believe it consists in frequenting of sermons do as if they should say they have a great desire to serve God but would fain be persuaded to it. Why should any man suppose that he pleases God by patiently hearing an ignorant fellow render religion ridiculous?

Men ought to do in religion as they do in war: when a man of honour is overpowered and must of necessity render himself up a prisoner, such are always wont to endeavour to do it to some person of command and quality, and not to a mean scoundrel. So since all men are obliged to be of some church, it is more honourable (if there were nothing else in it) to be of that which has some reputation than such a one as is contemptible and justly despised by all the best of men.

God made Adam in Paradise but one woman, and yet she betrayed him by holding correspondence with his only enemy the Devil against him. Then what are his fallen posterity like to suffer that have so many?

Virtue as it is commonly understood in women signifies nothing else but chastity, and honour only not being whores, as if that sex were capable of no other morality but a mere negative continence. Those who have this virtue believe it is sufficient to compound for any fault or defect whatsoever, and are commonly so humorous and uneasy upon that account as if they had parted with their right and resolved to repair themselves some other way; or had taken out letters of reprisal to recover their losses upon all they can light upon, and revenge themselves, as eunuchs do their disabilities, with ill-nature and the hatred of all mankind; when no virtue can be sullen and proud upon its own account but it degenerates into something worse than that which it strove to avoid.

humorous: peevish, capricious.
repair themselves: make amends.

There was never any ingenious man in the world that utterly forbore drinking, that is[n] commonly the greatest vice of very witty men or very fools—as all extremes use to meet—but seldom falls upon the middle sorts of both, of whom their sobriety renders multitudes worse than natural fools and perpetually makes the virtuosi or learned sorts of men naturally turn pedants, which the freedom of conversation in drinking as naturally redeems them from. And therefore the ancient Greek philosophers and modern German mechanics have been found to improve their inventions and parts that way more than any other, and to outdo all the soberer persons and nations in the world; for the more abstemious Italians and Spaniards are not more inferior to them in drinking than they are in all other arts and sciences.

All the gallantry of clothes began with fig-leaves and was brought to perfection with mulberry leaves.

Great persons of our times do, like Absalom when he rebelled against his father, commit iniquity upon the tops of houses that all people may see and take notice of it.

This age will serve to make a very pretty farce for the next, if it have any wit at all to make use of it.

I do now begin to find myself naturally inclined to cast up an account with death what the true value of anything really comes to.

Absalom . . . : II Samuel 16:22.

Notes

Hudibras

The First Part. Canto I

p. 1   The name of the hero is taken from Spenser, *Faerie Queene*, II. ii. 17:

> He that made love unto the eldest dame
> Was hight Sir Huddibras, an hardy man;
> Yet not so good of deeds as great of name,
> Which he by many rash adventures wan
> Since errant arms to sue he first began.
> More huge in strength than wise in works he was,
> And reason with fool-hardise over-ran;
> Stern melancholy did his courage pass,
> And was, for terror more, all armed in shining brass.

Butler's Hudibras, like Spenser's, is rash, foolhardy, severe, and subject to extremes of emotion.

p. 1   The phrase 'jealousies and fears' was used so frequently by the Puritans in their political tracts and manifestos that it became a slogan used to signify their suspicions of Charles I and his advisers. 'Fears and jealousies', says Clarendon, 'were the new words which served to justify all indispositions and to excuse all disorders' (*History of the Rebellion*, ed. W. D. Macray, Oxford, 1888, iv. 167).

p. 2   'When I am playing with my cat, who knows whether she have more sport in dallying with me, than I have in gaming with her?' (Montaigne, *Essays*, II. xii; trans. Florio, 3 vols., 1965, ii. 142.)

p. 3   Cf. Butler's note on logicians, p. 275.

p. 3   Aristotle uses this proposition to demonstrate relative properties (*Topica*, V. i).

p. 3   After Parliament had seized power from the King, committees were set up to take over and sell lands owned by the Church and the Royalists. The lands were transferred into the possession of parliamentary trustees and sold to produce revenue for Parliament. These trustees were frequently accused of abusing their authority to their own financial advantage.

p. 5   One of the duties of a justice of the peace was the inspection of weights and measures.

p. 5   The reference in Butler's footnote is to Seneca, *Epistolae Morales*, lxxxii. 24.

p. 6   The definition of truth given in Butler's footnote is substantially repeated in one of his commonplace books. See p. 272.

p. 6   For the source of Butler's note, see Raleigh, *History of the World*, 1614, 43.

p. 7   Johannes Goropius Becanus (1519–72), physician to Queen Maria of Hungary, maintained that High Dutch or Teutonic was the original language (*Hermathena*, *Opera*, Antwerp, 1580, p. 204).

p. 7   Sir Thomas Browne, whom Butler satirizes quite frequently in *Hudibras*, discusses the question of Adam's navel in *Pseudodoxia Epidemica*, v. v.

p. 8   The contradictions which Butler observed in the conduct and attitudes of the Presbyterians are set out more fully in his Character of 'An Hypocritical Nonconformist'.   See especially p. 247.

p. 8   The Puritans condemned as pagan the traditional celebration of Christmas. By a Parliamentary Ordinance of 1647 Christmas and other popular festivals were declared illegal. The passing of this ordinance provoked riots and was lamented in popular ballads.

p. 8   Mahomet was said to have been taken to heaven on a kind of mule known as an alborak. Butler substitutes 'ass and widgeon' for 'alborak and pigeon' since the former were colloquialisms for 'fools'.

p. 10   Gaspare Tagliacozzo (1545–99), Professor of Anatomy at Bologna, was the first person to practise plastic surgery scientifically. He published an account of his methods in his *De Curtorum Chirurgia per Insitionem*, Venice, 1597. The philosopher Robert Fludd gives an account, to which Butler here alludes, of a nobleman whose damaged nose was repaired from the flesh of one of his servants. According to Fludd, the operation was successful until the moment when the servant died, at which point the nobleman's nose 'did gangrenate and rot' (*Doctor Fludd's Answer unto M. Foster*, 1631, ii. vii. 132).

p. 10   *Aeneid*, ii. 705–29.

p. 11   Don Quixote (I. ii. ii) remarks that there is no record in the chivalric romances that knights errant ever ate except when a banquet was held for them.

p. 14   'A Spaniard, under the lash, made a point of honour of it not to mend his pace for the saving of his carcass, and so marched his stage out with as much gravity as if he had been upon a procession' (Roger L'Estrange, *Fables and Stories*, cxlii. 132).

p. 15   Virgil, *Aeneid*, i. 367–8.

p. 15   Virgil, *Aeneid*, vi. 187 ff. 'Hell' was the colloquial term for the waste-box under the tailor's counter.

p. 16   Ninepenny pieces were formerly bent and given to a sweetheart as a love token.

p. 17   i. i. 523–72 describe Ralpho's addiction to the hermetic philosophy and have many similarities with Butler's Character of 'An Hermetic Philosopher'. The *Hermetica* is a collection of mystical writings composed in the form of Platonic dialogues. They were named after Hermes Trismegistus, a legendary figure once supposed to have been a contemporary of Moses. In fact the dialogues are the work of many hands and were composed at various times during the first three centuries A.D. They enjoyed a considerable vogue during the Renaissance and were revered for the occult wisdom they appeared to contain.

p. 17   Both the *Hermetica* and the *Cabala* were thought to originate from the time of Moses. The phrase 'green breeches' is taken from the Geneva translation of Genesis 3 : 7, where Adam and Eve are said to have 'sewed fig-leaves together and made themselves breeches'.

p. 17   The 'intelligences' were the spirits thought to preside over and rotate the planets. Hermetic beliefs included the idea that, by the use of spells and incantations, the intelligences could be made to influence human temperament and actions. The 'ideas' are the Platonic ideas found in the 'intelligible world' and the 'influences' are the powers of the stars over human character and conduct. A satirical account of the intelligible world is given in *Hudibras*, ii. iii. 225–34.

p. 17   Raymond Lully or, as he was actually named, Raimon Lull (c. 1235–1315) was a Spanish theologian, mystic, and Arabic scholar. The treatises on alchemy formerly attributed to him are now regarded as spurious. Heinrich Cornelius Agrippa of Nettesheim (1486–1535) was the author of *De Occulta Philosophia*, a popular work which made hermetic beliefs widely known. An English translation appeared in 1651.   In a later work, *De Incertitudine et Vanitate Scientiarum*, he renounced his faith in magic and professed an intellectual scepticism.

p. 17   'The author of *Magia Adamica*' is Thomas Vaughan.

p. 18 'Anthroposophus' is Thomas Vaughan (1622–66), the author of *Anthroposophia Theomagica*, twin brother of the poet Henry Vaughan, and one of the chief writers in the hermetic tradition in England. Robert Fludd (1574–1637) was an English physician, mystic, and prolific writer of philosophical works. Jacob Boehme (1575–1624) was a German philosopher, mystic, and alchemist.

p. 18 William Camden describes the superstitions of the Irish in his *Britannia*, 1610, pp. 145–6.

p. 18 The occult society of the Rosicrucians was supposedly founded in the fifteenth century by one Christian Rosenkreuz. The little that is known of their beliefs has much in common with the ideas of the hermetic philosophers.

p. 18 'First matter' was, according to hermetic doctrine, the universal substance out of which all things were originally created. Thomas Vaughan describes a vision in which he beheld first matter (*Lumen de Lumine, Works*, p. 1919, 247).

p. 18 Thomas Vaughan describes the chaos as 'that limbus or huddle of matter wherein all things were so strangely contained' before the creation of the world (*Anthroposophia Theomagica, Works*, p. 18).

p. 21 In the preface to his poem *Gondibert*, Sir William Davenant remarks that Homer 'often interrogates his muse, not as his rational spirit, but as a familiar, separated from his body' (Spingarn, *Critical Essays*, 1908–9, ii. 2).

p. 21 George Wither (1588–1667) was a very prolific author of poems and tracts. He was a strong supporter of Parliament and sold his estate to raise a troop of horse on their behalf. William Prynne (1600–69) wrote a large number of violently Puritan tracts. John Vickars (?1580–1652) was a Presbyterian poet and author of attacks on the bishops, Catholics, and protestant sectarians. He also translated the *Aeneid*. James Harrington, to whom Butler alludes in his footnote, also translated six books of the *Aeneid* into English and was the author of the political romance *Oceana*.

p. 22 The customs used at bear-baitings are here ironically compared to the ceremonials at jousts and tournaments. At the latter a herald used to proclaim that 'no man . . . shall approach the lists nearer than four foot in distance' (Segar, *Booke of Honor and Armes*, 1590, viii. 79). At the bull-running at Tutbury in Staffordshire the spectators were warned to 'give way to the bull, none being to come near him by forty foot' (Plot, *Natural History of Staffordshire*, 1686, p. 439).

p. 23 These ideals were very frequently invoked in the Ordinances and political tracts during the early part of the Civil War. In 1643, for example, Parliament issued an Ordinance for the levying of money to maintain the army 'for the saving of the whole kingdom, our religion, laws and liberties from utter ruin and destruction'.

p. 23 In the Solemn League and Covenant between England and Scotland the parties agreed to preserve the Presbyterian Church in Scotland and to reform religion in England 'according to the word of God, and the example of the best reformed churches'.

p. 23 Parliament frequently accused the Jesuits of influencing Charles I and of attempting to subvert the established religion and government. The common soldiers, according to Clarendon, were persuaded that 'the King was in truth little better than imprisoned by evil counsellors, malignants, delinquents and cavaliers (the terms applied to his whole party)' (*History*, vi. 31).

p. 24 In ll. 755–63 Butler lists some of the main causes for which the Puritans claimed to be fighting. Breach of parliamentary privilege was the chief complaint made against Charles I by the five members of Parliament whom he accused of high treason in 1642. There was also said to be 'a malignant and pernicious design of subverting the fundamental laws and principles of government' ('The Grand

Remonstrance', 1641). In the Protestation, 1641, Parliament voted to defend 'the true reformed Protestant religion . . . as also the power and privilege of parliaments'. 'Liberty of conscience', says Clarendon, was, in 1647, 'the common argument and quarrel'.

p. 25   Socrates in Xenophon's *Memorabilia* (I. iv. 12) remarks that man, unlike the animals, has no fixed season for procreation.

p. 26   The torture of Christians by dogs is described in Tacitus, *Annales*, xv. xliv.

p. 28   Although the precise incident mentioned here has not been identified, there are several records of the killing of bears by Puritan officers as a result of the prohibition of bear-baiting by Parliament. The most notorious episode of this kind was the slaughter of some bears by Colonel Pride when he was High Sheriff of Surrey. See *The last Speech and dying Words of Thomas Pride; being touched in Conscience for his inhuman Murder of the Bears* (*Harleian Miscellany*, 1808–13, iii. 136). This document also mentions 'another lord of ours' who killed five bears and five fiddlers.

p. 29   In the blank space Butler refers to Sir Samuel Luke (d. 1670), the member for Bedford in the Long Parliament, who was captain of a troop of horse in the Civil War and scoutmaster-general to the Earl of Essex. Apparently as a consequence of the allusion in this line, the legend evolved that Butler was once actually employed by Luke. This idea, which is not mentioned by Butler's earliest biographers, John Aubrey and Anthony à Wood, first appeared in the anonymous life of the poet appended to the 1704 edition of *Hudibras*. The so-called 'Key to Hudibras', published as an appendix to the largely spurious *Posthumous Works* of Butler in 1715, identifies the hero of the poem with Luke and this very dubious hypothesis has often been accepted as a fact.

Hudibras

The First Part. Canto II

p. 30   The 'sage philosopher' is Empedocles of Acragas, who held that matter was composed of four 'roots', earth, air, fire, and water. They were set in motion and united or divided by two other substances which he called respectively 'love' and 'strife'.

p. 31   The Tartars were said to kill any stranger who lodged with them and who 'seemed of good presence and parts', 'supposing that those good parts of that man might abide afterwards in that house' (Purchas, *Pilgrimes*, 1625, III. I. iv. 92).

p. 31   There is a proverbial expression, included in some editions of the *Adages* of Erasmus, 'Amicus Plato, amicus Socrates, sed magis amica veritas' ('A friend to Plato, a friend to Socrates, but a greater friend to truth').

p. 31   Sir Thomas Browne writes that animals move '*per latera*, that is, two legs of one side together, which is tollutation or ambling; or *per diametrum*, lifting one foot before, and the cross foot behind, which is succussation or trotting' (*Pseudodoxia Epidemica*, IV. vi).

p. 31   This is possibly an allusion to the opening of Hobbes's *Leviathan* where the author suggests that man is capable of manufacturing an artificial animal: 'For seeing life is but a motion of limbs . . . why may we not say that all *automata* (engines that move themselves by springs and wheels as doth a watch) have an artificial life?'

p. 32   This is possibly an allusion to Descartes's *Discours de la méthode*, v, where he points out that, if there were machines with the outward appearance of a monkey or some other animal without reason, 'we should not have any means of ascertaining that they were not of the same nature as those animals.'

p. 32 This is an allusion to Lucan, i. 38:

> diros Pharsalia campos
> inpleat et Poeni saturentur sanguine manes.

'Let Pharsalia heap her awful plains with dead and the shade of the Carthaginian be glutted with carnage.'

p. 32 The authors mentioned in Butler's footnote who discuss the significance of the word 'penguin' include Sir Humphrey Gilbert, in his *True Report of the Late Discoveries of the New-found Landes*, 1583, iii, and David Powel in his *Historie of Cambria*, 1584, p. 229.

p. 34 Robert Plot records that when the Earls of Lancaster entertained many guests at Tutbury, musicians came to entertain them, 'amongst whom (being numerous) some quarrels and disorders now and then arising, it was found necessary after a while they should be brought under rules . . . and a Governor appointed them by the name of a King' (*Natural History of Staffordshire*, 1686, pp. 435–6). The bull-running alluded to in ll. 135–6 had no connection with the appointment of the minstrel king, but was held after his election, on the morning of the Assumption (Plot, pp. 439–40).

p. 34 Darius conspired with six other Persian noblemen to destroy the usurper Smerdis. They agreed that, after the death of Smerdis, the man whose horse was the first to neigh at sunrise should be king (Herodotus, iii. 85).

p. 34 Pegu is a town and district north-east of Rangoon. Elizabethan travellers returned from the East with tales of the great wealth, power, and cruelty of the kings of Pegu.

p. 35 A writ of error is brought to procure the reversal of a judgement in a court of law on the ground of error. A demurrer is a plea which, while admitting for the moment the facts as stated by the opponent, denies that he is legally entitled to relief and thus stops the action until this point can be determined by the court.

p. 35 ll. 175–98 refer to a passage in Trajano Boccalini's *Ragguagli di Parnasso*, quite a popular work, allusions to which would be recognized by Butler's readers. The episode describes how ambassadors arrived at the court of Apollo on behalf of all the gardeners of the world, complaining against the increase of weeds. They explained that they were encouraged to consult him having observed 'the miraculous instruments of drum and trumpet, at the sound whereof . . . pernicious plants of unuseful persons do of themselves willingly forsake the ground, to make room for . . . useful herbs of artificers and citizens'. Apollo replied that 'the instrument of drum and trumpets were granted for public peace' sake to princes, the sound whereof was cheerfully followed by such plants as took delight in dying' (*Advertisements from Parnassus*, trans. Henry Earl of Monmouth, 1657, Cent. I, Adv. xvi). Butler is apparently alluding at the same time to the petition by the House of Commons to Charles I that 'the kingdom might be put into a posture of defence'. The King refused to accede and would not approve an Ordinance drawn up for the raising of a militia. Finally Parliament claimed that 'his majesty . . . did by several messages invite them to settle the same by Act of Parliament' and on this authority a militia was raised (Clarendon, *History*, v. 118).

p. 36 This is one of several satirical references in the poem to belief in what is now called sympathetic magic. Robert Fludd describes a sympathetic ointment which would cure wounds when applied to a cloth dipped in the blood of a wounded man (*Doctor Fludd's Answer unto M. Foster*, 1631, p. 131). Sir Kenelm

Digby discusses sympathetic effects generally in his *Late Discourse . . . Touching the Cure of Wounds by the Powder of Sympathy*, 1658.

p. 37   The punishment of offenders by the sympathetic power of a red-hot poker is described by Digby (*Late Discourse*, pp. 126–7).

p. 38   George Sandys (*Travels*,1 673, 39) mentions a tribe which formed part of the army of the Grand Turk 'whose dead bodies do serve the Janizaries to fill up ditches'.

p. 39   The *corona civica* was awarded to men who had saved the life of a fellow-citizen in war.

p. 39   Ajax contended with Ulysses for the armour of Achilles and, having failed to win it, went mad with anger. He slaughtered a flock of sheep, imagining them to be the Greeks who had awarded the prize to Ulysses. Don Quixote mistook a flock of sheep for two contending armies and charged amongst them, killing those he supposed to be the enemy (I. iii. iv).

p. 40   'English Merlin' may not be the magician of Arthurian legend but the astrologer William Lilly who used this pseudonym when publishing almanacs.

p. 40   The sieve and shears were used for divination. The sieve was suspended from a pair of shears and a spell spoken over it. It was thought that the sieve would then turn when the name of a guilty person was mentioned.

p. 41   Aristotle declares that 'there is a type of manly valour; but valour in a woman, or unscrupulous cleverness, is inappropriate' (*Poetics*, xv). This view was developed during the Renaissance into the theory of 'propriety' of character.

p. 41   Pliny (*Natural History*, XL. xlix. 109) records that the males are stronger than the females in all animal species with the exception of panthers and bears.

p. 42   In the preface to *Gondibert* (1650), Davenant argues that the chief aids to government (religion, arms, policy, and law) are defective but can be strengthened by the power of poetry.

p. 42   In his Postscript to *Gondibert* (1651), Davenant claims, 'I intended in this poem to strip nature naked and clothe her again in the perfect shape of virtue.'

p. 45   The blank space in l. 498 should be filled with the name 'Waller'. After the Battle of Roundway Down near Devizes in 1643, Sir William Waller blamed the defeat of his forces on the Earl of Essex who, he said, had neglected to bring help 'out of envy at the great things he had done, which seemed to eclipse his glories' (Clarendon, *History*, vii. 120).

p. 45   In the early stages of the Civil War troops were raised by Parliament 'for the defence of the kingdom and of the King's person'.

p. 46   Early in 1642 Charles I went in person to the House of Commons to demand the submission of the five Members and Lord Kimbolton, whom he had accused of high treason. Having failed, the King withdrew and the accused men returned to Westminster in triumph. As they processed through the streets 'the pikemen had fastened to the tops of their pikes, and the rest in their hats or their bosoms, printed papers of the Protestation' (Clarendon, *History*, iv. 199).

p. 46   In ll. 527–80 the hero looks back on the early days of the Civil War. Clarendon records how the London mob assembled outside the House of Lords crying out 'No bishops, no popish lords' (*History*, iv. 111). On another occasion the people came near the two Houses, 'took out papers from their pockets and . . . would read the names of several persons under the title of "disaffected members of the House of Commons" ' (ibid. iv. 119).

p. 46   The Puritans objected to the use of vestments by ministers of the Church, on the ground that it was not enjoined in the Scriptures. The Presbyterians opposed the Anglican liturgy contained in the *Book of Common Prayer* and in 1645 Parliament decided to replace it by the *Directory for Public Worship*.

p. 47   In order to finance the militia Parliament issued propositions for bringing in money and plate, promising that those who supplied them should be repaid with interest of 8 per cent, 'for which they did engage the public faith' (Clarendon, v. 337).

p. 47   The Indians were said to catch wild elephants by luring them with tame female elephants (Purchas, *Pilgrimes*, II. x. iv. 1714).

p. 48   In 1647 the army presented a petition to Parliament demanding their arrears of pay and the assurance that they would not be subject to future conscription.

p. 48   In their attempts to persuade Charles I to raise a militia, Parliament arranged for petitions to be signed by the people, supporting their demands.

p. 48   The Solemn League and Covenant was drawn up in the name of the 'noblemen, barons . . . and commons of all sorts'. In it they declared their intention 'each one to go before another in the example of a real reformation'.

p. 49   The subscribers to the Solemn League and Covenant swore to undertake the reformation of religion 'according to the word of God, and the example of the best reformed churches'.

p. 49   At the Convocation of Canterbury in 1640 the clergy agreed to resist the alteration of the government of the Church by 'archbishops, bishops, deans, and archdeacons, etc.'. The vagueness of the concluding 'etc.' was deliberately misinterpreted by the Puritans as a mandate for any kind of repression the Anglicans might choose to introduce.

p. 51   An Ordinance of 1643 appointed committees of sequestrators to seize the lands of Royalist supporters and sell them to raise money for the Parliamentarian forces.

p. 55   In *Don Quixote* the hero's squire, Sancho Panza, is pulled from his ass and tossed in a blanket (I. III. iii).

p. 58   By the Self-Denying Ordinance of 1645 it became unlawful for 'any member of either House of Parliament to hold any office or command in the army, or any place or employment of profit in the state'.

p. 58   The nine worthies were often represented in Elizabethan pageants and shows, as in the last act of *Loves Labour's Lost*. The nine heroes who qualified for this honour varied from one pageant to another but most frequently included Joshua, Hector, David, Alexander the Great, Judas Maccabæus, Julius Caesar, King Arthur, Charlemagne, and Guy of Warwick.

p. 61   After his notorious victory at Drogheda in Ireland, Cromwell executed the whole garrison 'not sparing those upon second thoughts to whom in the heat of the action they promised and gave quarter' (Clarendon, *View of the Affairs of Ireland*, lxxxii. 96).

p. 63   'Like hermit poor in pensive place' is the opening line of a popular lyric attributed to Raleigh, and printed in *The Phoenix Nest*, 1593.

p. 63   Sir Bernard Gascoigne, a Florentine, originally named Guasconi, fought with the Royalists until his capture in 1648. His fellow prisoners were all executed but Gascoigne was spared and returned to his friends. His captors had decided that, if he were executed, 'their friends or children who should visit Italy might pay dear for many generations' (Clarendon, *History*, xi. 107).

Hudibras

The First Part. Canto III

p. 64   The opening of this canto is a parody of the opening of *The Faerie Queene*, I. viii:

> Ay me, how many perils do enfold
> The righteous man, to make him daily fall?

p. 64   Thomas Campion wrote a very popular lyric with the opening lines:

> What if a day, or a month, or a year
> Crown thy delights with a thousand sweet contentings?
> Cannot a chance of a night or an hour
> Cross thy desires with as many sad tormentings?

p. 66   The ballad of Chevy Chase includes the stanza

> For Witherington needs must I wail
>   As one in doleful dumps,
> For when his legs were smitten off,
>   He fought upon his stumps.

p. 67   These lines are a parody of Virgil's description of the female warrior Camilla who is said to have run faster than the winds and been able to skim over the corn without harming it (*Aeneid*, vii. 808–11).

p. 68   When he was an infant, Achilles' mother plunged him in the river Styx and made every part of his body invulnerable, apart from the heel by which she held him.

p. 68   William Prynne, a barrister, John Bastwick, a doctor, and Henry Burton, a cleric, were convicted of seditious libel in 1637, and were condemned to prison and to have their ears cut off in the pillory (Clarendon, *History*, iii. 58, 62).

p. 68   The 'authors' referred to are, in fact, one author, Virgil, and these lines are adapted from *Aeneid*, i. 691–4.

p. 69   The echo-device, to which Butler alludes and which he later parodies, had been used by Ovid in the *Metamorphoses* (iii. 380–92), was a popular device in the English masque—for example, Jonson's *Cynthia's Revels*—and may be found in poems by George Herbert and Lord Herbert of Cherbury.

p. 82   It is said that, on his death, the body of Richard III was thrown on to a horse and carried off the battlefield into a monastery at Leicester (Grafton, Continuation of Hardynge's *Chronicle*, 1812, p. 547).

p. 85   Scipio is reported as saying that he would rather save a single citizen than slay a thousand foes ('Life of Antoninus Pius', *Historia Augusta*, ix. 9).

p. 85   Virgil's Camilla, of whom Trulla is in part a parody, also plunders the dead for spoils (*Aeneid*, xi. 781–2).

p. 89   The 'Amazon' Radigund, having overcome Artegall, also makes him wear women's clothing as a mark of shame (Spenser, *Faerie Queene*, v. v. 20).

p. 91   In ll. 1013–38 Butler parodies the principles of the Stoics. Seneca declares that the mind is independent of the body, can never suffer exile, and is at home anywhere in the world. The body, in which the soul is imprisoned, is tossed hither and thither, whereas the soul cannot be harmed (*Ad Helviam Matrem de Consolatione*, xi. 6–7).

p. 92   On being told of Democritus' opinion that there was an infinite number of worlds, Alexander the Great cried out in despair that he had conquered only one (Valerius Maximus, viii. xiv). Diogenes is said to have told Alexander that he himself was superior to the King, for whereas he had no needs, Alexander was never satisfied (Cicero, *Tusculan Disputations*, v. xxxii. 92).

p. 92   The distinction between and relative claims of the active and the contemplative life was a traditional subject for debate. It appears to have originated with the Stoics (e.g. Seneca, *Epistolae Morales*, xciv. 45).

p. 95   Commissioners and Triers were appointed by Parliament in 1646. The Triers were appointed to ensure that only men fitted for the office should be elected as elders of the Presbyterian Church in each parish.   The Commissioners were required to judge people accused of 'scandalous offences' and, if necessary, to suspend them from the holy sacraments.

p. 96   'Smeck' is an abbreviation of 'Smectymnuus', the pseudonym formed from the initials of five Presbyterian divines. They were joint authors of *An Answer to a Book entitled An Humble Remonstrance*, 1640, an attack on episcopacy which provoked several replies and initiated a celebrated public controversy in which Milton defended the authors.

p. 96   There is here an ironic reversal of the traditional concept that 'dominion is founded in grace' and that kings are entitled to temporal power because they are elected by God. Butler implies that, once they had power, the Presbyterians could freely lay claim to divine grace.

p. 97   Both Gregory VII and Boniface VIII succeeded in enlarging the temporal power of the papacy. The allusion, however, is to the office in general rather than to any specific popes.

p. 98   On succeeding Solomon as king, Rehoboam was advised to say to his people 'My little finger shall be thicker than my father's loins . . . My father chastised you with whips, but I will chastise you with scorpions' (I Kings 12 : 10–11).

p. 99   It was said that, in order to avoid the error of electing a woman pope, as was thought to have happened in the case of Pope Joan, the sex of the successful candidate was examined. 'When any pope is first placed in the porphyry chair, which has a hole made for the purpose, his genitals are handled by the youngest deacon' (Baptista Platina, *Lives of the Popes*, 1688, p. 165).

p. 100   Aristotle often uses the name Socrates when indicating, for purposes of argument, a particular man.

p. 100   Aristotle defines a man as an animal that walks on two feet (*Topica*, v. i; vi. 3).

p. 100   It was a common belief, derived from ancient times, that bear cubs were born formless and were literally licked into shape by their parents.

p. 102   Before he set out to fight Goliath, David put on the armour of Saul, 'and David said unto Saul, "I cannot go with these, for I have not proved them." And David put them off him' (I Samuel 17 : 39).

Hudibras

The Second Part. Canto I

p. 104   Butler's description of Fame is a parody of Virgil's description of Rumour (*Aeneid*, iv. 173 ff.). Like Butler's Fame, Rumour flies with wings and is covered with eyes, tongues, and ears. She is also the bearer of both false and true reports.

p. 105   It was the custom to hang a whetstone about the neck of notorious liars as they stood in the pillory; hence the proverbial expression 'He lies for the whetstone' (*ODEP* 882).

p. 105   This couplet is a parody of *Aeneid*, iv. 196–7, where Rumour incenses King Iarbas.

p. 107   An allusion to the ghostly drummer who is said to have haunted the house of one John Mompesson (Joseph Glanvill, *Sadducismus Triumphatus*, 1681, ii. 89).

p. 108   Hudibras again resorts to Stoic principles in order to console himself.

p. 109   John Frederick, Duke of Saxony (1503–54), was notoriously fat. The bishop mentioned in Butler's footnote is Archbishop Hatto of Mainz who, according to popular legend, massacred the poor people of his country and, as a punishment, was devoured by mice.

p. 112   According to Sir Kenelm Digby, wine ferments violently during the period when the vines are in flower. This is another allusion to Digby's belief in sympathetic magic (*Late Discourse . . . Touching the Cure of Wounds*, 1658, p. 79).

p. 112   The Romans were thought to have devised a sepulchral lamp which burned perpetually without fresh supplies of oil. These lamps were the subject of speculations by members of the Royal Society and were discussed by Fortunius Licetus in *De Lucernis Antiquorum Reconditis*, Venice, 1621.

p. 114   On his dissolution of Parliament in 1653 Cromwell told the House that its members were 'whoremasters' and 'corrupt and unjust men' (Bulstrode Whitelock, *Memorials*, Oxford, 1853, iv. 5).

p. 114   Bonaventure tells how the devil tempted Saint Francis with lustful desires, whereupon the saint plunged naked into the snow and piled up seven heaps of it. ' "Behold," saith he, "this larger heap is thy wife, these four be two sons and two daughters, the other twain be a serving man and maid, that thou must needs have to serve thee. Now bestir thee and clothe them, for they be perishing with cold. But if manifold cares on their behalf trouble thee, do thou be careful to serve the one Lord." Then the tempter departed, routed' (*Life of St. Francis*, v. 4).

p. 115   A hymn written by Robert Wisdom, appended to the metrical versions of the psalms and included in many seventeenth-century editions of the Bible, contained the verse:

> Preserve us Lord, by thy dear word,
> From Turk and Pope defend us, Lord,
> Both which would thrust out of his throne
> Our Lord Christ Jesus, thy dear Son.

p. 115   If a husband were out of the kingdom or, as the law expressed it, *ex quatuor maria* ('outside the four seas') for nine months or more, the children born to his wife during that time were legally considered to be bastards (Blackstone, *Commentaries on the Laws of England*, 4 vols., 1809, I. xvi).

p. 116   In the manufacture of charcoal, bundles of wood were set up in the shape of a cone and covered with turf.   Holes were left at the bottom of the cone to let in the air. Combustion could be controlled by blocking the holes.

p. 119   The Indians were said to have such thick skulls that, if they were hit on the head with a sword, the sword would break, leaving the head unharmed (Purchas, *Pilgrimes*, III. v. iii. 993).

p. 119   For the source of Butler's footnote, see Francis Bacon, *Sylva Sylvarum*, x. 957.

p. 120   It was a Roman custom, when drinking the health of a mistress, to pour into the glass a certain quantity of wine for each letter in her name (Martial, *Epigrams*, I. lxxi).

p. 124   The law required a man who found cattle straying on his land to announce at the local market that he had them. If they were not claimed within a year and a day they belonged to the finder. As long as he kept them he was bound to supply them with provisions.

p. 125   Butler's note refers to Sir Kenelm Digby's *Treatise of Bodies*, *Two Treatises*, Paris, 1644, pp. 247–8.

p. 126   The Prince of Cambay was said to have consumed so much poison that he put people to death by spitting on them, and killed his concubines by copulating with them (Purchas, *Pilgrimage*, 1625, V. viii. i. 537).

p. 127   In ll. 817–24 there are references to the punishment inflicted on rogues and vagabonds. The offenders were whipped and escorted to the parish where they were born, having been given a testimonial signed by a justice of the peace certifying that they had been punished.

p. 129   Allusions in popular ballads suggest that the 'certain lady' is the wife of William, Lord Monson, Lord Chief Justice of Common Pleas. There are references to his whipping in 'A Proper New Ballad of the Old Parliament' and 'Chips of the Old Block', both included in *A Collection of Loyal Songs*, vol. ii.

Hudibras

The Second Part. Canto II

p. 131   Jean Baptiste van Helmont (1577–1644), the Belgian chemist and physician, engaged in violent controversy with the theological faculties at Louvain and Cologne, and with his greatest enemy, a certain van Heer. Thomas White (1593–1676), a Catholic theologian and philosopher, was involved in continual controversy against the Protestants and earned the censure of his own Church. Tully is Marcus Tullius Cicero whom Butler presumably includes because of his orations and polemical writings.

p. 131   Butler's notion that large numbers of people were killed in academic disputes is derived from a misreading of Diogenes Laertius who actually wrote (*Zeno*, vi) that the philosopher Zeno used to discourse in the same colonnade where, at the time of the Thirty, 1,400 Athenian citizens had been put to death.

p. 132   In the *Epistolae Morales* (cxiii. 2), the Stoic philosopher Seneca argues that virtue (*bonum*) is a living thing. The Latin word he uses for 'living thing' is *animal*.

p. 135   Plate was brought in after the publication of 'Propositions for the bringing in of money or plate' to maintain the army and 'for the preservation of the public peace', 1642. In these propositions reference was made to the 'Protestation', sworn a year earlier, to defend 'the true reformed Protestant religion'.

p. 135   The subscribers to the 'Protestation' swore to defend 'the true reformed Protestant religion expressed in the doctrine of the Church of England' and 'to defend His Majesty's royal person and estate'. Both these oaths were subsequently broken.

p. 135   The terms of the 'Solemn League and Covenant' (1643) were contradicted by those of the 'Engagement' (1649). In the former the subscribers vowed to preserve the person and authority of the King, whereas in the latter they swore to defend the parliamentary resolution to establish the country as a republic 'without King or House of Lords'.

p. 136   In 1642 both Houses voted that 'an army should be raised for the safety of the King's person . . . That the Earl of Essex should be their general, and that they would live and die with him' (Clarendon, *History*, v. 388). Three years later Essex was compelled to resign his commission as a consequence of the 'Self-Denying Ordinance'.

p. 136   In several of its resolutions during the early 1640s, including, for example, the 'Protestation', Parliament swore to 'defend the lawful rights and liberties of the subjects'.

p. 136   'The defence of both Houses of Parliament' was a phrase frequently included in parliamentary ordinances at the beginning of the Civil War. Yet in 1649 the Commons abolished the House of Lords in the belief that it was 'useless and dangerous to the people of England to be continued' (Clarendon, *History*, xi. 247).

p. 136   During the disputes between the army and Parliament in 1647 Cromwell was accused of stirring up hostility towards the government among his troops while at the same time assuring the House that the army would disband peaceably if it were so commanded (Clarendon, x. 88).

p. 136   In 'Pride's Purge' of 1648, the troops commanded by Colonel Pride blocked the entrance to the Commons and prevented the admission of Members who were unsympathetic to Cromwell's party.

p. 137   Priscian was a celebrated Latin grammarian. 'To break Priscian's head' was a proverbial expression meaning 'to violate the rules of grammar' (*ODEP* 82). Butler here alludes to the Quakers' strict usage of 'thou' and 'thee' rather than 'you' for the second person singular.

p. 138   There was a belief, challenged by Sir Thomas Browne, that every creature in the sea had its equivalent on land. The dogfish and sea horse were obvious examples (Browne, *Pseudodoxia Epidemica*, III. xxiv).

p. 140   In his edition of *Hudibras* (1793) T. R. Nash commented on this obscure allusion 'Our ancestors, when they found it difficult to carve a goose, a hare, or other dish, used to say in jest, they should hit the joint if they could think of the name of a cuckold.'

p. 140   A commonly practised form of witchcraft consisted in making an effigy of one's victim out of clay, wax, or wood and tormenting it with nails in the belief that the wounds would be transmitted to the victim by sympathetic magic.

p. 142   The 'glass drops' were a subject of much speculation by the members of the Royal Society shortly after the Restoration. Molten glass was dropped into cold water and allowed to solidify. It was noticed that, if the thin end of the glass drop were snapped off, the whole piece broke into many small fragments (Robert Hooke, *Micrographia*, 1667, vii. 33).

p. 145   Edmund Bonner, Bishop of London in the reign of Mary, became notorious for his violent persecution of Protestants. His conduct is described in John Foxe's *Acts and Monuments*, 1596, pp. 1853–4.

p. 146   The New Model Army, formed after the Self-Denying Ordinance of 1645, was commanded largely by Independent Sectarians, of whom Ralpho is a representative.

p. 146   The Assembly of Divines, which had been constituted in order to draw up a reformed system of church government and worship, remained in session for over five and a half years.

p. 148   The procession encountered by Hudibras and Ralpho is a Skimmington, an English folk ceremony, now extinct. It was inflicted on unpopular members of the community, particularly shrewish or unfaithful wives. It generally consisted of a procession with drums and rough music, leading in two people on horseback, a woman impersonating the wife seated in front and facing forwards, and a man impersonating the husband, facing backwards and seated behind the woman. There is a description of a Skimmington in Marvell's 'Last Instructions to a Painter'; it is discussed in E. K. Chambers's *Medieval Stage*, i. 153, and occurs in a central episode of Hardy's *Mayor of Casterbridge*.

p. 148   The Swedish cavalry, reorganized by Gustavus Adolphus, was arranged three or four ranks deep and charged at a gallop independently of the infantry. These tactics were introduced into the Royalist army by Prince Rupert and were in turn adopted by Cromwell in the New Model Army.

p. 152   In a ceremony held annually on the feast of the Ascension, the Duke of Venice was betrothed to the sea by going out together with the principal officers of the city and throwing a ring into the waves as a token of his lordship over them.

Hudibras

The Second Part. Canto III

p. 157   Birds used to be caught by means of a bell, a light, and a net. The sound of the bell and the brilliance of the light is said to have induced the birds to remain still while the net was placed over them.

p. 158   The Roman augurs foretold good or ill fortune by observing the flight of certain birds. The auspices taken from the feeding of chickens was used on military expeditions. If the birds refused to eat the sign was unfavourable; if they ate eagerly the sign was good.

p. 160   By a Parliamentary Ordinance of 1645, persons discovered consulting a 'witch, wizard or fortune-teller' were to be suspended from the sacrament of the Lord's supper.

p. 161   Matthew Hopkins, the notorious 'witchfinder' of Suffolk, boasted that in one year he had brought sixty witches to the gallows, among whom was John Lowes, Vicar of Brandeston, to whom Butler alludes in his footnote. See Matthew Hopkins, *Discovery of Witches*, 1647, and Notestein, *History of Witchcraft*, Washington, 1911, p. 164.

p. 161   One method used by Hopkins for enforcing confessions of witchcraft was to place his prisoner cross-legged and bound in the middle of a room and to keep her without food, drink, or sleep for at least twenty-four hours. Reduced to a weakened condition by this treatment, his victim would then confess.

p. 161   The notion that Hopkins was 'swum' and, since he floated, was subsequently hanged gained considerable currency. It was denied by Hopkins himself in his *Discovery of Witches* published shortly before his death.

p. 161   During a stay in his castle on the Wartburg in Germany, Luther is said to have been many times tempted by the devil whom he firmly resisted (*Colloquia Mensalia, or the Familiar Discourses of Martin Luther*, 1791, p. 342).

p. 162   François Perreaud, a Calvinist minister of Mascon, describes the haunting of his house by an evil spirit which sang obscene songs. The account of this incident is given in 'L'Antidémon de Mascon', appended to his *Démonologie*, Geneva, 1653.

p. 162   Edward Kelly was employed by the astrologer and mathematician John Dee (1527–1608) as a medium for establishing contact with the world of spirits. Dee kept a record of his conversations with the spirits, a large part of which was published with a Preface by Meric Casaubon, prebend of Canterbury and son of the classical scholar Isaac Casaubon, to whom Butler alludes in his footnote.

p. 162   In 1634 Urbain Grandier, a priest of Loudun, was burned for witchcraft and diabolical possession. He was accused by the Ursuline nuns of Loudun of having caused them to be possessed of devils. Two years earlier an attempt had been made to exorcize the nuns, in the course of which conversations took place between the exorcists and the devils by whom the nuns were possessed. The

'French book' mentioned in Butler's note is presumably Père Tranquille's *Véritable Relation . . . de la possession des Ursulines de Loudun*, Paris, 1634.

p. 162 Butler here seems to identify Sidrophel with the astrologer William Lilly, who was employed by Parliament on several occasions, notably at the siege of Colchester, where he predicted a speedy victory for the Parliamentarian forces.

p. 164 The hermetic philosophers adapted from Plato the doctrine of the world of ideas, attributing to it the power of governing matter in the physical world. 'Every species', writes Cornelius Agrippa, 'hath its celestial shape, or figure that is suitable to it, from which also proceeds a wonderful power of operating, which proper gift it receives from its own *idea*' (*Occult Philosophy*, 1651, pp. 26–7).

p. 164 The Elizabethan astrologer John Dee published a Preface to Billingsley's translation of Euclid's *Elements*, 1570. His 'preface before the devil' is presumably the account of his communication with supernatural powers (see note to II. iii. 163). Edward Kelly was his assistant. The two men were for a time entertained by Albert Laski, Count Palatine of Siradia, who hoped that their experiments might lead to the discovery of the philosopher's stone. They were later received at the court of the Emperor Rudolph II of Austria. Butler's source is again Casaubon's Preface to Dee's *True and Faithful Relation*, 1659.

p. 166 In the Servile War of 134 B.C. Eunus, a Sicilian slave, gained the leadership over his fellow slaves by breathing fire from his mouth and claiming to have the gift of prophecy. He did so by concealing a nut inside his mouth, filled with sulphur which he ignited.

p. 166 The philosopher and alchemist Paracelsus claimed to have discovered that human sperm, enclosed in a glass vessel and suitably treated, would develop into a human being of diminutive size (*Of the Nature of Things*, trans. J. F., 1650, pp. 8–9).

p. 166 In ll. 305–22 Butler satirizes recent observations made with the microscope, particularly those carried out by Robert Hooke and subsequently described in Hooke's *Micrographia*, 1665. Hooke gives an account of the pulsing of a louse's blood and mentions the 'many small milk-white vessels which crossed over the breast'. Elsewhere he describes the 'proboscis or probe' which he observed between the feelers of a flea, the mites which live on putrefying substances, and the 'eels' which he perceived in vinegar (*Micrographia*, pp. 210–17).

p. 167 Some commentators, assuming that Sidrophel is a portrait of the astrologer William Lilly, have identified Whachum with John Booker, another astrologer who was for a time associated with Lilly. The early lines do seem to refer to Booker's career as a scrivener. Lilly records that Booker 'wrote singularly well both Secretary and Roman' and that he became clerk to an alderman of London (*History of his Life and Times*, 1715, p. 28). The whole portrait, however, is general rather than personal.

p. 167 The almanacs, prepared by astrologers and sold in the streets, generally contained short verses describing the astrological features of each month. Lilly comments that John Booker wrote 'excellent verses upon the twelve months' (*Life and Times*, 1715, p. 28). Most almanacs also included a table showing the dates when the law terms began and ended, and a list of 'return days' when the sheriff had to make a return to the courts declaring how far he had carried out their instructions.

p. 169 The bird of paradise was thought to have no legs and therefore to remain constantly in flight throughout its life. In heraldry the martlet is generally represented without feet.

p. 170 Descartes discusses the experiment with the cannon ball several times in his letters, published in Paris between 1657 and 1667.

p. 171   William Sedgwick (?1610–?69), a Puritan mystic, was chief preacher in Ely. He became convinced that the day of judgement would fall on a certain date and retired to a house in the country to prepare for it. (Wood, *Athenae Oxonienses*, 1813–20, iii. 894).

p. 175   Le Blanc records that, in his travels, he saw a magician who, observing that a storm was approaching, made a hole in the ground, urinated into it, and spoke certain words, after which the storm moved elsewhere (*The World Surveyed*, 1660, p. 302).

p. 176   Cornelius Agrippa was accused of necromancy by Paulus Jovius (*Elogia Doctorum Virorum*, Basle, 1556, p. 237) who charged him with keeping an attendant devil in the shape of a black dog. Agrippa was defended against this accusation by Thomas Vaughan ('the author of *Magia Adamica*' of Butler's footnote) in the Preface to his *Anima Magica Abscondita*, 1650.

p. 176   Zoroaster, Pythagoras, and Apollonius of Tyana were all considered to be 'prisci magi' or precursors of the hermetic philosophy. All three were mystics and were said to have possessed the powers of divination and healing. Their relationship to this tradition is discussed in E. M. Butler, *Myth of the Magus*, Cambridge, 1948.

p. 178   The source of the story of the mother of Cyrus is Herodotus, i. 107–8.

p. 181   When Rome was attacked by the Gauls in 390 B.C., the Capitol was saved by the cackling of the geese in the temple of Juno. They woke the guard who roused his comrades and warded off the attackers (Livy, v. xlvii. 4).

p. 185   In his translation of Horace's *Epodes* Sir Richard Fanshawe rendered the Latin *idus* as 'Michaelmas' and *calendae* as 'our Lady' (the names of the quarter-days). See *Selected Parts of Horace . . . put into English*, 1652, p. 64.

p. 188   In the anonymous and spurious Second Part of *Hudibras*, published in 1663 between Butler's own First and Second parts, the hero visits Kingston-on-Thames where he inveighs against the May Games, much in the same way as he had attacked the bear-baiting in the First Part. He is again attacked by a mob and later set upon by dogs (*Hudibras, The Second Part*, 1663, p. 15; p. 70).

p. 188   In the second canto of the spurious *Hudibras* the knight meets a French mountebank who is attempting to sell quack medicines and who subsequently robs Hudibras as he lies asleep.

p. 189   The pendulum experiment was performed by Sir Christopher Wren at a meeting of the Royal Society in 1662, on the basis of which he proposed to establish a universal standard of measurement.

p. 192   The story of the fox which, in order to save itself from the hounds, hung by its teeth on a gallows, is told by Sir Kenelm Digby. Digby affirms that the fox's ingenuity is not the effect of reason, but a result of impressions received upon the animal's organs of sense (*Two Treatises*, Paris, 1644, pp. 312–17).

The Elephant in the Moon

p. 195   Date of composition: most probably during the 1670–1 controversy between the Royal Society scientists and Henry Stubbe (see l. 431). Lines from the poem recur in 'An Heroical Epistle of Hudibras to Sidrophel' (pub. 1674). Butler rewrote 'The Elephant' in heroic couplets, making a few interesting additions, but losing the conciseness of the short verse. Butler draws on John Wilkins's *Discovery of a World in the Moon*, 1638 (enl. 1640), and through Wilkins—or perhaps directly—on Johannes Kepler's *Somnium*, 1634. There are significant parallels in *The Virtuoso*, 1676, by Thomas Shadwell, who apparently knew Butler and thus perhaps 'The Elephant'. Whatever their original conception, the

finished portraits do not point unambiguously to particular members of the
Royal Society.

p. 195   The 'Down Survey' of Ireland in 1655–6 was conducted by Sir William
Petty, who was later acquitted of a charge that he had 'stolen' nearly 20,000
acres for himself and accepted bribes. Petty was an early member of the Royal
Society.

p. 196   'Pythagoreans . . . did affirm . . . that those living creatures and plants
which are in her exceed any of the like with us in the same proportion as their
days are longer than ours: *viz.* by 15 times' (Wilkins, *Discovery*, p. 81). Kepler
had argued that such large men could not find sufficient stones to build houses,
and must therefore live in vast underground caverns (Wilkins, p. 124).

p. 197   Sir Kenelm Digby had speculated on the interchangeability of senses
(*Treatise of Bodies*, 1644, ch. xxviii). Butler attributed seeing with ears to the
Rosicrucians in 'An Hermetic Philosopher' and in *Hudibras*, III. iii. 15–16.

p. 197   'The Arcadians . . . were esteemed of great antiquity, and it was usually
said they were before the moon' (Browne, *Pseudodoxia*, VI. i.).

p. 198   The speaker draws for his hypothesis on traditional beliefs that the
Arcadians were the most rustic and the most musical of the Greeks.

p. 198   The Royal Society planned 'what is to be observed in the production,
growth, advancing, or transforming of vegetables; what particulars are requisite
for collecting a complete history of the agriculture which is used in several parts
of this nation' (Thomas Sprat, *History of the R. S.*, 1667 (fac. 1958), p. 156).
John Evelyn published *A Philosophical Discourse of Earth* (1676) and, earlier,
Pomona . . . concerning Fruit-Trees in relation to Cider (1664). *Pomona* included
papers by five other Society members, and Butler alludes to the work in l. 116.

p. 199   The argument runs: Arcadia and Epirus were both parts of Greece;
the people of Epirus used elephants; 'hence' the Arcadians used elephants.
The Privolvans use elephants; 'hence' the Privolvans are Arcadians.

p. 200   An opinion urged by Giordano Bruno (1548–1600), and taken up by
Butler himself (see p. 272).

p. 200   Thales and Anaximander (sixth century B.C.) believed that the stars were
points at which the empyreum or sphere of pure fire broke or shone into the
enclosed sphere of air.

p. 200   A reference to the Society's blood transfusions, the first of which was
performed between two dogs in November 1666. The following year a mangy
dog was bled into a sound one, and the French reported reviving an old dog
with blood from a young one.

p. 201   An elder tree, on which Judas was reputed to have hanged himself, was
supposed to have magic powers, and elder twigs were carried in the pockets of
riding breeches to prevent chafing. See Browne, *Pseudodoxia*, I. viii. 4; II. vii. 8.

p. 205   Butler left the first half of this line blank (and, in Thyer's opinion,
intended it to remain blank); 'At last prevailed' is introduced from the long-
verse 'Elephant'.

p. 206   The speaker appropriates an argument from the Society's opponents,
who invoked from Genesis 3 the archetypal equation of knowledge with undoing.
Cf. *Paradise Lost*, ix. 1070 ff.

p. 208   'Some Wiltshire rustics, . . . seeing the figure of the moon in a pond,
attempted to rake it out' (Grose, *Provincial Glossary*, s.v. 'Wiltshire').

p. 208   The formula 'Strange News from . . .' was a favourite with pamphleteers;
e.g. *Strange and Terrible News from Cambridge*, 1659.

Satire upon the Royal Society

p. 209 Date of composition: probably about the same time as 'The Elephant'; fairly certainly later than Sprat's *History* (1667). Sprat records that the Fellows 'have composed queries and directions what things . . . are to be taken notice of towards a perfect history of the air and atmosphere and weather. . . . They have prescribed exact inquiries, and given punctual advice, for the trial of experiments of rarefaction, refraction, and condensation; . . . of the loadstone; . . . of currents; of the ebbing and flowing of the sea . . .' (p. 156). It is interesting that some of the problems which Butler mocks in this poem he gave serious thought to in his 'miscellaneous observations' (see pp. 270–2).

p. 209 The Royal Society collected 'histories' of the 1664 comet, and the astrologer William Lilly forecast (correctly) war and plague.

p. 210 See 'An Essay of Dr. John Wallis, Exhibiting His Hypothesis about the Flux and Reflux of the Sea', *Philosophical Transactions*, i (1666), 263–89.

p. 210 For Newton's theory of colours, see *Phil. Trans.* vi (1672), 3075–87; but Butler need only have read Robert Boyle's hypothesis that 'the beams of light, modified by the bodies whence they are sent (reflected or refracted) to the eye, produce there that kind of sensation men commonly call colour' (*Experiments and Considerations touching Colours*, 1663, I. v. 5).

p. 210 Butler himself could imagine no adequate source for springs unless underground rivers ran uphill to feed them (see p. 272). The physics of this process had been expounded by J. C. Scaliger (*De Subtiltate* 1557, ex. xlvi).

p. 210 Demonstrated by Samuel Colepress (*Phil. Trans.* ii. (1667) 500–1).

p. 211 Xenophanes (sixth century B.C.) held that the moon was quenched and rekindled every month.

p. 211 For Robert Boyle's report on weighing air, see *Phil. Trans.* iii. (1668) 845–50.

p. 211 On reviving flowers, see Sir Thomas Browne, *Religio Medici*, I. xlvii, and Joseph Glanvill, *Vanity of Dogmatizing*, 1661 (fac. 1931), p. 46.

p. 211 In such cases as the stick in water appearing bent it was a question whether deceptive refraction occurred in the sense mechanism or in the phenomena perceived.

Satire upon our Ridiculous Imitation of the French

p. 212 Date of composition: most probably in the early 1670s. Petticoat breeches were shortened after 1670 (ll. 19–22), and the oath *jarnie* (*jernie*, l. 123) is favoured by the modish Monsieur de Paris in Wycherley's *The Gentleman Dancing Master* (1672). Butler had visited, and disliked, France in 1670. Finally, there are similarities between this poem and the 'Duval' ode (written 1670–1).

To the Happy Memory of the most Renowned Duval

p. 216 Date of composition: the highwayman Duval was hanged on 21 Jan. 1670. In the same year was published an anonymous prose pamphlet, *The Memoires of Monsieur Du Vall*, written (tongue in cheek) by Dr. Walter Pope. From this Butler took the idea, and some details, for his ode, pub. 1671 ('By the Author of *Hudibras*'). The manuscript used by Thyer for the *Genuine Remains* incorporated minor alterations; the present edition uses Thyer's version. (For a facsimile of ed. 1671, see Samuel Butler, *Three Poems*, ed. A. C. Spence, 1961.)

Claude Duval was born in Normandy in 1643, and first came to England at the Restoration as a servant of the Duke of Richmond.

p. 216   Marco Polo records the custom of burning with the corpse pictures of whatever will be needed in the after-life (*Travels*, I. xxxvii *ad fin.*).

p. 219   The Excise and the Hearth Tax were the most unpopular sources of Charles II's revenue, and farming them out to private collectors made them more odious still. Excise was levied on beer, ale, cider, aqua vitae, tea, coffee, chocolate, and sherbet; Hearth Money was 2*s*. per annum on each fire-hearth or stove.

p. 219   Punctuation of ll. 120–5 follows the sense of ed. 1671. Thyer's punctuation in *Genuine Remains* implies: the lawyer had been sentencing meaner criminals than Duval, but his giving Duval quarter involved the lawyer's own doom once he left his garrison.

p. 220   See, e.g., Pliny, *Natural History*, VIII. xxxviii. 91.

p. 221   For Butler's parody of the heroic conflict between love and honour, see 'Cat and Puss'.

p. 221   In place of ll. 194–6, ed. 1671 reads:

> They life itself began to hate,
> And all the world besides disdain. . . .

Repartees between Cat and Puss

p. 223   The heroic play is explained by Dryden in his Preface (1672) to *The Conquest of Granada* (acted 1670–1), in which the love debates between Almanzor and Almahide are a good example of the rhetoric Butler parodies. The Duke of Buckingham's heroic parody, *The Rehearsal*, was acted in 1671, and Butler may have been one of his employer's coauthors. This would have been an appropriate moment for the composition of 'Cat and Puss'; but there is no certain evidence, and heroic plays were in vogue from the mid-1660s to the mid-1670s.

Upon Critics who Judge of Modern Plays

p. 227   Butler's MS., ff. 124^r–125^r; Thyer's title. Date of composition: following Thomas Rymer's *Tragedies of the Last Age*, pub. late summer 1677. In that critique Rymer fell upon the 'incorrect' plays of Beaumont and Fletcher, and a few weeks later he published a tragedy of his own, *Edgar*, to which Butler could allude in his closing lines. See also Dryden's 'Heads of an Answer to Rymer'.

p. 227   'The poet here very wittily considers the muse under the tyrannous direction of critics as a person found idiot or lunatic by a jury, who is not at liberty to act for himself but as his guardian shall order' (Thyer).

p. 227   Cf. p. 284–5 and 'Upon the Royal Society', l. 87. Torricelli's barometric experiment was performed by the Royal Society 'with water in a glass cane thirty-six and forty feet high . . .' (Sprat, *History of the R.S.*, p. 220).

p. 227   The story is that Whittington's cat was bought by the king of Barbary for a vast sum to rid his land of rats and mice. Thus the poor scullion became a rich man and Lord Mayor of London. A Whittington play, by Thomas Payver, was entered in the Stationers' Company Register in 1604. See also note to p. 250.

p. 227   Tragedy 'through pity and fear effects the purgation of those emotions' (Aristotle, *Poetics*, vi. 2. 1449^b).

p. 227   'So Euripides' Hippolytus is to be destroyed because Venus took pet at his being too chaste' (Thyer).

p. 228   Thyer suspects that Butler has Oedipus in mind. Here and in the lines following Butler refers to Aristotle's definition of the tragic hero as a man between extremes of good and bad, whose misfortunes result from some error or flaw of character (*Poetics*, xiii. 2–3. 1453ᵃ).

p. 228 Butler links the Welsh lawgiver king Howel the Good (d. 950) with 'an old superstitious custom of marriage's being looked upon as allowable at certain times, and not allowable at others' (Thyer). See J. H. Blunt, *Dict. of Doctrinal and Historical Theology*, s.v. 'Marriage vi'.

p. 229 Cf. Dryden, Prologue to *Secret Love*, ll. 28–31.

p. 229 Including Dryden, who had used Corneille extensively in his *Essay of Dramatic Poesy*. Lope de Vega fits least easily into the critical genealogy, but his plays provided copious source material for later dramatists (see p. 284).

A Ballad

p. 230 Butler MS., ff. 84ᵛ–85ʳ; hand no later than mid-1660s. The face caricatured is that of Oliver Cromwell (who is also the subject of a second ballad). Date of composition: Cromwell would hardly have attracted this attention before 1644, whereas the last stanza would exclude any date after the execution of Charles I in January 1649.

p. 232 Thyer suggests the clothes 'insinuate that a monster of Cromwell's enthusiastic cast must needs be begotten by some puritanic or fanatic preacher'.

A Speech Made at the Rota

p. 234 The Rota was a club formed by James Harrington for the discussion of political theories. The club was so called after the revolving contrivance used for receiving votes, and because Harrington advocated rotation in the offices of government. The Rota was active at the end of 1659, and held its last recorded meeting on 20 February 1660, by which time it was apparent that republicanism had no future. The fate of the Rump Parliament was in question throughout these weeks (up until General Monck's declaration for a free parliament on 11 February). This would be the most probable time for Butler's composition; yet *Hudibras* III. ii covers the same period, and was not published until 1677.

p. 234 'All government is founded upon overbalance in property. If one man hold the overbalance unto the whole people in property, his property causeth absolute monarchy. If the few hold the overbalance unto the whole people in property, their property causeth aristocracy or mixed monarchy. If the whole people be neither overbalanced by the property of one nor of a few, the property of the people or of the many causeth democracy or popular government' (Harrington, *The Rota*, 1660, p. 3).

p. 234 The Rota met at Miles's coffee-house, the Turk's Head, in New Palace Yard.

p. 234 See Henry Blount, *A Voyage into the Levant*, 1636, p. 105. Alternatively 'the *jus nigrum*, or black broth of the Spartans . . . was made with the blood and bowels of an hare' (Browne, *Pseudodoxia*, III. xxv).

p. 234 'For in fact the flaps of the tunic worn by their maidens were not sewn together below the waist, but would fly back and lay bare the whole thigh as they walked' (*Lycurgus and Numa*, trans. B. Perrin, 1914, iii. 4). 'They [boys] steal, too, whatever food they can, and learn to be adept in setting upon people when asleep or off their guard. . . . For the meals allowed them are scanty, in order that they may take into their own hands the fight against hunger, and so be forced into boldness and cunning' (*Lycurgus*, trans. Perrin, xvii. 3–4).

p. 235   Luz was the Aramaic name for the *os coccyx*, or 'nut' of the spinal column. It was a belief among the Jews that this bone was indestructible and would form the nucleus of the resurrected body.

p. 235   The Rump Parliament, which remained after Pride's 'purge' of the Long Parliament in 1648, was dissolved by Cromwell in 1653. It was recalled again by the army in 1659, shortly before the fall of Richard Cromwell, expelled by Lambert and his troops later in the same year, reassembled in December, and finally dissolved in 1660.

An Occasional Reflection on Dr. Charleton

p. 238   Here Butler ridicules both R[obert] B[oyle] and the Royal Society, of which Boyle was a prominent member. In 1659 Boyle had published *Some Motives and Incentives to the Love of God pathetically discoursed of in a Letter to a Friend*, or (in the running-title) *Seraphic Love*; he calls the friend 'Lyndamor'. In 1665 he published *Occasional Reflections upon Several Subjects*; here he extracts pious lessons from, e.g., '*the sight of N. N. making of syrup of violets*'. Walter Charleton (1619–1707) expounded atomism and other hypotheses in a highly eccentric style. He was an enthusiastic member of the Royal Society, which met at Gresham College. On 15 March 1665 Pepys recorded: 'Anon to Gresham College, where, among other good discourse, there was tried the great poison of Macassar upon a dog, but it had no effect all the time we sat there.' A further experiment was conducted on 19 April. Butler would probably have written this topical piece fairly soon afterwards. Swift too parodied Boyle in *A Meditation upon a Broom-Stick*.

p. 238   The dog, having failed to detect a scent on two of three possible paths, concludes without testing it that he must follow the third. See Montaigne, *Essays*, ii. 156; Sir Kenelm Digby, *Treatise of Bodies*, xxxvi. 7.

p. 239   Charleton removed the poison at the end of the meeting on 8 March 1665, returned it before 15 March, and was called to account 29 March. See Thomas Birch, *History of the R.S.*, 1756–7 (fac. 1968), ii. 21, 23, 28.

p. 239   The description of Sir Robert Murray by Samuel Sorbière in his *Relation d'un voyage en Angleterre*, 1664 (trans. *A Voyage to England*, 1709, p. 30).

p. 240   '*Of a Louse:* This is a creature so officious that 'twill be known to everyone at one time or other, so busy and so impudent that it will be intruding itself in everyone's company, and so proud and aspiring withal that it fears not to trample on the best, and affects nothing so much as a crown; feeds and lives very high, and that makes it so saucy as to pull anyone by the ears that comes in its way, and will never be quiet till it has drawn blood . . .' (Robert Hooke, *Micrographia*, 1665 (fac. 1961), p. 211).

Characters: An Hypocritical Nonconformist

p. 241   Date of composition: 'As most of these characters are dated when they were composed, I can inform the curious that they were chiefly drawn up from 1667 to 1669 . . .' (Thyer); four characters surviving in the Butler MS. (ff. 235–6) bear dates in October 1667. But the MS. suggests later work on (at least) one of his long characters, 'A Modern Politician' (ff. 228–9); likewise 'A Duke of Bucks' implies a continuing interest in the genre when Butler worked for Buckingham in the early 1670s.

p. 242   'This character, though fairly transcribed by our author, by lying in too damp a place has received some little damage, which will account for several hiatuses which appear in it' (Thyer).

Characters: A Fifth Monarchy Man

p. 248 The Fifth Monarchy Men hoped for the return of Christ to earth as King, and the establishment of the fifth kingdom foretold by the prophet Daniel, 'which shall never be destroyed: and the kingdom shall not be left to other people, but it shall break in pieces and consume all these kingdoms, and it shall stand for ever' (Daniel 2:44). The other four kingdoms were identified as the Assyrian, the Persian, the Greek, and the Roman. See L. F. Brown, *Baptists and Fifth Monarchy Men*, 1912, pp. 12 ff.

p. 249 In January 1661 Thomas Venner, with 40–60 accomplices, set up the Fifth Monarchy in the streets of London. Thirteen were later executed, Venner and Roger Hodgkin being hanged, drawn, and quartered.

p. 250 According to one story, Whittington ran away from his master, but

> as he went along
> In a fair summer's morn,
> London bells sweetly rung,
>   'Whittington, back return!'
>
> Evermore sounding so
>   'Turn again, Whittington;
> For thou in time shall grow
> Lord Mayor of London.'

See note to p. 227.

Characters: A Sceptic

p. 252 Horace argues that whereas the bad poet offers as his theme the entire Trojan War, Homer is more modest; he does not begin with the hatching from eggs of Leda's children by Zeus (*Ars Poetica*, 136–7, 147). These children were Castor and Pollux, and also Helen.

Characters: A Small Poet

p. 259 It is not inappropriate that the Small Poet should now materialize as Edward Benlowes (1602–76), author of the lengthy religious poem *Theophila* (1652); for Benlowes exhibits both the 'metaphysical' excesses and the facility for borrowing which Butler has already mocked.

p. 260 On the various devices mentioned in this paragraph see Addison, *The Spectator*, nos. 58–63 (7–12 May 1711).

p. 261 'When the smallest poet displays such excesses, a nobler poet ought to surpass him.' But the metaphor is obscure: (i) Thyer notes an apparent defect in 'more the most'; (ii) Butler may refer to 'throwing the bar' in trials of strength, the throws being measured in lengths of the bar; (iii) less plausibly, he may refer to a dice game, 'cut' and 'bar' each being a name for a false die.

p. 261 Thyer prints 'we'.

Characters: A Romance Writer

p. 265 'This alludes to some kind of a puppet performance in those times, as I find the name "Janello" in another imperfect piece of Butler's, introduced as belonging to a famous operator in that art' (Thyer).

Characters: A Modern Critic

p. 266   Whereas the writers should be entitled to (benefit of) clergy, the critic treats them as the law would if they were illiterate, or had previous convictions, or were accused of (serious) offences which had been deprived of clergy by statute.

Characters: A Duke of Bucks

p. 266   George Villiers, second Duke of Buckingham (1628–87), was Butler's employer at least between 1670 and 1673, but the contrast of moral temperament between the two men is manifest. Cf. Dryden's portrait of Buckingham as Zimri in *Absalom and Achitophel* (i. 543–68), and also Burnet, *History of his Own Time*, ed. Airy, 1897–1900, i. 182–3.

Miscellaneous Observations

p. 268   These 'miscellaneous observations' have been selected from the Butler MS. (B.M. Add. 32625). They have been rearranged so as to follow in this sequence: politics—nature—theory of knowledge—reason and faith—theory of literature—specific literary criticisms—general reflections. They have been selected from the MS. folios as follows:

p. 268	f. 184^r			204^r
	155^r	p. 280	f. 202^r	
	232^r			227^r
	190^v			166^v–167^r
	191^r	p. 282	f. 198^r	
	143^v	p. 283	f. 165^v	
p. 269	f. 161^v			165^r
	158^r			145^r
	175^v			199^r
p. 270	f. 181^r	p. 284	f. 204^r	
p. 271	f. 181^v			199^r
p. 272	f. 178^v			202^r
	219^v			204^v
	144^r			199^r
	169^r			210^r
p. 273	f. 169^v–170^r	p. 285	f. 202^v	
p. 274	f. 179^r			208^v
	177^r			148^v
	224^r			188^r
p. 275	f. 151^v			210^r
	171^r	p. 286	f. 165^v	
	153^v			159^r
	148^r			189^r
	200^r			189^r
p. 276	f. 170^v	p. 287	f. 159^v	
	169^{r-v}			156^r
p. 277	f. 146^v			156^r
	147^r			163^v
	170^r			172^r
p. 278	f. 152^r	p. 288	f. 227^r	
	154^v			208^v
	196^r			142^v
	214^r			142^v
p. 279	f. 214^v			226^r
	197^r			

p. 268   In *Leviathan* (1651) Hobbes argues that the only alternative to political submission is a primal anarchy in which there can be no security whatever because all men are equal in ability to destroy one another (I. xiii; II. xvii). Hobbes declares that the rights of a prince cannot be extinguished but that, in cases where he lacks power of enforcement, the obligations of subjects may be; the commonwealth being in effect dissolved, men are at liberty to seek other protection (II. xxix *ad fin.*). If they submit to one who already has the power, that is 'sovereignty by acquisition'; if they contract to establish a ruler, and covenant their rights to him, that is 'sovereignty by institution'. This contract is invalid as soon as made inasmuch as by transferring all rights to him they cease to be a party. It is further imaginary in that Hobbes did not regard a multitude as a legal entity; individuals can agree among themselves to cede rights to a ruler, but only in him, when he assumes power, do they become a corporate body (II. xviii and *De Cive*, chs. v–vi).

p. 268   The Test Act of 1673 required that all office-holders under the Crown take the oaths of allegiance and supremacy, and also declare disbelief in transubstantiation.

p. 269   The contest in 1673 lasted from 5 February to 7 March, when Charles cancelled his Declaration of Indulgence. The bishops opposed the Declaration. Assemblies of Protestant dissenters were indeed the most immediate threat to conformist congregations, and a part of the episcopate was often credited with Catholic sympathies; but Butler's charge of open support is probably a misreading of the bishops' manoeuvres against a Commons bill in favour of Protestant dissenters alone.

p. 269   Many believed that the disasters of 1665–6 were God's judgements. See E. N. Hooker, 'The Purpose of Dryden's *Annus Mirabilis*', *H.L.Q.* x (1946), 49–67.

p. 270   The most famous statements of this theory were published (1705–29) by Bernard Mandeville; for the seventeenth-century background see F. B. Kaye ed., *The Fable of the Bees*, by B. Mandeville, 1924, I. xxxviii ff.

p. 277   Butler writes 'health and death'.

p. 277   Two points are maintained by Butler in this sentence: (i) a man must have enough reason to understand what an unverifiable message is about before he can have faith in that message specifically; (ii) if he can go further and verify the message, then his faith in it is superseded by knowledge of it. So some reason is a prerequisite for faith, and some ignorance a co-requisite. The construction of the sentence is confusing because with the words 'for no man' Butler shifts his ground from (i) to (ii).

p. 278   This passage clearly links Butler with the liberal Anglicanism of such theologians as William Chillingworth, John Hales, and John Tillotson. Chillingworth asserts 'faith is not knowledge—no more than three is four—but eminently contained in it; so that he that knows believes and something more, but he that believes many times does not know; nay, if he doth barely and merely believe, he doth never know' (*The Religion of Protestants*, 1638, p. 325). This argument opposed both Catholic fideism and Sectarian 'new light'.

p. 282   For similar critical assessment see Dryden, *Selected Criticism*, ed. Kinsley and Parfitt, Oxford, 1970, pp. 58, 102–3; Richard Flecknoe, 'A Short Discourse of the English Stage', in *Critical Essays of the Seventeenth Century*, ed. J. E. Spingarn, 1908–9, ii. 93–4.

p. 284   The poetry of Edmund Waller (1606–87) was highly praised for its 'turns' either on words, by patterned repetition, or on thoughts, as in the lines:

> The sign of beauty *feeds* my *fire*.
> No mortal *flame* was e'er so cruel
> As this, which thus survives the *fuel*!

('On the Discovery of a Lady's Painting', quoted by W. L. Chernaik, *The Poetry of Limitation*, 1968, p. 215). See further Chernaik, pp. 56–9, 214–19, and cf. Butler, 'Cat and Puss' (esp. ll. 117–18).

p. 284   Dryden, in his *Essay of Dramatic Poesy*, defends the verisimilitude of rhymed plays 'by distinguishing betwixt what is nearest to the nature of comedy, which is the imitation of common persons and ordinary speaking, and what is nearest the nature of a serious play: this last is indeed the representation of nature, but 'tis nature wrought up to an higher pitch' (*Selected Criticism*, ed. Kinsley and Parfitt, p. 71). Yet he had used rhymed couplets in two comedies, *The Rival Ladies* and *Secret Love* (if only in places where the serious side of the action was being 'raised').

p. 284   Butler most probably refers to Dryden's comparing Shakespeare, Beaumont and Fletcher, and Jonson in *An Essay of Dramatic Poesy* (*Selected Criticism*, pp. 56–8).

p. 285   Dryden is most critical of Jonson in his Epilogue to the Second Part of *The Conquest of Granada*. In his 'Defence of the Epilogue' he specifies Jonson's borrowing 'very much from Plautus' (*Selected Criticism* p. 127). Butler may recall 'forty' from an unrelated quotation in Dryden's next paragraph. For criticism of Dryden's 'thieving', see Gerard Langbaine (*Critical Essays of the Seventeenth Century*, ed. Spingarn, iii. 110–47).

p. 285   Butler writes 'that it is' and in the next line 'extreme', here emended to 'extremes'.

Index